Narrative Beginnings

FRONTIERS OF NARRATIVE *Series Editor:* David
Herman, Ohio State University

Narrative Beginnings

Theories and Practices

Edited by Brian Richardson

UNIVERSITY OF NEBRASKA PRESS
LINCOLN AND LONDON

© 2008 by the Board of Regents of the
University of Nebraska. All rights reserved.
Manufactured in the United States of America

Library of Congress
Cataloging-in-Publication Data

Narrative beginnings : theories and
practices / edited by Brian Richardson.
p. cm. — (Frontiers of narrative)
Includes bibliographical references and index.
ISBN 978-0-8032-3974-6 (pbk. : alk. paper)
1. Narration (Rhetoric) 2. English
literature—History and criticism—Theory, etc.
3. Literature—History and criticism—Theory, etc.
I. Richardson, Brian, 1953–
PR149.N27N38 2008
808—dc22   2008025271

Set in Sabon by Bob Reitz.
Designed by Ashley Muehlbauer.

This volume is dedicated to Hazard Adams, R. Brandon Kershner, Peter Rabinowitz, Monika Fludernik, and James Phelan: teachers, mentors, and colleagues who were there at many different beginnings.

Contents

Editor's Preface ix
Acknowledgments xi
Introduction Narrative Beginnings 1
BRIAN RICHARDSON

Part One: Origins, Paratexts, and Prototypes 11

1. To Begin with the Beginning Birth, Origin, and Narrative Inception 15
   NIELS BUCH LEANDER

2. Before the Beginning Nabokov and the Rhetoric of the Preface 29
   MARILYN EDELSTEIN

3. Stories, Wars, and Emotions The Absoluteness of Narrative Beginnings 44
   PATRICK COLM HOGAN

4. September 1939 Beginnings, Historical Narrative, and the Outbreak of World War II 63
   PHILIPPE CARRARD

Part Two: Beginnings in Narrative Literature 79

5. "The More I Write, the More I Shall Have to Write" The Many Beginnings of *Tristram Shandy* 83
   TITA CHICO

6. Virginia Woolf and Beginning's Ragged Edge 96
   MELBA CUDDY-KEANE

7. A Theory of Narrative Beginnings and the Beginnings of "The Dead" and *Molloy* 113
   BRIAN RICHARDSON

8. *Heartbreak Tango* Manuel Puig's Counter-Archive   127
   CARLOS RIOBÓ

9. Lost Beginnings in Salman Rushdie's *Midnight's Children*   137
   GAURA SHANKAR NARAYAN

10. Recessive Origins in Julia Alvarez's *Garcia Girls* A Feminist Exploration of Narrative Beginnings   149
    CATHERINE ROMAGNOLO

11. Curtain Up? Disrupted, Disguised, and Delayed Beginnings in Theater and Drama   166
    RYAN CLAYCOMB

12. Where to Begin? Multiple Narrative Paths in Web Fiction   179
    JESSICA LACCETTI

Part Three: Beginnings and/as Endings   191

13. The Beginning of *Beloved* A Rhetorical Approach   195
    JAMES PHELAN

14. Connecting Links Beginnings and Endings   213
    ARMINE KOTIN MORTIMER

15. "Mr. Betwixt-and-Between" The Politics of Narrative Indeterminacy in Stevenson's *Kidnapped* and *David Balfour*   228
    OLIVER BUCKTON

16. Maculate Reconceptions   246
    SUSAN WINNETT

    Further Reading on Narrative Beginnings   263
    Contributors   267
    Index   271

Editor's Preface

Beginnings are one of the most important topics of narrative theory, textual analysis, and the study of fiction. They are frequently thematized within modern literary narratives; to take a recent example, the first sentences of J. M. Coetzee's *Elizabeth Costello* run as follows, "There is first of all the problem of the opening, namely, how to get us from where we are, which is, as yet, nowhere, to the far bank. It is a simple bridging problem, a problem of knocking together a bridge," an opening that gestures toward the problems and possibilities of narrative openings. Beginnings are also among the most critically neglected subjects: despite seminal books on the subject by Edward Said and A. D. Nuttall, and despite the widely acknowledged importance of beginnings, for the most part the critical literature on the subject consists of these two books plus a few journal articles.

The essays in this volume attempt to rectify this situation by providing sixteen analyses of the most important authors, texts, and approaches on the subject. They tend to focus on British, American, and postcolonial literature from 1770 to 2006 but also include major European and South American fiction. The texts analyzed include important works by Laurence Sterne, Balzac, R. L. Stevenson, James Joyce, Virginia Woolf, William Faulkner, Vladimir Nabokov, Samuel Beckett, Manuel Puig, Salman Rushdie, Georges Perec, Toni Morrison, and Julia Alvarez. Together, these essays trace the full arc of modern literary history, going from the eighteenth century to nineteenth-century realism and on to modernism, postmodernism, and hypertext fiction. All the essays are fully versed in relevant areas of narrative theory and the theory of the novel, and each is comfortable addressing larger cultural and ideological issues, including gender, race, and empire. Indeed, these ideological issues are central concerns in the essays on postcolonial, feminist, U.S. ethnic, and third-world authors. In addition to studies of beginnings in nineteenth-and twentieth-century fiction, the essays include interdisciplinary approaches that analyze beginnings in historical narratives, hypertexts, plays and performance art, and human cognition.

The essays fall into three groups: part 1, "Origins, Paratexts, and Prototypes," includes studies of the genesis or inspiration of specific works, the prefatory textual matter before the narrative proper, and widely disseminated cultural prototypes of originary narratives; part 2, "Beginnings in Narrative Literature," includes detailed studies of the act, theme, and function of beginnings present in a single, compelling text as well as more expansive accounts of beginnings in the history of the novel, as well as essays devoted to the place of beginnings in narrative theory; and part 3, "Beginnings and/as Endings," probes the many curious relations between beginnings and endings, especially the ways in which both concepts are symmetrical, changeable, somewhat arbitrary, or even reversible.

The contributors represent a wide range of critical positions, including feminism, postmodernism, cognitive science, postcolonial studies, narratology, U.S. ethnic studies, historiography, psychoanalysis, poststructuralism, performance studies, and hypertext studies. Each essayist is theoretically informed, critically sophisticated, and ideologically sensitive. Together, the authors bring about a thorough transformation of the ways in which narrative beginnings are conceptualized.

Acknowledgments

Thanks to Cathy Romagnolo for many years of rich discussion on the topic of narrative beginnings, and to the Society for the Study of Narrative Literature, which approved two panels on beginnings and endings for the 2005 MLA convention—papers that provided the origin of this anthology. Thanks to Jennifer Wellman for editorial advice. Thanks also to the following publishers for granting permission to reprint: Clemson University Digital Press, for several pages of Melba Cuddy-Keane's chapter, "Virginia Woolf and Beginning's Ragged Edge"; Ohio University Press, for Oliver Buckton's chapter, "Mr. Betwixt-and-Between: The Politics of Narrative Indeterminacy in Stevenson's *Kidnapped* and *David Balfour*," which originally appeared in Buckton's book *Cruising with Robert Louis Stevenson: Travel, Narration, and the Colonial Body* (2007); and The Ohio State University Press, for James Phelan's chapter, "The Beginning of *Beloved*: A Rhetorical Approach," a longer version of which appears in Phelan's book *Experiencing Fiction: Judgments, Progressions, and the Rhetorical Theory of Narrative* (2007).

Narrative Beginnings

INTRODUCTION

Narrative Beginnings

The beginning is a foundational element of any narrative, fictional or nonfictional, public or private, official or subversive. The full importance of beginnings, however, has long been neglected or misunderstood and is only recently becoming known. Currently, only a handful of studies address this surprisingly rich and elusive subject. Others, many of them represented in this volume, are now starting to give beginnings the historical, theoretical, and ideological analysis they require.

This critical and theoretical neglect is particularly surprising given the power beginnings possess for the act of reading. There is no doubt that even casual readers remember for decades salient beginning sentences, as the following memorable openings confirm: "It is a truth universally acknowledged, that a single man in possession of a good fortune must be in want of a wife"; "Call me Ishmael"; "All happy families resemble one another, but each unhappy family is unhappy in its own way"; "Longtemps, je me suis couché de bonne heur"; "Mrs Dalloway said she would buy the flowers herself"; "I am an invisible man"; "Lolita, light of my life, fire of my loins." Such a list (which could be extended considerably) attests to the conceptual and emotional power concentrated in resonant opening lines of works that move us. Or even that no longer move us: although Camus is rapidly falling out of the canon, the first words of *The Stranger* continue to reverberate: "Aujourd'hui, maman est morte."

Two key moments in the history of literature continue to resonate among narrative beginnings: one is Tristram Shandy's unfortunate conception, birth, and christening, which dooms him to be out of order for the rest of his life. This is accompanied by the nonchronological presentation of the rest of the story, including an array of temporally anterior episodes that threaten to undermine the possibility of establishing a fixed beginning point in the story, or *fabula*. This regressive narration is in turn paralleled by the unconventional placement of normally prefatory paratextual material throughout the text (most notoriously, the author's preface appears in the middle of the third volume). Sterne's practice would rapidly become an irresistible model for subsequent authors who played with chronology and beginnings, from Lord Byron and Alexander Pushkin to Salman Rushdie and Alasdair Gray.

The second key moment is the famous pause before the first stroke of Lily Briscoe's paintbrush in *To the Lighthouse*:

> She took her hand and raised her brush. For a moment it stayed trembling in a painful but exciting ecstasy in the air. Where to begin? that was the question; at what point to make the first mark? One line placed on the canvas committed her to innumerable risks, to frequent and irrevocable decisions. All that in idea seemed simple became in practice immediately complex; . . . Still the risk must be run; the mark made. With a curious physical sensation, as if she were urged forward and at the same time must hold herself back, she made her first quick decisive stroke. (Woolf 157–58)

Woolf here articulates key psychological and compositional implications of beginning an artwork; intriguingly, they do not match up at all with her own inspired beginning of *To the Lighthouse* (she wrote the first twenty-two pages "straight off in less than a fortnight" [Lee 471]) but correspond better with the difficult beginning of *Mrs Dalloway*, which required several drafts.

A brief glance at the variety of beginnings that have been deployed in the history of literature will help frame the essays that follow. Examples from drama can offer a helpful vantage point to view the range of possible beginnings: a Chekhov play will begin in the most ordinary, even undramatic manner; alternatively, an audience may be plunged deeply in medias res, as in the opening lines of Webster's *The Duchess of Malfi*, where the protagonist, Bosola, walks onstage and shouts, incredulously, "Banished?!" A more or less creaky scene to provide the necessary exposition may be produced, as in the beginning of Sheridan's *The Rivals*, where one character asks the other to explain what he is doing in the town of Bath. Such artificial expositions may be parodied, as in the overly elaborate and needlessly confusing opening of Shakespeare's *Cymbeline*. Frame plays have introduced the main drama ever since the time of Seneca; after Thomas Kyd's *The Spanish Tragedy*, the framing characters have frequently remained onstage to watch the play their dialogue has introduced or engendered. False beginnings are also possible, as in Genet's *The Maids* or Stoppard's *The Real Thing*, where the first scene presented to the audience turns out to be a play enacted by the characters, who then resume their "real" selves. At the beginning of Lanford Wilson's *Talley's Folly*, the protagonist enters, addresses the audience, and provides expository information about the play. After a few minutes of this, he stops, goes back to the beginning, and partially repeats the material he has just narrated, presumably for the benefit of spectators who arrived a bit late to the theater. In Caryl Churchill's "Heart's Desire," the brief opening scene is reenacted onstage about a dozen times, each new version providing a partial repetition and different development of the story.

Drama has its own set of enacted paratextual devices. These include the spoken summary of Roman plays prior to their performance, the often elaborate Elizabethan induction, the Restoration and eighteenth-century prologue, the Sanskrit invocation and prologue, and the direct address to the audience at the beginning of Tennessee Williams's *The Glass Menagerie* or Jack Gelber's *The Connection*. And on more popular stages with potentially angry spectators, the star is routinely given a scene at the beginning so the audience knows that the actor they paid to see is indeed in the house. The printed versions of these plays contain considerably more paratextual material that is not presented onstage, most notoriously Bernard Shaw's elaborate prefaces and endless stage directions. Avant-garde and contemporary drama regularly tamper with the conditions of theatrical presentation, as Ryan Claycomb's essay in this volume demonstrates.

Similarly, a glance at typical beginning strategies during the last major periods of the history of the novel help to situate the studies that follow. Before the rise of modernism, most authors discursively framed the opening of the text and ensured that the first pages conveyed a sense of the beginning. The more a work aspired to a totality, the more natural and definitive the beginning would be made to appear. For a paradigmatic instance we may look at Fielding's *Tom Jones*. The first chapter is constituted by the author's address to the reader concerning the appropriate expectations of the narrative that follows. The next chapter provides salient background material concerning the earlier history of Squire Allworthy and his sister, Bridget. It is only in the third chapter that the arrival of the foundling is described. Several chapters then follow that depict the youth of Tom Jones. Every element pertinent to the origin of the story is here set forth except those key facts that will not be revealed until the conclusion of the work.

A favorite strategy of nineteenth-century realists is to begin the narrative from an entirely external perspective in which all the powers of omniscience are withheld; Turgenev's *On the Eve* (1859) begins, "In the shadow of a lofty lime, on the banks of the river Moskva, not far from Kuntsevo, on one of the hottest days in the summer of 1853, two young men were lying on the grass. One of them, who appeared to be about twenty-three years old, and was tall, swarthy, with a sharp and rather crooked nose." Often the region is described first in some detail, as if by someone who had just happened on the scene; *The Return of the Native* (1879) begins with a twelve-paragraph opening chapter devoted exclusively to a depiction of Egdon Heath; the second chapter starts, "Along the road walked an old man. He was whiteheaded as a mountain." Other nineteenth-century novels begin with a more direct account of the first figure depicted and thereby thrust the reader into the drama at hand: "One fine morning in the full London season, Major Arthur Pendennis came over from his lodgings, according to his custom, to breakfast at a certain club at the Pall Mall, of which he was a chief ornament." Thackeray's *Pendennis* begins with a compressed characterization of the man, his society, and the setting of the events about to unfold.

Modernist texts, by contrast, typically begin with a plunge into the middle of an action of deceptive casualness. Nothing significant seems to be occurring; no conflict is exposed. Marcel rolls over in his bed, Buck Mulligan jests and shaves, Mrs Dalloway decides to buy the flowers herself, Lena Grove walks down a dusty road; this tendency is exemplified by the opening of Musil's *The Man without Qualities*, as announced in the title of its first chapter, "From which, remarkably enough, nothing develops." The setting of the first page of the modernist novel corresponds to familiar diurnal or biological rhythms of morning or evening: shortly after dawn, just after waking, right around breakfast, as in *Ulysses*, *Mrs Dalloway*, *The Trial*, and *The Waves*, or at dusk, often just before going to sleep, as in "Heart of Darkness," *The Death of Virgil*, and *In Search of Lost Time*. Faulkner is the main exception here, preferring to begin his novels in the hot, lambent, summer afternoon in Mississippi, where nothing moves very fast. As a modernist novel continues, the careful reader soon learns the thematic, symbolic, and architectural reasons for the deceptively unremarkable opening; the first paragraphs of any modernist fiction are always dense with submerged meaning. At the same time, modernist narratives rarely pretend to begin at the beginning of a story; there is typically a "ragged edge," as Melba Cuddy-Keane points out, that stretches beyond and before the *fabula* proper. The artifice of the textual beginning is thus contrasted to the unbounded plenum of events it partially circumscribes.

Postmodern texts, by contrast, frequently foreground the first passages of the narrative, often in a stark or paradoxical manner. The first words of Raymond Federman's *Double or Nothing* appear in a section whose heading reads "This is Not the Beginning." We might draw many examples from Beckett—such as "Birth was the death of him" from Fizzle 4—that contest the ordinary function of the beginning, as I will discuss later in this volume. In Flann O'Brien's early proto-postmodern text, *At Swim-Two-Birds*, the narrator states, "One beginning and one ending was a thing I did not agree with. A good book may have three openings entirely dissimilar and inter-related only in the prescience of the author" (9), and this novel has in fact four beginnings, as Brian McHale has discussed (109). Daniel Handler's *Watch Your Mouth* (2002) similarly has four beginnings, in homage to "Beethoven, whose only opera clears its throat with not one but four possible overtures" (5).

Nabokov's *Ada* begins allusively and parodically: "'All happy families are more or less dissimilar; all unhappy ones are more or less alike,' says a great Russian writer in the beginning of a famous novel (*Anna Arkadievitch Karenina*, transfigured into English by R. G. Stonelower, Mount Tabor Ltd., 1880). That pronouncement has little if any relation to the story to be unfolded now." Alasdair Gray redeploys a number of Shandean strategies in *Lanarck*: the novel begins with book 3, which is followed, a hundred pages later, by the prologue and book 1. In *Midnight's Children*, Salman Rushdie is constantly interrogating national, individual, and novelistic beginnings, as Gaura Shankar Narayan's essay in this volume discloses, and the novel contains numerous false beginnings as well: at the beginning of the chapter 11, the narrator, Saleem Sinai, pretentiously refers to Valmiki's dictation of the *Ramayana* to the god Ganesh. He is, however, mistaken; it was in fact Vyasa who is said have dictated the *Mahabharata* to Ganesh at the beginning of that other Sanskrit epic.

Italo Calvino hardly goes beyond the beginning in *If on a winter's night a traveler*, a book mostly composed of first chapters of different novels. As the narrator states: "The romantic fascination produced in the pure state by the first sentences of the first chapter of many novels is soon lost in the continuation of the story: it is the promise of a time of reading that extends before us and can comprise all possible developments. I would like to write a book that is only an incipit, that maintains for its whole duration the potentiality of the beginning, the expectation still not focused on an object" (177).

The transformations of beginning strategies in narrative are appropriately depicted by Gertrude Stein at the start of "Composition as Explanation": "There is nothing that makes a difference in beginning and in the middle and in ending except that each generation has something different at which they are all looking" (21).

Beginnings have always been part of critical discourse, though often in a way that belied the complexities and ramifications of this deceptively rich and elusive topic. In antiquity, two statements stand out. The first is Aristotle's overly simple observation in the *Poetics* that "a beginning is that which does not itself follow anything by causal necessity, but after which something naturally is or comes to be" (§7.3), a claim that most authors in this volume will show to be much more problematic than Aristotle imagined. Later in the *Poetics*, Aristotle states that the drama's "complication is composed of what has happened offstage before the beginning of the action which is there described, and in part from what happens onstage" (§18.1), thereby suggesting that establishing the precise point where the narrative begins may be less simple than his earlier formulation suggests. The other famous claim from antiquity is Horace's injunction to begin the telling in the middle of the story, in medias res, rather than from the strict beginning; Homer, he notes approvingly, begins the *Iliad* with the wrath of Achilles near the end of the Trojan War, not with Leda's egg (ab ovo) from which Helen emerged. With this, the opposition between the beginning of the story (*fabula*) and the beginning of its telling (*syuzhet*) first emerges in literary criticism.

Other classical critical traditions offer additional insights. In the *Natyashastra*, Sanskrit poetician Bharata devotes several lines to the proper arrangement of the preliminary stage matter and prologues of classical Indian dramas as found in plays such as Kalidasa's *Shakuntala*. This type of recessed opening entered Western drama after being incorporated into the triple beginning (dedication, prelude in the theater, prologue in heaven) of Goethe's *Faust*, as Ekbert Faas remarks (161–62). Concerning the events of the story, Bharata defines the beginning (*prarambha*) as the part of the play that creates a curiosity about the attainment of the major objective (379), in which the seed of the plot (*bija*) is created and "scattered in small measure" (381); this produces the opening (*mukha*) and provides the source of the play's many objects, events, and sentiments (384).

Up to the end of the nineteenth century, subsequent work on beginnings did not advance much beyond Aristotle's comments. In his essay "Of the Three Unities," Corneille points out that although tragedy shows only one action onstage, and that it must have a beginning, a middle, and an end, "not only are these three parts separate actions which find their conclusion in the principal one, but, moreover, each of them may contain several others with the same subordination" (219). Each part, that is, may be more variegated and autonomous than was otherwise imagined. Interestingly, John Dryden, who loved to combine extremely divergent elements into a single whole, reformulates this idea in his "Essay of Dramatic Poesy": "There ought to be one action, says Corneille, that is, one complete action that leaves the mind of the audience in full repose; but this cannot be brought to pass but by many imperfect actions, which conduce to it" (233).

Gustav Freytag takes up the subject in 1863 in *The Technique of the Drama*. He identifies five parts of every drama: the introduction, the rise, the climax, the fall, and the catastrophe. The introduction presents all the background information necessary for the understanding of the play: the place and time of the action, the social and personal relations of the protagonist, and the general environment of the drama. A classical prologue, detached from the drama proper, is hazardous, he asserts, since "the poet who treats it as a separate piece is compelled to give it an exposition" and divide it into segments which themselves must have "an introduction, a rise, a proportionate climax, and a conclusion" (117). Freytag also affirms that as a rule it is expedient to quickly establish a defining thematic keynote, a finished scene, and a short transition to the first moment of the rising action (121).

But it is Henry James who deserves the last word (for now) on this subject. In the preface to *Roderick Hudson* he writes: "Really, universally, relations stop nowhere, and the exquisite problem of the artist is eternally to draw, by a geometry of his own, the circle within which they shall happily appear to do so" (171). Here is the first articulation modern thinking about the difficulty of establishing compelling and convincing beginnings.

Finally, it must be noted that beginnings are if anything even more important in many nonfictional texts. Most institutions and every nation have an official narrative with a decisive point of origin, and where that beginning is established and what it includes will have a considerable effect on the history that follows. Edward Said is reputed to have observed that the situation of the Palestinians was harmed by their lack of a compelling story of their origins. Religion is the other great storehouse of beginning narratives; indeed, it may be a central function of religion to fabricate such stories. The exception seems to be the Inuit, who appear to be the only society that has no creation myth. This paucity is more than counterbalanced by Hindu conceptions, with their numerous (and often contradictory) creation myths. This cosmology is also the one that stretches furthest into the past: the period from Brahma's creation to the destruction of the world is 4,320,000,000 years; this cycle of creation and destruction is repeated 36,000 times.

The Judeo-Christian narrative of creation in Genesis notoriously juxtaposes two different and often contradictory accounts: in the first chapter, the birds and the beasts of the earth are created on different days before Adam and Eve are formed on the sixth day; in the second chapter, Adam is created first, then the fowl and beasts appear, and finally Eve is formed out of Adam's rib. In addition to this confused official version, there is another, unauthorized shadow version, which includes the episode of the creation of Lilith prior to the creation of Eve. Accounting for the origin of woman seems to have been particularly troublesome for the Bible's authors. Gnostic and Kabbalah traditions produced still other variants, such as "The Raising of Adam from the Mud by Eve." Furthermore, many of the early biblical stories have their origin in Sumerian myths that precede them by a millennium.

Different cultures will also define beginnings differently, especially when those beginnings involve alternative notions of what constitutes their subject. Thus, Native American autobiographies often begin with accounts of prior family members that far transcend the family genealogies typical of modern biography. As Hertha D. Sweet Wong notes, one Yukon Native begins the story of her life with a history of her nation, the origin myth of her people, and the histories of her mother and other relatives: "She does not even get to her own birth until page 52" (174). Similarly, Geronimo begins his autobiography with an account of the creation of the world and goes on to relate the mythic account of the origin of his people. Many of the essays that follow discuss social and ideological aspects of beginning strategies. In doing so, they disclose the cultural and political importance of official or accepted origin stories.

Works Cited

Adams, Hazard, ed. *Critical Theory since Plato*. New York: Harcourt Brace Jovanovich, 1971.

Aristotle. *Poetics*. Adams 48–66.

Bharata-Muni. *The Natyasastra: A Treatise on Ancient Hindu Dramaturgy and Histrionics*. Ed. and trans. Manomohan Ghosh. Rev. ed. 2 vols. Calcutta: The Asiatic Society and Granthalaya, 1956–67. Vol. 1.

Calvino, Italo. *If on a winter's night a traveler*. Trans. William Weaver. New York: Harcourt Brace Jovanovich, 1981.

Corneille, Pierre. "Of the Three Unities of Action, Time, and Place." Adams 219–26.

Dryden, John. "An Essay of Dramatic Poesy." Adams 228–57.

Faas, Ekbert. *Tragedy and After: Euripedes, Shakespeare, Goethe*. Montreal: McGill-Queen's University Press, 1984.

Freytag, Gustav. *Freytag's Technique of the Drama*. Trans. Elias J. MacEwan. 2nd ed. Chicago: S. C. Griggs, 1896.

Handler, Daniel. *Watch Your Mouth*. New York: HarperCollins, 2002.

James, Henry. *Theory of Fiction*. Ed. James E. Miller Jr. Lincoln: University of Nebraska Press, 1972.

Lee, Hermione. *Virginia Woolf*. New York: Random, 1996.

McHale, Brian. *Postmodernist Fiction*. London: Methuen, 1987.

O'Brien, Flann. *At Swim-Two-Birds*. New York: NAL, 1976.

"The Raising of Adam from the Mud by Eve." *The Other Bible*. Ed. Willis Barnstone. New York: Harper and Row, 1984. 69–70.

Stein, Gertrude. *Look at Me Now and Here I Am*. London: Penguin, 1971.

Wong, Hertha D. Sweet. "First Person Plural: Subjectivity and Community in Native American Women's Autobiography." *Women, Autobiography, Theory: A Reader*. Ed. Sidonie Smith and Julia Watson. Madison: University of Wisconsin Press, 1998. 168–78.

Woolf, Virginia. *To the Lighthouse*. New York: Harcourt Brace, 1981.

PART ONE

Origins, Paratexts, and Prototypes

Three major areas of research have emerged since 1975 that theorize beginnings before the narrative proper gets under way. These are rhetorical situation, paratextual apparatuses, and ideological positioning. Peter Rabinowitz's important study *Before Reading: Narrative Conventions and the Politics of Interpretation* is a comprehensive analysis of the literary and cultural presuppositions that the reader brings to the text prior to its actual processing, or the implicit contract that exists between author and reader. Rabinowitz identifies four main types of preexisting narrative conventions, several of which have direct implications for our processing of the opening sections of the text. The first of these conventions are rules of notice, which help establish a hierarchy of importance among the many clusters of words that make up a novel. Among the rules of notice are rules of positioning, which suggest that titles, epigraphs, descriptive subtitles, and the first and last sentences of most texts are accorded a privileged import. He goes on to identify, second, rules of signification, which "tell us how to recast or symbolize or draw significance from the elements that the first set of rules has brought to our attention" (44). The third set, rules of configuration, helps the reader "assemble disparate elements in order to make patterns emerge" (44). In more formulaic works, we need only look at the opening scene to get a good sense of what is likely to follow. Fourth are rules of coherence, which suggest that we read a text as a purposive whole; these rules help us deal with textual disjunctures and inconsistencies "by transforming them into metaphors, subtleties, and ironies" (45). Taken together, these rules describe the interpretive conventions that readers draw on as they approach a text for the first time.

For Gérard Genette, the paratext is the means by which a text makes a book of itself and proposes itself as such to its readers. The paratext includes titles, dedications, epigraphs, prefatorial material, notes, appendixes, and other contextualizing practices. It is a threshold, an undecided zone between the inside and the outside, a "fringe" that attempts to direct the book's reception. As Genette asks, how would we read Joyce's *Ulysses* if it were not called *Ulysses*? Although the ways and means of the paratext change constantly over time, Genette suggests there has never existed a text without a paratext. He classifies the varieties of paratext in a series of comprehensive categories. Spatially, the materials that come with the work proper (preface, titles, postscripts) are the peritext, while those that appear outside the volume (correspondence, interviews, subsequent essays) constitute the epitext. Temporally, one may differentiate between the original paratext, which appears when the book is first published, and anterior ones, which precede its publication, as well as subsequent, belated, and posthumous paratexts. Genette also identifies factual paratextual matters, such as indications of the author's age, race, gender, or sexual orientation; examines the paratext's illocutionary force (conveying information, intention, and interpretation); and discusses the pragmatic status of this entity, addressing questions like who precisely is the addressee of the paratext. The value of such a meticulous survey reveals itself at several points, such as the seemingly simple issue of the author's name on the cover, which Genette clarifies in his reflections on pseudonymity and anonymity. Werner Wolf and Walter Bernhart have recently assembled an anthology, *Framing Borders in Literature and Other Media,* that takes up these and related issues from a variety of contemporary perspectives.

A number of scholars have begun to scrutinize a particular part of the paratext: the title. Genette provides a thorough overview of the varieties and functions of titles, noting, among other things, the many purposes a title can perform. Rabinowitz analyses the different expectations that would be have been produced if Jane Austen, as she originally intended, had called her book *First Impressions* rather than *Pride and Prejudice* (60). Jacques Derrida, in his discussion of frames and framing, deconstructs the opposition of an inside and outside to a work. The frame does not demarcate the two but is rather "a hybrid of inside and outside"; it is "an outside which is called to the inside of the inside in order to constitute it as inside" (63). Several other theorists have recently taken up the question of titles. Jerrold Levinson sees the title as an integral or even essential part of an artwork; for him, the "title-slot" for a work of art is never devoid of aesthetic potential, and how it is filled, or that it is not filled, is always aesthetically relevant. John Fisher argues that titles are names whose purpose is hermeneutical and whose function is to guide interpretation. Hazard Adams, by contrast, sees titles as synechdoches of the work, as tokens of authorial ownership, and as the point where the historical author fuses with the implied author (or "authority," as he terms it). Experimental fiction has also played with the title; J. G. Ballard has even written a story that consists exclusively of a title and the footnotes that explain each of its words ("Notes towards a Mental Breakdown").

In his seminal book on beginnings, Edward Said draws attention to a number of paradoxes with which the concept is entwined. Beginnings seem always predetermined, yet they also appear to mark a distinct break from that which precedes them. Said approvingly quotes Valéry's remark: "We say that an author is original when we cannot trace the hidden transformations that others underwent in his mind" (15). Although the notion of genuine originality is fallacious, the artist may produce an intentional beginning act that "authorizes" the work. Said goes on to identify two types of works that center on beginnings. In one, the starting point is "hysterically deliberate" (e.g., *Tristram Shandy*); "the beginning is postponed, with a kind of encyclopedic, meaningful playfulness" (44). The other category includes *Paradise Lost* and *The Prelude*; in both of these instances, "what was initially intended to be the beginning became the work itself" (44). Said also differentiates the human, secular, consciously intentional, and ceaselessly reexamined concept of beginnings from the idea of origins, which are instead theological, mythical, and privileged: "an origin centrally dominates what derives from it" (373), while the beginning encourages nonlinear development, relations of adjacency, and a movement toward dispersion.

In her 1999 essay "Epics and the Politics of the Origin Tale," Susanne

Wofford addresses ideological issues in both genres. She observes that origin stories regularly expose and naturalize violent change at the foundation of a society or nation, whereas epics tend to occlude originary causes and evade the kinds of revelations that the origin story presents. In this volume, Catherine Romagnolo, Jessica Laccetti, and Susan Winnett explore the imbrication of narratological and ideological issues once gender comes into play.

The studies in this volume open with Niels Buch Leander's wide-ranging overview of the presumptive opposition of artificial and "natural" beginnings and his examination of the trope of birth as a figure of beginning. It is followed by Marilyn Edelstein's attempt to move beyond Genette's formulations in his concept of the paratext by analyzing the unusual relation between a fictional peritext and a genuine though curious epitext in Nabokov's *Lolita*. These essays are followed by two examinations of the discourse of beginnings in ostensibly nonfictional narrative histories of war. Patrick Colm Hogan sifts through a number of such instances, while Philippe Carrard scrutinizes several distinct types of beginnings in his account of histories of World War II. In these works, the authors disclose the powerful cultural and political significance of official or accepted origin stories as well as their surprising fragility.

Works Cited

Ballard, J. G. "Notes towards a Mental Breakdown." *War Fever*. New York: Farrar Strauss and Giroux, 1991. 161–70.

Derrida, Jacques. *The Truth in Painting*. Trans. Geoff Bennington and Ian McLeod. Chicago: University of Chicago Press, 1987.

Rabinowitz, Peter. *Before Reading: Narrative Conventions and the Politics of Interpretation*. 1987. Reprint. Columbus: Ohio State University Press, 1999.

Said, Edward. *Beginnings: Intention and Method*. New York: Basic Books, 1975.

1

To Begin with the Beginning

Birth, Origin, and Narrative Inception

NIELS BUCH LEANDER

To Astrid, my firstborn child

> Men can do nothing without the make-believe of a beginning.—GEORGE ELIOT, from the opening of *Daniel Deronda*

The ancient distinction between art and nature has generally caused scholars to distinguish between artificial and natural beginnings. This vocabulary has, however, the unfortunate consequence of insinuating that beginnings in art do not really take place. Strictly speaking, *artificial* means "made as a copy of something natural" (*OED*), a meaning that a scholar like Anthony Nuttall accepts when he asserts that "the formality of an artificial opening necessarily simulates the validity and force of natural beginnings" (23). By contrast, I claim that this vocabulary misleads us into thinking of beginnings in art as mere replicas; books and other narratives, however, really do begin. In the following pages I argue that if a literary opening echoes a "natural" creation, it does not do so by way of mere imitation or simulation, but rather by establishing a pragmatic authority that deviates from recognized natural beginnings.

I discuss the notion of origin in order to separate it from the idea of beginning involved in a literary opening, and I apply these reflections to openings that, for one reason or another, replicate a birth as the sign of origin. I wish to show that the narrative beginning involving birth is controversial: first, it appears that the opening does not lend authority from the notion of birth; and second, birth has become problematic in terms of an indication of origin, which is why twentieth-century fiction seems to have abandoned the analogy between birth and the literary opening. In other words, the literary "pun" on reproduction has been abandoned as the ultimate instigator of narrative, while the literary parameters of creation have become more phenomenological and, should I say, less phallocentric.

To begin with I wish to insist on the necessity of differentiating origins from beginnings more generally speaking. Indeed, when we think of beginnings, we may not have noticed that two directly opposed ideas are at stake. On the one hand, a beginning can be thought of as a capacity to commence something new and undertake an initiative. A beginning in this sense serves as an internal indication of change, which helps underline the agent's essential freedom and potential, no matter how small the enterprise: "I begin to walk," "I begin this article," and so forth. On the other hand, a beginning can be read as the external event that originally constituted an object, situation, or being (e.g. "modernity began with industrialization," "the beginning of the universe," etc.). In this way, a beginning traces and institutes an origin, thereby allowing us to make sense of why and how something turned out the way it did— or, typically, how *we* turned out the way we did. Understood as origin, a beginning is intended to provide explanation. This in turn circumscribes our present potential: such a beginning is generally meant to *determine* the present situation. In other words, beginnings confront us with, on the one hand, a radical contingency—through the will to act and conceive—and, on the one hand, a reassuring determinism—through the desire to explain and resolve.

Despite their diverging implications, these two aspects of beginnings—let me call them "a start" and "an origin"—are surprisingly easy to confuse, especially in English, where "beginning" is both a noun (e.g., "the beginning") and a participle (e.g., "she is beginning"). After all, their major difference lies in the temporal positioning. A start could be seen as what one day could constitute the origin of something or someone, just as God's creative start in Genesis is taken in the Judeo-Christian tradition as the origin of the human race. Origins could be described as insights into a previous moment's starting potentialities that were now "closed" and determined by time's passing.

How closely these two aspects of beginnings—starts and origins—are associated is a matter of considerable historical fluctuation. Indeed, eras with a limited belief in genuine change tend to conflate the distinction altogether. In the Middle Ages, for instance, the two aspects of beginnings seemed almost inseparable due to a conceptual readiness to encompass each and every formation under one instigating act of creation (Smith xx). A start was consequently perceived more like an origin in present time, as it did not indicate a window of change but instead a continuation of a previous motion. In contrast, modern writers tend to differentiate sharply between starts and origins, especially in the twentieth century, when the differentiation was a prerequisite to a systematic critique of origins. In this way Foucault is careful to set apart origins from beginnings generally, which he instead characterizes as the *termini a quo* (e.g., temporal thresholds) of temporal events (339–46).

The distinction between these two forms of beginnings plays a pivotal role in the formulation of the human sciences in the twentieth century. It stands, for instance, at the very heart of the poststructuralist rejection of a foundational, humanist interpretation. In his seminal text "La structure, le signe et le jeu," Jacques Derrida associates the notion of origin closely with humanism's traditional metaphysical or "onto-theological" perspective (427). The distinction between "start" and "origin" could therefore explain what Derrida in this text pinpoints as the fundamental divide in the human sciences. Whereas the human sciences traditionally sought interpretations that served as origins and thus put "an *end* to the [interpretative] game," the alternative mode of interpretation, which Derrida clearly advocates, is no longer concerned with reassuring origins but attempts instead to go beyond humanism by "affirming the game" (427, emphasis added). Beginnings that do not semantically "end" are hence used anti-theologically.

The theoretical approach to literary openings is in this respect just as important and illustrative as any other beginning. Georges Poulet and other members of the so-called Geneva School, for instance, have attempted to relocate origins in literature by seeing them in the extratextual form of authorial consciousness. Poulet's friend and intellectual heir, J. Hillis Miller, was the first American to write on literary openings when his chapter on the opening of Dickens's *Bleak House* appeared in 1958. Miller's analysis is not as such a stylistic one, but focuses instead on the spatial and temporal location of the reader. In accordance with Poulet's phenomenological criticism, Miller treats the opening of *Bleak House* as an origin, as a mental moment gathering momentum and spreading through the rest of the novel: "The entire novel seeks to explain, by a retrospective reconstruction going counter to the forward movement of the novel, how the world came to be in the befogged, mud-soaked, fragmented, and decomposed state presented in the initial paragraphs" (168). The initial characters and spaces serve as pieces that simply need to be put together: "In a sense all the novel is present in the initial moment and is only explicated or pieced together by the events which follow" (168). From Poulet and Miller's vocabulary we sense that the literary work is treated quasi-theologically—the opening is really an authorial genesis. Miller, however, seems to take no notice of Dickens's ironic play on religious connotations. Instead, he sees the work as a parallel to cosmological creation, which elevates, first, the work to a world unto itself and, second, the author to a creating consciousness of a conspicuously theological sort.

It is in this context that Derrida's anti-theological vocabulary should be understood. We tend to think of Derrida, Foucault, and also Barthes as essentially critical anti-biographical theorists, but their anti-theological vocabulary indicates that we should rather think of them principally as anti-phenomenological thinkers. For instance, a closer inspection of Barthes's manifesto "The Death of the Author" reveals that the notion of author is not meant to be dismissed altogether but rather that the notion is to be freed from theologically loaded concepts such as "origin." The central schism in twentieth-century human sciences can hence be explained as simply a controversy over how to understand beginnings. Foucault, Derrida, and other theorists of the human sciences wish to separate the connotations of "origin" from the concept of "beginning" in order to release the present human potential through its own beginnings. The ironic consequence is, however, that they need to take the human dependence upon origins more seriously than if they had not set up this sharp dichotomy in the first place. The form of beginning that they envisage is based precisely on a renunciation of the dependency upon origins. Foucault, for instance, portrays origins as both alienating and inescapable, a frustrating dynamics that will elicit human creativity (340). The renunciation of the origin is in this way a narrative that sets new beginnings in motion.

My point is here to argue that there can be no beginning independent of the particular narrative we bring to it. In the recent past one can hardly discern a beginning from the event itself: "I started reading this book" is at times indistinguishable from "I am reading this book." Yet the beginning labels the event, and this is crucial because, epistemologically speaking, we never describe an event as such; we only describe an event *under a certain description*. Sartre is therefore only half right—or half wrong—when he writes in *La nausée* that "in life there is never any beginning" (57). In life there are temporal events, but a beginning is an event under a certain description that needs to be established. That does not imply that beginnings are pure fictions; they exist in time, but simply cannot be located independently of us. It is, for instance, not enough to explain a beginning by the temporal interval between a beginning and an end: that interval simply cannot be defined without the description of the interval itself. In other words, a beginning requires a supporting narrative, which can describe the beginning *as* event. At the logical scale, it can be observed that a beginning already contains narrative components because, as analytic philosophers have shown, sentences that include beginnings will automatically be narrative sentences (Danto, *Analytical Philosophy* 157). When undertaking a beginning, we must therefore begin, not at "the beginning," but by the description under which we wish to place the event.

"To begin at the beginning" is therefore at best a useless tautology. When the befuddled white rabbit in *Alice in Wonderland* asks where to begin his account, and the King of Hearts very gravely orders him to "begin at the beginning . . . and then go on till you come to the end: then stop," we easily pick up on this tautological humor (Carroll 94). Despite the evident truth of the King's suggestion, the rabbit is no better off: because where does the account indeed begin? Under what description does the account, and hence its beginning, fall? Without this descriptive component, the beginning eludes us. A beginning simply cannot be understood in itself, or as Hegel puts it, a beginning is "an unfulfilled immediacy which cannot be analyzed [Nichtanalysierbar]" (qtd. in Steiner 22). In other words, a beginning is what philosophers call an epistemological "primitive"—a building block that cannot or should not be scrutinized and upon which other knowledge is therefore constructed.

For this reason, the inaccessibility of the beginning and its dependency on a narrative component do not preclude the human reliance on beginnings. On the contrary, "men can do nothing without the make-believe of a beginning," as we learn in the first line of George Eliot's *Daniel Deronda* (1876), which I chose as the epigraph of my essay:

> Men can do nothing without the make-believe of a beginning. Even Science, the strict measurer, is obliged to start with a make-believe unit, and must fix on a point in the stars' unceasing journey when his sidereal clock shall pretend that time is at Nought. His less accurate grandmother Poetry has always been understood to start in the middle; but on reflection it appears that her proceeding is not very different from his; since Science, too, reckons backwards as well as forwards, divides his unit into billions, and with his clock-finger at Nought really sets off *in medias res*. No retrospect will take us to the true beginning; and whether our prologue be in heaven or on earth, it is but a fraction of that all-presupposing fact with which our story sets out.

Eliot's credo does not dismiss the human belief in beginnings. On the contrary, it is the very impossibility of arriving at a "true beginning" that prompts us to believe even more firmly in beginnings. We cannot be taken to the true beginning, but will have to rely on an "all-presupposing fact" that will set everything in motion. To Eliot, all human inquiry is "obliged to start with a make-believe unit" in order to measure other things and get its interpretation under way. In this way, each human endeavor shares some of its structure with literature, namely its narrative aspect. All modes of inquiry rely on their own narrative of beginning, and literature's more explicit reliance on make-believe therefore helps conceptualize beginnings in general. What Eliot makes clear is that a beginning's *foundational* quality cannot be separated from its *fictional* quality. The designation of a beginning is a requirement of narrative, but a beginning in itself requires a narrative.

Common sense may always recommend locating a "natural" beginning, but as I have shown, the designation of such a beginning is highly problematic. I maintain that literary works have always shown an inherent resistance to the commonsensical approach to beginnings. If we revert to the oldest example of a critical assessment of a specific literary opening, we notice, for example, that it addresses precisely this problem of "natural" beginnings. In *Ars Poetica*, Horace defies the Greek logos and eulogizes Homer for opening in medias res with "Sing, goddess, of the Wrath of Peleus' son Achilles" (127).

To Horace, what makes Homer the greatest of poets is precisely that "he doesn't begin the Trojan War from the twin egg (*ab ovo*)," that is, the conception of the twins Clytemnestra and Helen (127). *Inception does not begin by conception.* To Horace, the *midway* becomes instead the very measure of the whole work: the poet "tells his fables and mixes truth with falsehoods in such a way that the middle squares with the beginning and the end with the middle." Horace's symmetrical dictum resounds throughout the history of composition, from Pierre de Ronsard's poetological advice "begin in the middle" (298) to the famous opening of Dante's *Divine Comedy*: "Halfway through the journey of my life."

In the Horatian line of thought, poetry should precisely show that the laws of art are unlike the laws of nature; this entails that the beginning of a poem should never fuse with an established beginning in nature. So accepted was Horace's principle that Lord Byron's resolve to "begin at the beginning" in his *Don Juan* could be nothing but deeply polemical:

Most epic poets plunge "in medias res"
(Horace makes this the heroic turnpike road),

That is the usual method, but not mine—
My way is to begin with the beginning. (21)

Lord Byron therefore opens by "narrating somewhat of Don Juan's father / And also of his mother, if you'd rather" (21).

Yet, the problem about beginning "with the beginning" is that even what we think of as the most "natural" of beginnings—birth and conception—quickly turn *artificial* rather than "natural." Intuitively, it seems natural to begin one's life story by one's birth. But, as Georges Perec explains in his semi-biographical text *Je suis né*, there is something deeply implausible about beginning a text with "I am born" (9–10). To see what Perec means, let us look at the humor involved when Dickens's David Copperfield begins his narrative in precisely that way:

> I am born. Whether I shall turn out to be the hero of my own life, or whether that station will be held by anybody else, these pages must show. To begin my life with the beginning of my life, I record that I was born (as I have been informed and believe) on a Friday, at twelve o'clock at night. It was remarked that the clock began to strike, and I began to cry, simultaneously.

Dickens's opening looks like a number of realist biographical narratives that situate themselves through the time of a birth. The trouble with Dickens's beginning is, however, its use of the present tense. Although it is standard in, say, French to use the present tense about one's birth, it is strictly speaking deeply illogical, and Dickens plays on this logical inconsistency. By beginning with "I am born" in the absence of temporal and spatial indications, Dickens manages to blend an almost abstract birth with the humor involved in imagining that one could witness one's own birth. When, therefore, the second line evokes an uncertainty about whom the hero of the narrator's life will be, we do also sense the presence of the narrator being born in the process and who now imagines whether the narration which in the third sentence turns into past tense will ever move ahead as expected and recapture the present tense. The birth appears to be double: the narrator tells the tale of his birth ("I was born on a Friday"), but the narrator is also born to us as readers in present time. The humor and implausibility of the opening passage obviously lie in the fact that one cannot witness one's own birth. The information that one will have of the birth could of course never have been obtained firsthand, and the narrator mitigates the provocative opening by adding, quite reasonably, that his information about the birth has been obtained through others. The irony continues, though, as the information he conveys is not accurate spatial and temporal information but the rather "useless" information that he was born "on a Friday" (most people, after all, never bother to ascertain what day of the week they born on). The rather implausible coincidence that Copperfield started crying exactly as the clock struck twelve further accentuates that the tale of his birth is reported through others and may not be meticulously accurate. Through this "inaccurate accuracy" the tale gains a symbolic power; the birth may not serve as a beginning in itself, but when the clock strikes twelve at the moment of birth, the birth is supported structurally by the beginning of a new day. The authority of the birth is hence undermined by the assertive beginning, which corresponds with Copperfield's ophanized standing, born exactly at twelve o'clock—"at Nought," as George Eliot wrote—and whose witnesses to the birth need to be declared rather than taken for granted.

What the opening of *Copperfield* shows is that even in saying "I" we rely upon previous tales, which together constitute our individuality. Without explicitly acknowledging these tales, we naturally take for granted that we are the continuation of the individual who, according to the record of our parents or of the registry office, was born at that precise time and in that precise place (cf. Eco). This identity of the narrating subject is, however, at the center of narrative theory, to such a degree that Alain Robbe-Grillet claims that "a book always begins by 'I am born'" (111–12). Yet in Robbe-Grillet's view this is precisely why the modern novel attempts to resist these three opening words. Textual beginning should no longer legitimize itself as an origin by evoking a birth.

There is, in other words, something paradoxically abrupt about announcing one's own beginning. The search for a natural beginning easily turns inconsistent and therefore humorous, as we are further reminded by one of the most brilliant openings in history, that of Laurence Sterne's *Tristram Shandy* (1759), where the narrator begins by recounting how he was conceived:

> I wish either my father or my mother, or indeed both of them, as they were in duty both equally bound to it, had minded what they were about when they begot me.

Sterne's opening is clearly positioned in the polemic surrounding the Horacian dictum, because Shandy soon exclaims: "right glad I am, that I have begun the history of myself in the way I have done; and that I am able to go on having everything in it, as Horace says, ab ovo" (38). But of course Shandy has not proven that a story can successfully begin ab ovo. Rather, he has taken the ab ovo dictum ad absurdum, and thereby proves that the true ab ovo beginning appears instead to begin in medias res. It is nevertheless important to realize that the absurdity involved in the opening scene stems not from Shandy's narrative mode but from his explanatory mode. As Nuttall has argued, Shandy's initial disorientation is established by commencing the retrospective counterflow of explanation before the narrative flow has properly begun (158). Our puzzled state shows that the world the person is born into is in need of further explanation; beginnings are part of an infinitely larger process, and something must precede even what seems to be an ideal beginning. The novel is, of course, also a mockery of the authorial omniscience: the exact moment that the narrator is conceived is of course not known even to the two "agents" who bring about his beginning, that is, to his parents reluctantly entangled in the bed of creation. The humor of the absurdity should not be forgotten; the absurdity is deliberately portrayed as fallacious.

The belief in literature's dependency on natural beginnings seems to rest on a neglect of this fundamental difference between the narrator's story and the way that story is presented. The "internal" perspective of the narrator cannot conform to the "external" perspective of the event. The problem in the case of natural beginnings like birth and conception is that they necessarily belong to the "external" perspective, and the reason why we laugh at the openings of *David Copperfield* and *Tristram Shandy* is that they mix the external perspective of birth or conception, which we believe can be verified by observation, with the internal perspective of the narrator who reports the event.

The literary insight into narrative perspective indicates the epistemological difficulty of explaining a beginning. This difficulty is accentuated in the case of biological beginnings, which explains why, throughout literary history, the biological beginning has been perceived with a great deal of suspicion and skepticism. The search for such biological beginnings will only end up in a dependency on other narrations—and each beginning will not only have to be narrated but will be a narration in itself.

Whereas the "natural" beginning of birth and conception ends up seeming rather artificial, humorous, and deliberately ironic, a beginning that deliberately limits the perspective of the first-person narrator to the present seems sincere and intuitive, as in the case of the opening of Eugène Le Roy's *Jacquou le croquant* (1899): "The first I can remember is 1815, the year that the strangers arrived in Paris . . ." In this case, the first memory of the narrating consciousness also becomes the opening of the novel. This limits the opening's dependency on secondhand sources, and the explicit indication of the narrator's limits opens for a different standard of reliability.

The reason for these perspectival complications is that modern literature, especially with the rise of the novel, tends to tell the tale of a single individual. From Cervantes's *Don Quixote* (1605–15), the novel has had to adapt to the challenges of narrating life-stories, as if the individual is now a world in itself, needing its own cosmology, as it were. The problem is however that a life is not narratively cohesive. Aristotle, for instance, praises Homer precisely for not recounting all the things that happen to one person. His explanation is that "a plot is not unified, as some suppose, if it concerns one single person. An indefinitely large number of things happen to one person, in some of which there is no unity. So too the actions of one person are many, but do not turn into a single action" (97). Nevertheless, modern literature tends precisely to situate an individual within a plot, thereby investigating alternative ways of establishing unity—the unity that *David Copperfield* and *Tristram Shandy* handle in their ironic ways.

We can conclude that unmediated beginnings are unknowable. Even one's own beginning cannot be ascertained without relying on other narratives. The inscrutability of beginnings calls for them to be narrativized, and a present start could be understood only as the abstract notion of origin begins to dissipate. I have therefore argued that one's fundamental approach to beginnings—whether one sees them as "starts" or as "origins"—has profound epistemological and ideological consequences, which can be traced in the central twentieth-century divide in the humanities between "theorists" and "philologists." Nevertheless, even a beginning that defies the notion of origin will have to establish its authority on an alternative narration. Therefore, when Virginia Woolf writes in *The Waves* that "if there are no beginnings and endings there are no stories" (qtd. in Danto, "Narrative Sentences" 155), we must not forget that the opposite also holds: if there are no stories, there are no beginnings.

The beginning of a story, whether cosmological or literary, will then also have to be the story of a beginning, a phenomenon that John Barth deliberately plays on in the opening of his *Lost in the Funhouse* (1969): "Once upon a time there was a story that began."

Without this narrative aspect of beginnings, an infinite regress would develop. The search for a beginning could extend infinitely backwards until the beginning becomes entirely unrecognizable and ineffectual. It is this infinite regress that *Tristram Shandy* explores through the absurd location of the moment of conception. Ultimately, only the origin of the world would do—unless something stops the regress. And this "something," I claim, can only be a narrative structure, which mediates the otherwise inaccessible beginnings.

My contention is therefore that "natural" beginnings are "artificial" in the sense that they, like literary manifestations, depend on narrative components. I therefore recommend that we do not distinguish in essence between artificial and natural beginnings but rather between beginnings that are *internally* grounded and beginnings that are *externally* grounded. This does not imply, as Nuttall fears, that natural beginnings are being reduced to mere "cultural fictions" that we read *into* the world, but never *off* it (201). This is a false dichotomy. We read beginnings into the world on the basis of real events, since these help us structure an otherwise unsystematic collection of events. The narrative component that we add enhances our ability to trace and define temporal beginnings—and it is therefore a fundamental instrument in our understanding also of the natural world. In this sense we comprehend life as if it were a narrative—but that, of course, does not *make* it fiction.

I wish to thank the Carlsberg Foundation of Copenhagen for my postdoctoral fellowship, during which I completed this essay.

Works Cited

Aristotle. "Poetics." Leitch 90–117.
Barth, John. *Lost in the Funhouse*. London: Secker & Warburg, 1969.
Barthes, Roland. "The Death of the Author." *Authorship*. Ed. Sean Burke. Edinburgh: Edinburgh University Press, 1995. 125–30.
Byron. *Don Juan*. London: John Lehmann, 1949.
Carroll, Lewis. *Alice in Wonderland*. New York: Norton, 1992.
Danto, Arthur C. *Analytical Philosophy of History*. Cambridge: Cambridge University Press, 1965.
———. "Narrative Sentences." *History and Theory* 2.2 (1962): 146–79.
Derrida, Jacques. "La structure, le signe et le jeu dans le discours des sciences humaines." *L'écriture et la différence*. Paris: Seuil, 1967. 409–28.
Dickens, Charles. *David Copperfield*. Oxford: Clarendon Press, 1981.
Eco, Umberto. "Fictional Protocols." *Six Walks in the Fictional Woods*. Cambridge: Harvard University Press, 1994. 117–40.
Eliot, George. *Daniel Deronda*. New York: Modern Library, 2002.
Foucault, Michel. "Le recul et le retour de l'origine." *Les mots et les choses: Une archéologie des sciences humaines*. Paris: Gallimard, 1966. 339–46.
Horace. "Ars Poetica." Leitch 124–34.
Leitch, Vincent B., ed. *The Norton Anthology of Theory and Criticism*. New York: Norton, 2001.
Le Roy, Eugène. *Jacquou le croquant*. Paris: Calmann-Lévy, 1981.
Miller, J. Hillis. "Chapter VI: Bleak House." *Charles Dickens: The World of His Novels*. Cambridge: Harvard University Press, 1958. 160–224.
Nuttall, Anthony David. *Openings: Narrative Beginnings from the Epic to the Novel*. Oxford: Clarendon Press, 1992.
Perec, Georges. *Je suis né*. Paris: Seuil, 1990.
Robbe-Grillet, Alain. "Un roman qui s'invente lui-même." *Pour un nouveau roman*. Paris: Minuit, 1963. 108–12.
Ronsard, Pierre de. "A Brief on the Art of French Poetry." Leitch 94–98.

Sartre, Jean-Paul. *La nausée*. Paris: Gallimard, 1938.
Smith, D. Vance. *The Book of the Incipit: Beginnings in the Fourteenth Century*. Minneapolis: University of Minnesota Press, 2001.
Steiner, George. *Grammars of Creation*. London: Faber and Faber, 2001.
Sterne, Laurence. *The Life and Opinions of Tristram Shandy*. London: Penguin, 1967.

2

Before the Beginning Nabokov and the Rhetoric of the Preface

MARILYN EDELSTEIN

The few narrative theorists who analyze beginnings typically assume that a narrative's beginning is to be found in its opening line, first paragraph, or first chapter. But what do we make of a work whose ostensible beginning (the beginning of the plot, of the primary narrative) is itself preceded by something else—specifically, a preface or foreword? Is a preface part of the text? It is, for instance, part of the physical book when it is included within the book's covers. It is part of the reader's experience of the text as a whole, and when the reader reads the preface first it serves as the point of entry into the narrative. What do we make of such a liminal text, a text that precedes, initiates, and influences the reader's experience of the subsequent narrative?[1] Examining the few works in narrative theory that address prefaces and analyzing some of Vladimir Nabokov's prefatory texts, especially in *Lolita*, can illuminate the difficulty of deciding when, where, and how a narrative actually "begins" and reveal much about authors' relations to their texts and their readers.

Prefaces to novels, while no longer oral, are like the exordia or proemia (introductions to speeches) in classical rhetoric—from which they derive—in that they allow manipulation of both the speaker/ author's ethos or persona as well as of the audience's reception of the text. Classical rhetorical treatises advise orators how to use the exordium or proem to make the audience attentive and receptive, to bring "the mind of the auditor into a proper condition to receive the rest of the speech" (Cicero 41; bk. 1, ch. 15). Prefaces to novels fulfill similar rhetorical functions,[2] serving as a site for the author to "make his own character *look* right and put his hearers . . . into the right frame of mind" (Aristotle 90; *Rhetoric*, bk. 2, ch. 1, lines 22–24, emphasis added). Few authors have been as skillful as Nabokov in cleverly crafting an ethos designed to shape readings of not only their literary texts but of "the author himself."

Prefaces to novels exist on the threshold of the fictional world and on the borders between literature and literary theory or criticism. Novel prefaces are part of what Susan Sniader Lanser calls the "extrafictional structure" and what Gérard Genette calls the "paratext." Lanser's 1981 book *The Narrative Act: Point of View in Prose Fiction* provided the first detailed analysis of the extrafictional and extratextual elements that shape reading of fictional narratives. In Lanser's schema, an author's preface would usually be extrafictional—outside the fictional world—but still intratextual—because a part of the total published text of the novel. Lanser distinguishes between the extrafictional author a reader "builds" from such information as titles or prefaces and any extratextual information a reader may discover about the real historical author (122–24).

In his 1987 book *Seuils* (translated into English in 1997 as *Paratexts: Thresholds of Interpretation*), which does not discuss Lanser's pioneering work in the United States, Gérard Genette coined the term "paratext" to designate all those "auxiliary" discourses that surround, serve, and present a text.[3] For Genette, the paratext includes both "epitext" and "peritext." "Epitext" refers to auxiliary elements that are not physically part of the text but nonetheless "frame" it, such as an interview with the author, which Lanser would call "extratextual."[4] "Peritext" refers to elements that are physically part of the text, such as titles or epigraphs, as well as prefaces (4–5), which Lanser would call "extrafictional."[5]

Many paratextual elements can influence readers' expectations of and responses to works of fiction, starting with the author's name on the book's cover—especially when readers are already familiar with the author's other works or even reputation. For instance, if the name on the cover of Vladimir Nabokov's *Lolita* were a woman's instead, say "Margaret Atwood," many readers might read *Lolita* as a scathing feminist critique of male objectification or consumption of Woman (or Girl)—a reading much less likely (but not impossible) with Nabokov's name on the cover.[6]

Some prefaces are "written" not by the author whose name appears on the novel's cover but by a fictional character created by the novelist. Such "fictional prefators" usually discuss the novel much as an "author-prefator" does—commenting on its origins, composition, purpose, or meaning.[7] Such a fictional prefator will be ontologically distinct from the narrator of the attached text, although the relation to the "real" author may be harder to discern.

Sometimes the preface is obviously written (and even signed) by the novel's author. For many readers—both amateur and professional—such a preface appears to be a direct (yet also somehow supplementary) communiqué from the author *in propria persona* about both the writing and reading of the novel that follows. An author's preface may appear in the novel's first edition or be added only to second or later editions in response to what the author believes have been critical (mis)readings. Genette calls such a paratext a "later preface" (174).

For some authors we have an entire collection of initial or, more commonly, later prefaces to shape our sense of "the author" as both novelist and critic-theorist, as with Henry James's prefaces for the New York Edition of his novels, or with the less formal "set" of Nabokov's added forewords to his translated novels. But should such author-prefators' critical claims be accepted as authoritative, especially in such a rhetorically powerful position as a preface? What is the relationship between the author-prefator, the implied author, and the "real" author?

The author's prefatory "voice" seems to occupy a narrative level somewhere between that of an implied author and a real (or historical) author—both of which seem to exist "above" or "below" (or perhaps "beside") the voice of the narrator(s). Most narrative theorists still use Wayne Booth's concept of the "implied author," first theorized in his 1961 classic *The Rhetoric of Fiction*. For Booth, this implied author is constructed by the reader, who views the literary work as "the product of" an "evaluating person" who "chooses, consciously or unconsciously, what we read; we infer him as an ideal, literary, created version of the real man [*sic*]." Booth argues that readers should distinguish "between the [real] author and his implied image" (74–75).

Lanser believes that the "extrafictional" voice—for example, that of the author-prefator (present in what Genette calls the "peritext")—is "the most direct textual counterpart for the historical author" (or what Booth, in *Critical Understanding*, calls the "*flesh-and-blood*" writer [268]) and that it "has the ontological status of historical truth." However, she does acknowledge that there will be various degrees of "'masking' which the historical author has consciously or unconsciously achieved" and which will make such a voice "more or less similar to the historical author's voice" (122–23).

Questions of masking, impersonation, and reliability are especially relevant to an understanding of the relationship between the foreword (by fictional "John Ray, Jr., Ph.D.") and the afterword (by Vladimir Nabokov, the actual author of the novel) in Nabokov's *Lolita*, and the relation of either to "Nabokov himself." Nabokov begins his afterword: "After doing my impersonation of suave John Ray, the character in *Lolita* who pens the Foreword, any comments coming straight from me may strike one—may strike me, in fact—as an impersonation of Vladimir Nabokov talking about his own book. A few points, however, have to be discussed; and the autobiographic device may induce mimic and model to blend" (313).[8]

Lolita's pedophilic, murderous, unreliable first-person narrator, Humbert Humbert, seems easily distinguishable from both its implied author and its real author—neither of whom seems to approve of either pedophilia or murder, or to be possibly insane, or to be dead when the novel is published. But figuring out the relationships among John Ray's views of the novel, those expressed by the "Vladimir Nabokov" of the afterword, and those expressed by the "real" Vladimir Nabokov elsewhere is much more difficult. Many critics consider Nabokov's forewords in particular as "autobiographical and autocritical writing" (Boyd 385). But who or what is the "auto-" or author not only writing but being written/constructed in these forewords, written by an author who tells us he may be "impersonating" himself?

Through a large body of multimedia interviews (orchestrated and then compiled and edited by Nabokov in *Strong Opinions*); through published letters, lectures, autobiographies, and criticism; and through his forewords—that is, throughout his paratext—Nabokov constructed a public persona (or a set of personae) as artful and powerful as his novels. Such personae are something like what Booth calls the "career-author," "these sustained characters who are the sum of the invented creators implied by all of the writer's particular works," but they are closer to what he wants to call "character" ("in the old sense of 'reputation'"): "the fictitious hero created and played with, by author and public, independently of an author's actual works" (*Critical Understanding* 270–71). Because of Nabokov's complex and not always consistent textual personae and his complex assertions of his presence within his novels, Nabokov criticism has been especially susceptible to authorial manipulation and control.[9] Particularly in his forewords to the translated novels, which Dale Peterson calls "those peculiar literary vestibules," Nabokov has proven a "notoriously intimidating receptionist" (824).

In these forewords, as in other paratextual sites, Nabokov repeatedly warns readers and critics against examining his works for any political, social, or ethical "messages," stressing instead the works' aesthetic qualities. For instance, he tells readers in the foreword to *The Eye* that his books are "blessed by a total lack of social significance" (ix), and he asserts in the introduction to *Bend Sinister* that he is not interested in politics or "the Future of Mankind" (vi). Thus, Page Stegner was not alone in his view of Nabokov when he titled his 1966 book—the first book-length study of Nabokov—*Escape into Aesthetics*.

Especially influential for critics has been Nabokov's almost ritual paratextual mockery of the "Viennese delegation" (as he calls Freudians in the foreword to *King, Queen, Knave* 8). He writes in *Bend Sinister*'s introduction that "all my books should be stamped Freudians, Keep Out" (xii). And, in effect, they all were. Psychoanalytic interpretations of Nabokov's work did not begin to appear until some years after his death in 1977 (e.g., an article by Jennifer Shute in 1984 and a book by Geoffrey Green in 1988).

Most discussions of Nabokov's prefatory texts have dealt with the forewords Nabokov wrote for the English translations of his Russian novels—the first in *Invitation to a Beheading* in 1959 and the last in *Glory* in 1970—which seemed to be in a recognizably and consistently Nabokovian "voice." Nabokov's only introduction in his own name to a novel originally written in English, *Bend Sinister*, was only published in the 1963 edition, sixteen years after the novel's first publication.[10]

"John Ray's" foreword to *Lolita* was the first preface Nabokov wrote, and it was also an integral part of the novel; the second such integral *and* fictional preface would be "Charles Kinbote's" to *Pale Fire*.[11] Ray's foreword appeared in the first edition of *Lolita*, by Olympia Press in 1955, and in all later editions. Nabokov wrote what is usually called the "Afterword" but is actually titled "Vladimir Nabokov On a Book Entitled *Lolita*" to accompany the substantial excerpts from the novel first printed in the United States in 1957, in the *Anchor Review*. The afterword was included in the first U.S. edition of *Lolita* (by Putnam in 1958) and has appeared in all printings and at least twenty-five translations of *Lolita* since (Appel 438). It has thus become as much a part of the text of *Lolita* as Ray's foreword or the first-person narrative by Humbert Humbert. Perhaps Nabokov's initial inability to get *Lolita*—his great American novel—published in the United States (where publishers were afraid it would be censored or banned) and its first publication instead by a French publisher of both soft-core pornography and controversial "Literature" prompted Nabokov to write his first commentary to one of his own novels, in what many readers have taken to be his own "voice" in the afterword.[12]

Lolita is unique in Nabokov's *oeuvre* in containing both a fictive "editor's" foreword—written by Nabokov but signed by "John Ray, Jr., Ph.D."—and an afterword, written and signed by Nabokov. *Lolita* thus has both a pre-text and a post-text framing the primary narrative, which is also framed by the entire Nabokovian paratext (and, even for "amateur" readers, by Lolita's and *Lolita*'s reputation). Nabokov's afterword is similar in tone, language, style, and ideas to much of this paratext, especially Nabokov's forewords to the translated novels and his interviews and lectures. Many Nabokov scholars have focused on the differences between Nabokov's views expressed in the afterword and Ray's views in the foreword. But in spite of their temporal and spatial separation in the total text of *Lolita*, both the foreword and the afterword fulfill many of the same typical prefatory functions and use many of the same rhetorical strategies.[13]

Both Ray and Nabokov comment on the origins of the work—Ray on how he came to edit Humbert's manuscript, Nabokov on the "initial shiver of inspiration" that prompted the writing of *Lolita* (313). Both comment on the work's circuitous route to publication (even though these are different routes for ontologically distinct "works"). Both discuss generic expectations and conventions, present some general aesthetic theory, and mention specific details of the text—details that mean nothing until the reader has finished the narrative; thus the afterword has an advantage over the foreword.

Both Ray and Nabokov also respond to specific real or imagined criticisms of *Lolita*; in this regard, the afterword is like those "later prefaces" authors add to subsequent editions of a work if they think critics have misunderstood it. Both justify the novel's sensuousness—Ray because it is "functional" in the development of the novel's moral lesson, Nabokov because "no writer in a free country should be expected to bother about the exact demarcation between the sensuous and the sensual" (316). Both also comment on Humbert's "character" (in both senses of the term)—Ray telling us that Humbert is "abnormal," desperately honest, but still a sinner, and Nabokov saying he disagrees with Humbert on "many things, besides nymphets" (317).

Yet the foreword, unlike the afterword, is not by the author of the novel *Lolita* but by the fictional editor of the supposedly real memoir by Humbert Humbert. Rare in the twentieth-century novel, the editorial pose was common in the seventeenth-, eighteenth-, and nineteenth-century novels (especially French and English), whose "editors" presented the attached narratives as actual memoirs, diaries, or letters (and *Lolita* includes and parodies elements of all of these). Early novelists could thus present their texts as "true" or historical and so circumvent then-current philosophical and ethical objections to the "merely fictional."[14] Although many early novel readers did believe the fictional prefator *was* an actual editor and the text that followed *was* a "true story," few readers in the mid-twentieth-century encountering *Lolita* would have believed in the reality of John Ray or of Humbert Humbert's "memoir," given that it is Vladimir Nabokov's name on the book's cover.[15]

Yet Ray does follow these early fictional prefators' practice of asserting the memoirist's historical reality, referring readers to newspaper accounts of Humbert's crime. Certainly, most readers will assume Nabokov is parodying such claims of authenticity; after all, he frequently asserts in his paratext that his novels have nothing to do with everyday "reality." Nabokov's parody of—and homage to—the editorial pose in the foreword reflects his and *Lolita*'s ambivalent relation to precursor texts and prior conventions.[16]

Most importantly, both Ray (fictional prefator) and Nabokov (author-prefator) become readers of the attached text, modeling and explicitly advising how to read it. Two readings, which also comment on and incorporate others' readings (and misreadings), are staged in the two liminal texts. Even when readers discern (fairly quickly in most cases) that "John Ray, Jr." is a rather amusing fictional creation by Nabokov, they cannot be entirely immune to Ray's commentary when they read his foreword *before* Humbert's narrative. But will Ray's reading of *Lolita* be confirmed, amended, or rejected as readers read the subsequent narrative—and then again as they read Nabokov's afterword? And is Nabokov's paratextual reading of his novel any more trustworthy than Ray's?

It is tempting to speculate that Nabokov creates Ray as a model of a bad reader and uses himself, in the afterword, as a model of a good reader. Many critics have, in fact, assumed that Ray's views are included in *Lolita* only to be ridiculed and that the afterword exists "to counteract the foreword" (Morton 80). Stegner asserts that Ray "is so obviously a parody of the psychopathologist, and his moralizing is so patently absurd, that it is difficult to understand how he could ever be taken seriously" (40).

Other critics have indeed realized that, as Andrew Field puts it, the foreword "is in large part a joke . . . but one should not be taken in—there are several very serious things said" (331). Ironically, those reading *Lolita* in the 1950s and early 1960s—before the publication of most of Nabokov's interviews, forewords, and lectures (and thus before the full development of his paratextual personae)—might have been fooled into taking at least some of Ray's claims (if not Ray's factual existence) seriously. Some later critics would be fooled into taking *none* of Ray's claims seriously, or taking them as diametrically opposed to claims Nabokov himself would make. Other, more astute critics have realized that, as Julia Bader puts it, "Nabokov does not simply endorse the obverse of John Ray's opinions" (65).

Readers cannot safely assume that all of Ray's claims—such as that *Lolita* is "a tragic tale" leading to a "moral apotheosis"—are ironic and that all of "Nabokov's" in the afterword—such as that *Lolita* "does not teach . . . anything" (316)—are entirely "sincere." Ray is even capable of understanding that *Lolita* is not only a "case history" but also a "work of art"; he refers to "old-fashioned readers who wish to follow the destinies of the 'real' people behind the 'true' story" (6). The quotation marks around "real" and "true" would seem to be Nabokov's watermarks.

But in spite of these similarities, Ray and Nabokov also suggest glaringly contradictory readings of *Lolita*, especially in regard to the relation between ethics and aesthetics in the text. The didactic claims (so common in eighteenth-century novel prefaces) Ray makes and Nabokov's anti-didactic claims in his afterword (and throughout his paratext) have had a significant effect on interpretations of not only *Lolita* but all of Nabokov's work (as well as of "Vladimir Nabokov" himself).

Few readers—especially those familiar with Nabokov's paratext—will be inclined to take seriously Ray's prefatory claim that *Lolita* will teach its readers to be better people through its "ethical impact" (7–8). In the afterword, Nabokov specifically counters some of his "creature" Ray's moral(istic) claims. Nabokov writes: "I am neither a reader nor a writer of didactic fiction, and, despite John Ray's assertion, *Lolita* has no moral in tow" (316). Ray notes the "general lesson" that "lurks" in "this poignant personal study" (7), while Nabokov writes of his "loathing of generalizations devised by literary mythists and sociologists" (316). And "John Ray, Jr., Ph.D." *is* a social scientist.

Those reading *Lolita* after having read any of Nabokov's paratextual statements (e.g., in interviews) or even having heard about his or *Lolita*'s reputation will be inclined to laugh at Ray's moral claims and believe Nabokov's dismissal, in *Lolita*'s afterword as elsewhere, of any general lessons or moral messages to be found in his fiction. After all, Nabokov said in a 1962 interview, "I have no social purpose, no moral message; I've no general ideas to exploit" (*Strong Opinions* 16). And he writes in his introduction to *Bend Sinister* that he is not "a didacticist" (vi). Many reviewers and critics writing about Nabokov's work have supported their assertion of the dominance of aesthetic concerns over ethical, political, or even "human" concerns in his fiction by quoting just such paratextual statements.

To consider the ethics of or in *Lolita*, readers must make their way through not only the rhetorical thickets of Ray's foreword and, later, Nabokov's afterword but through Humbert's narrative. Perhaps Ray's foreword prepares us to be properly suspicious readers of Humbert's "Lolita," warily interpreting his scattered claims of deep regret or the final scene in which, while listening to playing children's voices drifting up from a valley, he states, "I knew that the hopelessly poignant thing was not Lolita's absence from my side, but the absence of her voice from that concord" (310).[17] Although in this oft-quoted passage Humbert acknowledges that the absence of Lolita's voice from this chorus of children is "hopelessly poignant," he does not state directly his responsibility for that absence. Here as elsewhere in his "memoir," Humbert, like a forensic orator delivering an exordium (and like Nabokov as both fictional prefator and author-prefator), has created an ethos and manipulated his audience (in Humbert's case, both literally and figuratively his jury) through his rhetoric.

Critics still debate whether or not Humbert, whom Nabokov refers to as his "vain and cruel . . . eidolon" (*Strong Opinions* 94), is genuinely repentant and "becomes" moral within the fictional world of the novel. So, although Ray tells us in the foreword that *Lolita* has a moral and "Nabokov" tells us in the afterword that it does not, readers cannot simply dismiss what Ray says and accept as authoritative what Nabokov says in this or any other paratext. For example, Nabokov writes in a letter to a fellow Slavicist that he "never meant to deny the moral impact of art which is certainly inherent in every genuine work of art," but only to criticize "the deliberate moralizing which to me kills every vestige of art in a work" (*Selected Letters* 56).

Even Nabokov's famous claim in *Lolita*'s afterword that "a work of fiction exists only insofar as it affords me what I shall bluntly call aesthetic bliss" is far more ambiguous than many critics have assumed.

Nabokov defines "aesthetic bliss" as "a sense of being somehow, somewhere, connected with other states of being where art (curiosity, tenderness, kindness, ecstasy) is the norm" (316–17). This equation of art with tenderness and kindness, especially, seems to bring a moral or ethical dimension to Nabokov's aesthetic. And Nabokov's paratextual statements condemning Humbert's narcissistic use and abuse of Lolita suggest an ethical stance. Much of Nabokov's fiction, including *Lolita*, does interrogate ethical questions even if it doesn't provide explicit ethical "messages."

Nabokov's paratextual rhetoric is often contradictory on the relations between ethics and aesthetics as well as between politics and art. Although in his paratexts Nabokov often insists on the irrelevance of politics and history to his fiction, he also refers in these same paratexts to such things as Soviet "propaganda" and Lenin's "tyranny" (*Eye* viii), to "idiotic and despicable regimes," to "Fascists and Bolshevists" practicing "tyranny and torture" (*Bend Sinister* vii). Perhaps we should be especially wary of how we interpret paratextual comments by an author who proclaims (in a paratext) "I am not 'sincere'" and refers (perhaps ironically) to "the fatal fatuity of my explications in this Foreword" (*Bend Sinister* vii). Only well after Nabokov's death did critics begin to analyze political and ideological subtexts in his fiction— for example, in Linda Kauffman's feminist analysis of *Lolita* and in David Larmour's recent edited collection *Discourse and Ideology in Nabokov's Prose*. Should the very frequency and intensity of Nabokov's paratextual claims that readers should not look for—or at—ethical, political, or psychoanalytic dimensions of his fiction have suggested to readers and critics that "the author" did protest too much?

Lanser notes "the potential for irony, masking or play at the extrafictional level," although she feels this does not negate the authority of the extrafictional voice, which she insists "must be treated as we treat a historical author rather than as we treat a fictional character" (128–29). However, the "Nabokov" we encounter in his prefaces and other paratextual appearances is no less, and only differently, a fictional construct than are John Ray, Charles Kinbote, or Humbert Humbert.

The existence of a preface at the entrance to a novel problematizes the time and experience of that novel's "beginning" and the reader's experience of the novel "itself." If, as in the case of *Lolita*, a novel not only has a "preludial" but also a "postludial" paratext (Genette 161), the author has even more opportunity to manipulate readers' interpretations of the novel as they both enter and later exit the text. Although readers' expectations of a text they are about to begin reading are shaped by a host of extratextual and paratextual elements that precede their picking up the book—such as knowledge of the author's other works or biography and of the historical, social, and cultural contexts in which the work was written—few such elements have as much immediate power to shape the reading experience as a preface or afterword that is part of the physical text itself. *Lolita*, with its two liminal texts, provides a rare opportunity to examine the dialogic relations in narrative between the fictional and extrafictional, the textual and paratextual, and, most importantly, between authors (implied, real, or "real") and their readers.

Notes

1. I focus here on prefaces written by authors of novels. I use the term *prefaces* to include prologues, forewords, and other similar texts.
2. For further discussion of the origins of novel prefaces in classical oratory and of common rhetorical strategies in prefaces, see Edelstein and Genette.
3. In the rare discussions of such textual elements as prefaces, recent narrative theorists and critics are much more likely to cite and apply Genette on the "paratext" than Lanser on the "extrafictional" and "extratextual."
4. Print, audiovisual, and Internet interviews with and appearances by authors have become increasingly common over the last century and deserve further study.
5. Lanser also notes the influence of author's name, book title, chapter titles, etc., on readers' textual expectations (124–25).
6. See Kauffman for an influential feminist analysis of *Lolita*.
7. Genette similarly refers to the "*authorial*, or *allographic*, preface" (178–79) and to the "fictive" preface.
8. All further references in the text to *Lolita* will be to the 1958 Putnam edition.

9. As McHale notes, postmodernist authors like Nabokov are apt to insert themselves into their texts, both "as the vehicle of autobiographical *fact* within the projected fictional world; and as the *maker* of that world, visibly occupying an ontological level superior to it" (202).
10. Nabokov wrote forewords (his most frequently used term) or introductions to works other than his novels: collections of short stories, a play, his autobiographical *Speak, Memory*, his translation of *Eugene Onegin*, etc. Occasionally, other types of prefatory matter (e.g., epigraphs) appear in his novels.
11. The degree to which even the integral prefaces/prefators are involved in the novel's action varies. Charles Kinbote, the "editor" who writes the foreword to *Pale Fire*, plays a major (in fact, *the* major) role in the total text of *Pale Fire*, which is ostensibly an edited and annotated version of John Shade's poem "Pale Fire." John Ray Jr. does not play a role in the primary narrative of *Lolita* (although the cousin who gave him Humbert's memoir to edit is mentioned once or twice in the novel).
12. See Boyd for a detailed discussion of the composition, publication history, and reception of *Lolita*.
13. Genette, too, considers the "postface" as a "variety of preface" since they share many features (161). See Edelstein for further analysis of prefatory strategies employed in *Lolita*'s foreword and afterword.
14. See, e.g., Nelson and Davis.
15. See, e.g., Mylne (esp. 71–76) on the gullibility of some eighteenth-century French readers of novels, and Davis on early English novel readers.
16. See, e.g., Frosch's fine analysis of parody in *Lolita*.
17. Tamir-Ghez effectively analyzes Humbert's rhetoric of repentance.

Works Cited

Appel, Alfred, Jr. "Notes." *The Annotated Lolita*. By Vladimir Nabokov. New York: McGraw-Hill, 1970. 321–441.

Aristotle. *The Rhetoric and The Poetics of Aristotle*. Trans. W. Rhys Roberts. New York: Modern Library, 1954. 1–218.

Bader, Julia. *Crystal Land: Artifice in Nabokov's English Novels*. Berkeley: University of California Press, 1972.

Booth, Wayne. *Critical Understanding: The Powers and Limits of Pluralism*. Chicago: University of Chicago Press, 1979.

———. *The Rhetoric of Fiction*. Chicago: University of Chicago Press, 1961.

Boyd, Brian. *Vladimir Nabokov: The American Years*. Princeton: Princeton University Press, 1991.
Cicero. *De Inventione*. Trans. H. M. Hubbell. Loeb Classical Library. Cambridge: Harvard University Press, 1960.
Davis, Lennard J. *Factual Fictions: The Origins of the English Novel*. New York: Columbia University Press, 1983.
Edelstein, Marilyn Joan. "At the Threshold of the Text: The Rhetoric of Prefaces to Novels." Diss. SUNY at Buffalo, 1984.
Field, Andrew. *Nabokov: His Life in Art; A Critical Narrative*. Boston: Little, Brown, 1967.
Frosch, Thomas. "Parody and Authenticity in *Lolita*." *Nabokov's Fifth Arc: Nabokov and Others on His Life's Work*. Ed. J. E. Rivers and Charles Nicol. Austin: University of Texas Press, 1982. 171–87.
Genette, Gerard. *Paratexts: Thresholds of Interpretation*. Trans. Jane E. Lewin. Cambridge: Cambridge University Press, 1997. Trans. of *Seuils*. Paris: Editions du Seuils, 1987.
Green, Geoffrey. *Freud and Nabokov*. Lincoln: University of Nebraska Press, 1988.
Kauffman, Linda. "Framing Lolita: Is There a Woman in the Text?" *Refiguring the Father: New Feminist Readings of Patriarchy*. Ed. Patricia Yaeger and Beth Kowaleski-Wallace. Carbondale: Southern Illinois University Press, 1989. 131–52.
Lanser, Susan Sniader. *The Narrative Act: Point of View in Prose Fiction*. Princeton: Princeton University Press, 1981.
Larmour, David H. J., ed. *Discourse and Ideology in Nabokov's Prose*. New York: Routledge, 2002.
McHale, Brian. *Postmodernist Fiction*. New York: Methuen, 1987.
Morton, Donald E. *Vladimir Nabokov*. New York: Ungar, 1974.
Mylne, Vivienne. *The Eighteenth-Century French Novel: Techniques of Illusion*. Manchester: Manchester University Press, 1965.
Nabokov, Vladimir. *Bend Sinister*. 1947. New York: McGraw-Hill, 1974.
———. *The Eye*. 1965. Trans. Dmitri Nabokov and Vladimir Nabokov. New York: Pocket Books, 1967.
———. *Glory*. Trans. Dmitri Nabokov and Vladimir Nabokov. New York: McGraw-Hill, 1971.
———. *King, Queen, Knave*. Trans. Dmitri Nabokov and Vladimir Nabokov. Greenwich: Fawcett Crest, 1969.
———. *Lolita*. 1955. New York: Putnam, 1958.
———. *Pale Fire*. New York: Putnam, 1962.

———. *Strong Opinions*. New York: McGraw-Hill, 1973.
———. *Vladimir Nabokov: Selected Letters, 1940–1977*. Ed. Dmitri Nabokov and Matthew J. Bruccoli. San Diego: Harcourt, 1989.
Nelson, William. *Fact or Fiction: The Dilemma of the Renaissance Storyteller*. Cambridge: Harvard University Press, 1973.
Peterson, Dale. "Nabokov's *Invitation*: Literature as Execution." *PMLA* 96 (1981): 824–36.
Shute, Jennifer P. "Nabokov and Freud: The Play of Power." *Modern Fiction Studies* 30 (1984): 637–50.
Stegner, Page. *Escape into Aesthetics: The Art of Vladimir Nabokov*. New York: Dial, 1966.
Tamir-Ghez, Nomi. "The Art of Persuasion in Nabokov's *Lolita*." *Poetics Today* 1.1–2 (1979): 65–83.

3

Stories, Wars, and Emotions
The Absoluteness of Narrative Beginnings

PATRICK COLM HOGAN

It has been a commonplace since at least Homi Bhabha's famous collection that nation and narration are intertwined. Nationhood, everyone now tells us, is inseparable from storytelling. The problem with this claim is that it is often obscure. To take a prominent instance, it is difficult to say just how Bhabha himself conceives of the relation. On the other hand, when writers do make clear what they have in mind, the result is often banal. Indeed, in these analyses, "narrative" often seems to encompass virtually every coherent causal sequence with human agents. Is it consequential that we do not have a sense of nationalism without a sense of causality and human action? A claim is consequential only if there is some competing theory that is contradicted by the claim. As far as I am aware there has never been a theory of nationalism that does not already acknowledge the importance of causal sequence and human action.

It does, of course, happen that writers on nation and narration consider stories in a narrower sense. But the implications of these studies are also unclear. For example, Monroe, Hankin, and Van Vechten ask how Serbian identity came to displace all other possibilities and lead to murder in Yugoslavia. They go on to specify their quandary in narrative terms, asking, "What stories were in most frequent public circulation, and how might these have precipitated violence?" (439). It is undoubtedly true that our behavior is influenced by stories. But it is influenced by many other things as well, including images, slogans, formal political arguments, ordinary conversations, scientific reports.

Stories, Wars, and Emotions   45

The important theoretical issue is whether there is some nationalist function that is specific to narrative. In a related way, Simon During sees narratives as producing models for behavior (144). This too is reasonable, but it too involves no clear theoretical implications regarding narrative per se. Similar problems arise in studies treating narrative and other political concerns. For example, the essays in Dennis Mumby's collection *Narrative and Social Control* (1993) help to explain such topics as the operation of conformity in the workplace and the social communication of racist belief, but they do not appear to have significant theoretical consequences for the relation between narrative as such (its particular forms, structural principles, etc.) and politics or social relations.

The problem I am pointing to has not gone unremarked. For instance, John Breuilly has outlined some main tendencies in narrative accounts of nationalism. He concludes his discussion by stating that "narrative must be theorized in order to provide an intelligible account of what is happening, in order for the reader to see why nationalism and nation-state formation (but not necessarily every nationalism and every conceivable nation-state formation) are such pervasive features of modernity" (158). Whether or not one agrees with Breuilly's own treatment of nationalism and its relation to modernity, his critical attitude toward narrative accounts of nationalism seems well justified.

And yet, I believe there is something extremely important in the narrative analysis of political issues. In other words, narrative is not only a matter of personal enjoyment and interest; it is deeply consequential for our social and political lives. In particular, I believe that nationalism is crucially linked with storytelling in a nontrivial sense. The development, organization, and specification of nationalist feeling and action are bound up with narrative structure, both in its general or schematic form and in its most prototypical specifications. This link becomes particularly urgent when we recognize the close relation between narrative and emotion. In each case, the emplotment of nationalism is inseparable from our emotional response, thus our motivations for action. Indeed, I would go so far as to say that nationalism cannot be understood in separation from narrative and that narrative cannot be understood in separation from our emotion systems.

In the following pages, I will argue that the human emotion system generates distinctive features of narrative structures, specifically narrative beginnings, and that these structures, in turn, guide our understanding of important social and political phenomena. Since I obviously cannot discuss all relevant social and political phenomena, I will focus on one, one that is, arguably, the most consequential of all nationalist actions and events—war. More precisely, I will begin by considering what is peculiar about the usual nationalist emplotment of war as this defines the beginning of conflict. I will then consider the ways in which this emplotment results from the general features of our emotion system—specifically, the ways in which our emotion system leads us to attribute and understand causal responsibility.

The Origin of the Conflict

What gave rise to the recent "War on Terror"? If you ask most Americans, I imagine you will be told "the terrorist attacks on September 11." What gave rise to the war in Afghanistan? Perhaps you will be told the same thing, or perhaps that the Taliban supported al Qaeda, the group responsible for September 11. What gave rise to the war in Iraq? Again, September 11 is a likely response, supplemented by Saddam Hussein's links with al Qaeda, and, of course, his weapons of mass destruction.

Beyond empirical issues of truth and falsity, several things are curious about the preceding questions and responses.[1] Perhaps most significantly, they assume absolute and, in effect, singular origins for wars. This is curious, since it is not clear what this would mean in causal terms. Causal sequences do not begin from nothing. They are multiple and continuous. To say that the World Trade Center bombings gave rise to the recent wars is, implicitly, to suggest that these wars did not develop out of preceding U.S. policies. It also involves treating the bombings themselves as if they were uncaused. In fact, al Qaeda articulated several reasons for the bombings. Bin Laden argued that the United States has been responsible for numerous crimes against Muslims, including the devastation of Iraq, the support of corrupt dictatorships in the Muslim world, and the underwriting of Israeli imperialism (see, e.g., the interview by Hamid Mir). Consider Israel further. Supporters of bin Laden are likely to see Israeli imperialism as an absolute origin,[2] but Israeli policies derive from many sources, shaped by a continuous history. One element that went into the formation of Israel was, of course, the Holocaust. This too is not without a history, including the devastation of Germany during and after World War I. In short, none of these cases really has a beginning. Any event results from the confluence of many earlier events. Yet, we assume that there is an isolable point of origin.

I suspect that, as I was outlining these causal histories, some readers may have worried that I was justifying heinous acts; indeed, opponents of the wars in Afghanistan and Iraq faced this objection repeatedly. But, of course, to say that a violent act has an historical explanation is not to say that it is justified. Indeed, that is part of the point. The continuity and complexity of history justify violent acts only in rare cases, and then only partially.

This leads us to a second curious feature of the preceding questions and answers. The assumption of an absolute and singular origin is widely taken to imply a particular moral evaluation. Specifically, in the case of destructive events, the initiating action is commonly taken to define who is morally culpable *for all subsequent events*; thus it assumes a sort of absolute moral culpability. This idea is strange. First, it presupposes that the situation prior to the initiating act was just or at least normal (i.e., a form of moral ordinariness undisturbed by large injustices). We form our sense of moral normalcy in the same way that we form our sense of causal or any other sort of normalcy. We form a prototype (roughly, a standard case) by weighted averaging over a set of instances. For example, we form our prototype for a bird by averaging over instances of birds—which is why our prototypical bird is close to a robin and not so close to an ostrich.[3] Once we have defined moral normalcy by way of prototypes, we judge moral deviation relative to those prototypes.

In the case of morality, prototype formation is almost certainly related to the triggering of emotion as well. Emotions are crucial because, here and elsewhere, they provide the motivational force for action. We do not set out to maintain or change a situation based solely on abstract evaluation. We act only when we are moved to do so. We are moved specifically by emotion. As Zajonc explains, "cognitions of themselves are incapable of triggering an instrumental process, unless they first generate an emotion that mobilizes a motivational state capable of recruiting action" (47). As writers such as Nussbaum have emphasized, emotions are crucial to ethical thought and action in particular, most obviously through compassion. Compassion is enabled by the fact that we have spontaneous empathic tendencies, derived in part from the "mirror neurons" in the brain (see Brothers 78). These tendencies help guide our moral judgments in the case of suffering.[4] Like other emotions, however, our empathic responses tend to decrease with habituation. This helps to explain why it is very easy for a society to drift toward repeated military aggression or toward other morally objectionable practices of corruption and cruelty. For example, when a practice such as torture is rigorously outlawed, we are unlikely to consider it morally normal, as it will not form part of our prototype for moral normalcy. Moreover, in these circumstances we are more likely to experience empathic pain at the thought of someone subjected to torture. However, once a society begins to practice torture, people begin to shift their sense of moral normalcy. The averaging of their experiences alters their moral prototypes, and they become emotionally habituated to the thought of the pain suffered by victims of, say, electrical shocks or near drowning.[5] This is one reason why it is crucial to stop such practices (not only torture, but military aggression, violation of the laws of war, etc.) early on. They very quickly become normalized, which makes them far more difficult to dislodge. Moreover, they are likely to have consequences throughout the social system (e.g., the habituation to the suffering of torture victims is likely to facilitate a much broader acceptance of cruelty). These tendencies are systematically worsened by the attribution of absolute moral culpability. Such attribution inhibits our inclination to imagine the experience of out-group members and thus inhibits our spontaneous empathic responses even without habituation.

Finally, the attribution of absolute moral culpability also presupposes that the (putatively) initiating act was a free and purely immoral choice, while the response was, in some sense, not free, but compelled by the initiating act. Thus the apparent immorality of the response does not taint the group responding, but accrues to the immorality of the initiating act. Consider again the idea that the bombings of September 11 gave rise to the war in Afghanistan. Those who accept this view are likely to assume that the pre–September 11 condition of, say, Iraq and Palestine was just or at least morally normal. They are also likely to assume that the September 11 bombings were a purely free and evil act, thus unaffected by preceding conditions. However, since the bombings were not just or morally normal, they compelled a violent response from the United States. In consequence, any suffering in Afghanistan is to be blamed on al Qaeda and their allies, not on the government actually dropping the bombs.

Of course, the problems we have been considering are not simply curious features of discourse about war; they are narrative features.[6] They suggest that, in treating war, we do not engage in strict causal analysis; rather, we tell stories. Stories certainly incorporate causal relations, but they do so in particular, cognitively biased ways. In technical terms, stories select, segment, and structure causal sequences.[7] One important result of this is that stories involve, as Aristotle put it, a beginning, a middle, and an end. Aristotle's point seems trivial, but the feeling of triviality fades as soon as one recognizes that causality in the real world does not involve such components at all. Stories only have a beginning, a middle, and an end because, when we tell stories or think in terms of stories, our minds pluck out causal sequences from the complex of events (selection), bound those sequences (segmentation), and bring them into comprehensible relations with one another (structuration).

Emotional Physics: How We Understand Causes

To understand stories, then, we need to consider causality, not in itself (as we do in natural science), but as it is spontaneously construed by the human mind. As writers such as Ed Tan have suggested, our response to stories is animated, first of all, by interest. Only some aspects of the world excite our interest and thus draw our attentional focus. How does this occur? We have a set of prototypes that guide our judgments of and expectations about what we experience. We understand and evaluate the world, first of all, in terms of the normalcy defined by these prototypes. Commonly, our attentional focus is drawn to properties of events or situations that violate these prototypes. We do not pay much attention if Jones is wearing a wristwatch on his wrist, but we are more likely to take note if he is wearing one on his ankle. On the other hand, our interest in difference alone may fade quickly. Interest is intensified and sustained by emotional arousal. If someone is wearing an unusual T-shirt I am likely to notice, but without further emotional involvement I am unlikely to keep the T-shirt active in working memory or to keep recalling it much past the initial perception. I am more likely to sustain interest if I find the shirt funny, angering, or embarrassing. This results from the close relation between emotion and attention circuits in the brain (see Adolphs and Damasio 32–33).

Emotional arousal not only sustains interest in one's environment but also focuses that interest; specifically, emotional arousal stimulates our concern to isolate its cause. For example, if I feel fear, I need to understand what has triggered the fear so that I can run away from it. It may seem that we just know what has caused an emotion, but this is not true. We need to infer the causes of our own emotions in more or less the same way that some third person would have to infer them (see Nisbett and Ross 226–27). Moreover, we are often mistaken in our attributions.

There are many empirical studies of this phenomenon. For example, research indicates that our general emotional state will vary with such things as the repetition of an experience (see Zajonc 55) or the day of the week. However, we are likely to attribute our feelings to more perceptually and mnemonically salient objects. As Clore and Ortony explain, "people tend to experience their affective feelings as reactions to whatever happens to be in focus at the time" (27). As Zajonc expresses the point, "If the person is unable to specify either the origin or the target of affect he or she is experiencing, then this affect can attach itself to anything that is present at the moment" (48).

Of course, this is not to say that our attributions are purely random. If I am sad, I am unlikely to blame my desk or the fact that my nose itches. Two factors contribute crucially to such causal attribution. Neither is a matter of abstract, rational inference; rather, both are bound up with the operation of our emotion systems. The first factor is perceptual. We have innate perceptual sensitivities to particular features of our environment—certain sounds, spatial relations, types of motion (or motion in general, as opposed to immobility), and so forth. These innate sensitivities are most often, perhaps always, potential emotion triggers or components of such emotion triggers. As Damasio explains, "We are wired to respond with an emotion, in preorganized fashion, when certain features of stimuli in the world or in our bodies are perceived" (131). However, even when such features are not the cause of a given emotion, our innate sensitivity to these features gives them prominence in causal attribution.

The second factor is a matter of memories, specifically emotion-congruent memories, both episodic and semantic. When we experience anxiety in a current situation, that activates memories of anxiety in earlier situations. Common properties of the current and former situations (e.g., the presence of the same person) become prominent, defining likely candidates for causal attribution. A current experience also activates prototypes of emotion causation from semantic memory. These guide our causal attributions as well.

A common example is attributing one's emotional excitation to a romantic partner when the arousal results from more diffuse somatic and environmental factors. As Gilbert and Wilson point out, citing empirical research on the topic, people "may mistakenly believe that a person is attractive when, in fact, their pounding pulse is being caused by the swaying of a suspension bridge" (183). A romantic partner is a likely candidate for causal attribution, and misattribution, for perceptual reasons (most obviously, the presence of emotion-triggering secondary sexual characteristics), memory-based reasons (due to personal recollections of romantic feelings in the past), and semantic reasons (as a romantic partner is a prototypical cause of emotional arousal).[8]

Simplicity and Feeling

In recent years, cognitivists have emphasized the adaptive function of emotion. For example, Panksepp states that "brain emotive systems were designed through evolutionary selection to respond in prepared ways to certain environmental events" (123). In order for emotion to have an adaptive function, it has to simplify. A crucial adaptive function of emotion is that it usurps rational deliberation. For example, fear causes us to run rather than trying to puzzle out our options, "lost in the byways of . . . calculation" (Damasio 172), as a predator approaches. One important aspect of emotional simplification is valencing. It is a commonplace of emotion research that ambivalent inputs tend to cycle through our emotion circuits, producing a valenced output. The inputs may be partially anger-producing and partially fear-producing, but the output is likely to be anger (with a confrontation response) or fear (with a flight response), not some combination of the two. As Ito and Cacioppo put it, "The affect system has evolved to produce bipolar endpoints because they provide both clear bivalent action tendencies and harmonious and stable subjective experiences" (69).

One aspect of this simplification that is not widely recognized occurs in causal attribution. Just as inputs may bear on different emotions, they may bear on different causes. Just as outputs tend to reduce ambivalence, outputs, it seems, tend to limit causal attributions as well. Anscombe has drawn a useful distinction between the cause of an emotion and the object of an emotion (16; I do not follow Anscombe's specific analysis of this distinction). The cause is what gives rise to an emotion, whereas the object is something toward which we direct the emotion. In these terms, the cause of an emotion may be diffuse and ambivalent, but the object of an emotion is likely to be singular and valenced. The point is related to "the restriction of range of cue utilization" in emotional states (Frijda 121), which enhances our tendency to "act upon, or base . . . judgments upon, easily available information and upon 'representative'—that is, somehow typical—information" (120–21).

Consider a hypothetical example. John has a range of experiences that include enough frustration to cycle through to, roughly, anger. Many of these experiences are minuscule frustrations (e.g., his shoe pinches). The most perceptually and mnemonically salient aspect of John's environment, and one of the most semantically prototypical sources of frustration, is his spouse, Jane. As a result, John blames her for his anger. This is largely true even when John is self-consciously aware that Jane is not to blame for his frustration. Higher cortical processes of inference allow John to understand that Jane is not the relevant cause, but the emotion systems are distinct from these inference systems. The latter may exert inhibitory control over the former, but they are not always fully successful (on the inhibitory operation of the cortex with respect to subcortical emotion systems, see LeDoux 165). This may be due in part to the fact that strong emotions tend to take control of attentional focus. Thus they tend to usurp the very aspects of working memory (in the lateral prefrontal cortex and anterior cingulate cortex [see LeDoux 277 and Damasio 71]) that would otherwise operate to inhibit the emotion systems. Weakness of inhibition seems particularly likely when there is no strong emotional commitment to the inhibition, which is to say when there is no countervailing emotion that pushes attentional focus toward the object's irrelevance (e.g., if John has no strong emotional motivation to see his wife as innocent).

It is worth noting that the same points apply to, for example, Americans who blame Saddam Hussein for the September 11 bombings, with the practical consequences this has for supporting the invasion of Iraq. It is quite possible that many of them know that Hussein was not connected with the bombings; however, media coverage of governmental statements has repeatedly drawn their attentional focus to terrorist threats against the United States and toward Saddam Hussein. This has triggered fear and/or anger responses that are associated with Hussein and thus tend to usurp or limit attentional focus when Hussein is under consideration. Moreover, few Americans have any emotions that would motivate attention to Hussein's innocence in these particular cases. As a result, inhibitory cognitive processes—processes that impede our emotional tendency to take Hussein as the object of fear or anger—are unlikely to be triggered.

In cases such as John and Jane, as well as Saddam Hussein, misattribution is facilitated by another feature of our cognitive architecture. For a particular set of emotions, we tend to attribute causality to intentional agency. Speaking of cognitive functioning more generally, Boyer notes that "it is part of our constant, everyday humdrum cognitive functioning that we interpret all sorts of cues in our environment, not just events but also the way things are, as the result of some agent's actions ... our agency-detection systems are biased toward overdetection" (145). The point applies a fortiori to emotion. Thus this sort of agency attribution is our default tendency for such basic emotions as anger, fear, and gratitude or attachment, which tend to be oriented toward an agent.

A crucial aspect of both emotional response and causal attribution is our assumption that agents have a dispositional attitude toward us. For example, we fear certain animals, and that fear is related to our view that they are disposed to eat us. Indeed, emotional responses seem to rest in part on a preliminary, unself-conscious categorization of agents into benevolent and malevolent.[9] We seem to have a bias toward the former, which may be overcome by familiarity.[10] The evolutionary advantage of this bias is obvious. There is a greater risk in underestimating threats than in underestimating opportunities for aid. Moreover, it is clear that malevolent/benevolent categorizations must initially apply to groups. If we had to rely on learning about individuals (e.g., individual lions or snakes), the selection advantage of the categorization would be lost or at least greatly diminished. Generally, we cannot wait to identify the particular intent of this lion or that snake. Indeed, categorization generally must precede any interaction with a particular object. Once the lion is eyeing me hungrily, it is already too late.

While this tendency seems largely unexceptional in the case of predatory animals, it becomes much more problematic when applied to other people. The function of such categorization is the same in the case of people as it is in the case of lions. However, in the case of lions (as well as blue jays, squirrels, etc.), the division is, first of all, a matter of species. That is obviously not the case with humans. We do not categorize unfamiliar people as benevolent or as malevolent based on identifying their species as human. In the case of humans, then, a subspecies distinction operates to perform an initial sorting into prima facie trustworthy and untrustworthy agents, potential enemies and potential friends. This is what social psychologists refer to as the division between in-groups and out-groups.[11]

Some in-group/out-group divisions are purely the result of

temporary, situational distinctions. These may have great significance in limited contexts. However, the most socially consequential divisions are long-standing. These are divisions that have been stabilized and elaborated through the development of racial, ethnic, religious, or other identity categories—including, of course, national categories. Depending on just how salient a particular identity category is, it may very strongly bias our emotional attitudes and our related moral/causal attributions. (As Herzfeld puts it, "Ethnic and national terms are moral terms in that they imply a qualitative differentiation between insiders and outsiders" [43].) In some cases, the bias may be so strong that it resists the familiarity effect. Oatley reports a disturbing experiment in which subjects were shown photographs of people from different racial backgrounds. Their emotional responses to the pictures were monitored using neuroimaging. Oatley summarizes the results, explaining that the familiarity effect operated for whites with respect to white faces and for blacks with respect to black faces, but not across races. "Whereas the faces of one's own ethnic group become less threatening with repeated viewing," Oatley explains, "those of another group may remain threatening" (73). One result is that our emotion system not only simplifies causal attribution but tends to cluster putative causes together into bundles of benevolence and malevolence, and it frequently relies on identity categories when it does the bundling.

Back to the Beginning

We can now give some explanatory account of story structure and our causally inadequate understanding of war. Our emotion system leads us to think of causal sequences in terms of stories, not in terms of the complex, interacting systems of natural science. This is because our emotion system creates interest in and focuses attention on perceptually and mnemonically salient, emotionally prototypical objects. It simplifies causal attribution in precisely the way that natural science tries to avoid. (As Boyer explains, "scientific activity is quite 'unnatural' given our cognitive dispositions" [321].) The result of this is an inclination toward the projection of singular and absolute origins.

This selection then combines with our tendency to segment and structure causes in terms of malevolent or benevolent intentions, with some bias toward malevolent categorization. One result is the common specification of narrative beginnings in terms of malevolent actions. We find this to some degree in the standard beginnings for all three cross-cultural narrative prototypes: romantic, heroic, and sacrificial tragicomic.[12] For example, in the standard romantic plot, the lovers are initially separated by an interfering parent. For our purposes, the most important of these three prototypes is the heroic, because our emplotment of wars is precisely an emplotment in terms of the heroic prototype. That prototype manifests the malevolent initiating moment most starkly. Moreover, it synthesizes our tendency to view causality as dispositional (i.e., to understand it in terms of benevolence or malevolence) with our parallel tendency to categorize human agents into in-groups and out-groups. Specifically, it sets out a malevolent attack by an out-group—usually an invasion by a foreign power—as the absolute and singular origin of the central narrative conflict.[13]

Beyond these matters, which bear directly on narrative beginnings, our cognitive dispositions have other consequences for our (narrative) understanding of and response to war as well. One result is that we tend to experience our own emotionally guided response to the "initiating event" as compelled by the event, thus not morally blameworthy. This is particularly true when we have no attentional focus on the harmful consequences of our acts (e.g., enemy casualties that would trigger empathy by way of mirror neurons). In contrast, we tend to see the malevolent actions of the out-group as chosen. They are not caused by prior events, but rather derive from group properties. Thus their actions are not only immoral in themselves but reveal an underlying immorality of shared character (racial, cultural, religious, national, or whatever).

A second result is that arguments against absolute and singular origins for conflict strike us as similar to the arguments of out-groups. Specifically, we tend to categorize such arguments as positing a different origin for conflict rather than as disputing origins per se. Because of the cognitive and affective constraints on our spontaneous causal understandings, we readily assimilate such arguments to justifications for the out-group actions. Simplifying somewhat, we might say that our spontaneous causal attributions give us two obvious alternatives—our own version of causal attribution and a parallel version offered by the out-group. If these are the two options, then any argument that is not of the former sort would seem to be of the latter sort. Of course, in many cases, attacks on antiwar arguments are duplicitous. Politicians know perfectly well that, for example, antiwar protestors are not supporters of Saddam Hussein. However, the point is that the objective illogic of their objections to protestors can be broadly persuasive due to our cognitive propensities.

The preceding point is enhanced by a final consequence of human emotion; specifically, insofar as they involve strong emotions, our spontaneous attributions of causality may remain at least partially impervious to our knowledge about actual causal relations. In other words, our emotion system may continue to spontaneously project a single, absolute, malevolent origin to conflict, even when higher cortical systems have inferred that this is not the case. Again, this results from two complementary factors. First, our emotional responses may usurp working memory, thus the very inferential processes that should inhibit our spontaneous causal attributions. Second, our lack of emotional involvement with alternative analyses (e.g., our lack of emotional involvement with the projected causal agents, thus the out-group) means that these alternative analyses receive no further attentional focus or elaboration and thus are unlikely to engage inhibitory processes.

As noted at the outset, it has become a commonplace in recent years that politics, at least in the form of nationalism, is bound up with narration. The preceding analysis suggests that this is true in a profound sense. It is not simply that nationalism is enhanced by novels and movies; rather, the way in which we think about the nation, particularly in such emotionally intense conditions as war, is inseparable from the ways in which our emotion system guides our causal understanding into stories. The point has, I believe, important consequences for our analysis of nationalism generally and war particularly. For example, one reason war propaganda is so effective is that it produces stories that our emotion system inclines us to accept. In connection with this, we see why responses to war propaganda may be effective when they offer an alternative story but tend to be ineffective when they try to undermine the story form itself. This is true however powerful the empirical support and logical rigor of the antiwar analyses.

An earlier version of this chapter was presented at the Modern Language Association Convention in Philadelphia, Pennsylvania, in December 2004. I am grateful to Brian Richardson for organizing the session, and to members of the audience for their stimulating comments and questions.

Notes

1. Though curious, they not at all unusual. Indeed, the same general features recur everywhere. See, e.g., Angelova on Bulgarian, Serbian, and Rumanian history textbooks (9).
2. Herman makes the same point about the Israeli side, explaining that, "since the occupation and ethnic cleansing are normalized and their results largely suppressed, and the violations of international law ignored, the propaganda system is able to make the causal force in the violence the suicide bombers, who seemingly came out of nowhere in an irrational assault on the peace loving Sharon and Israeli people."
3. For a fuller account of prototypes see Hogan, *Mind* 57–62, 80–98, and citations. The averaging is weighted in that not all instances count equally. Among other things, distinctive instances within some encompassing category count more heavily. For example, within the encompassing category "food," diet foods are distinguished by having fewer calories. As a result, the prototypical diet food has far fewer calories than the average diet food (see Kahneman and Miller 143). Similarly, our prototype for a woman will give greater weight to instances that are more "feminine," thus more different from men, than the average. As a result, our prototypical woman is more feminine than the statistically average woman. Similarly, our prototypical man is more masculine (i.e., more sharply differentiated from women) than the statistically average man. The same point holds for ethnic, religious, national, and other prototypes.
4. On empathy and the cognitive sources of moral development, see, e.g., Blair.
5. On torture in the U.S. "War on Terror" see Hajjar and citations.
6. At a very general level, some of these connections have been recognized

by earlier authors. For example, Bennington remarks generally on "the faith in origins and ends which narration perpetuates" (132). Similarly, Breuilly notes that "the narrative form, with its assumption of a beginning, middle and end, could actually become an important component of the national movement" (157). However, these observations are rarely developed with explanatory adequacy or descriptive thoroughness.

7. On these cognitive processes see Hogan, *Cognitive* 14–17, 38–40.
8. It may seem odd that the emotionally crucial issue initially is the violation of prototypes, while the emotionally crucial issue subsequently is the conformity to prototypes. The difference results from the fact that we are dealing with different sorts of prototypes, which themselves have different relations to emotion. Initially, we respond to a series of experiences with situation prototypes. Those situation prototypes carry with them certain expectations. Our "action readiness" (i.e., what we are prepared to do) is inseparable from those expectations. When there is a deviation from our expectations, that necessarily changes our action readiness. Frijda argues that an emotion is centrally a change in action readiness (5). At the very least, such a change brings with it certain emotion tendencies that themselves refocus our attention. Thus, in the case of situation prototypes, emotions are most commonly triggered by deviations. However, once an emotion is triggered, our attentional focus is shifted to environmental features that are consistent with relevant emotion prototypes. Consistency with these prototypes then serves to sustain or enhance the emotion and the relevant attentional focus.
9. For further discussion see Hogan, *Mind* 254–55.
10. The positive effect of mere familiarity is well attested in psychological research. For example, Zajonc explains that "when a particular stimulus is shown over and over again . . . it gets to be better liked" (35). This is most obviously explained by a categorization bias toward assumed malevolence (or, more generally, danger, for the effect is not confined to agents). If we see something many times and it invariably proves innocuous, this tends to work against a malevolent or threatening categorization. If we assume an initial neutral categorization, the ameliorative effect of familiarity would be more difficult to explain.
11. On the research treating in-groups and out-groups see Hogan, *Culture* 96–100 and citations.
12. On prototypical stories and on the three cross-cultural narrative prototypes see Hogan, *Mind*.
13. There are two narrative strands in the heroic plot; I am addressing only one strand here.

Works Cited

Adolphs, Ralph, and Antonio Damasio. "The Relationship between Affect and Cognition: Fundamental Issues." *Handbook of Affect and Social Cognition*. Ed. Joseph Forgas. Mahwah NJ: Erlbaum, 2001. 27–49.

Angelova, Penka. "Narrative Topoi nationaler Identität: Der Historismus als Erklärungsmuster." *Narrative Konstruktion nationaler Identität*. Ed. Eva Reichmann. St. Ingbert, Germany: Röhrig Universitätsverlag, 2000. 83–106.

Anscombe, G. E. M. *Intention*. 2nd ed. Ithaca: Cornell University Press, 1963.

Bennington, Geoffrey. "Postal Politics and the Institution of the Nation." Bhabha 121–37.

Bhabha, Homi K., ed. *Nation and Narration*. New York: Routledge, 1990.

Blair, R. J. R. "A Cognitive Developmental Approach to Morality: Investigating the Psychopath." *Cognition* 57 (1995): 1–29.

Boyer, Pascal. *Religion Explained: The Evolutionary Origins of Religious Thought*. New York: Basic Books, 2001.

Breuilly, John. "Approaches to Nationalism." *Mapping the Nation*. Ed. Gopal Balakrishnan. London: Verso, 1996. 146–74.

Brothers, Leslie. *Friday's Footprint: How Society Shapes the Human Mind*. Oxford: Oxford University Press, 1997.

Clore, Gerald L., and Andrew Ortony. "Cognition in Emotion: Always, Sometimes, or Never?" *Cognitive Neuroscience of Emotion*. Ed. Richard D. Land and Lynn Nadel with Geoffrey L. Ahern, John J. B. Allen, Alfred W. Kaszniak, Steven Z. Rapcsak, and Gary E. Schwartz. Oxford: Oxford University Press, 2000. 24–61.

Damasio, Antonio R. *Descartes' Error: Emotion, Reason, and the Human Brain*. New York: Avon, 1994.

During, Simon. "Literature—Nationalism's Other? The Case for Revision." Bhabha 138–53.

Frijda, Nico. *The Emotions*. Cambridge and Paris: Cambridge University Press and Editions de la Maison des Sciences de l'Homme, 1986.

Gilbert, Daniel T., and Timothy D. Wilson. "Miswanting: Some Problems in the Forecasting of Future Affective States." *Feeling and Thinking: The Role of Affect in Social Cognition*. Ed. Joseph P. Forgas. Cambridge: Cambridge University Press and Paris: Editions de la Maison des Sciences de l'Homme, 2000. 178–97.

Hajjar, Lisa. "In the Penal Colony." *Nation* 7 Feb. 2005.

Herman, Edward S. "Road Map to Sustainable Ethnic Cleansing." *Znet* 5 July 2003. http://zmag.org.

Herzfeld, Michael. *Cultural Intimacy: Social Poetics in the Nation-State.* New York: Routledge, 1997.

Hogan, Patrick Colm. *Cognitive Science, Literature, and the Arts: A Guide for Humanists.* New York: Routledge, 2003.

———. *The Culture of Conformism: Understanding Social Consent.* Durham NC: Duke University Press, 2001.

———. *The Mind and Its Stories: Narrative Universals and Human Emotion.* Cambridge and Paris: Cambridge University Press and Editions de la Maison des Sciences de l'Homme, 2003.

Ito, Tiffany, and John Cacioppo. "Affect and Attitudes: A Social Neuroscience Approach." *Handbook of Affect and Social Cognition.* Ed. Joseph Forgas. Mahwah NJ: Erlbaum, 2001. 50–74.

Kahneman, Daniel, and Dale T. Miller. "Norm Theory: Comparing Reality to Its Alternatives." *Psychological Review* 93.2 (1986): 136–53.

LeDoux, Joseph. *The Emotional Brain: The Mysterious Underpinnings of Emotional Life.* New York: Touchstone, 1996.

Mir, Hamid. "Osama Claims He Has Nukes: If US Uses N-Arms It Will Get Same Response" (interview with Osama Bin Laden). *Dawn* 10 Nov. 2001. http://dawn.com.

Monroe, Kristen Renwick, James Hankin, and Renée Bukovchik Van Vechten. "The Psychological Foundations of Identity Politics." *Annual Review of Political Science* 3 (2000): 419–47.

Mumby, Dennis K., ed. *Narrative and Social Control: Critical Perspectives.* Newbury Park CA: Sage, 1993.

Nisbett, Richard, and Lee Ross. *Human Inference: Strategies and Shortcomings of Social Judgment.* Englewood Cliffs NJ: Prentice-Hall, 1980.

Nussbaum, Martha C. *Upheavals of Thought: The Intelligence of Emotions.* Cambridge: Cambridge University Press, 2001.

Oatley, Keith. *Emotions: A Brief History.* Malden MA: Blackwell, 2004.

Panksepp, Jaak. *Affective Neuroscience: The Foundations of Human and Animal Emotions.* Oxford: Oxford University Press, 1998.

Tan, Ed S. *Emotion and the Structure of Narrative Film: Film as an Emotion Machine.* Trans. Barbara Fasting. Mahwah NJ: Erlbaum, 1996.

Zajonc, Robert B. "Feeling and Thinking: Closing the Debate Over the Independence of Affect." *Feeling and Thinking: The Role of Affect in Social Cognition*. Ed. Joseph P. Forgas. Cambridge: Cambridge University Press and Paris: Editions de la Maison des Sciences de l'Homme, 2000. 31–58.

4

September 1939 Beginnings, Historical Narrative, and the Outbreak of World War II

PHILIPPE CARRARD

As James Phelan has observed in his overview of the scholarship bearing on how novels open and close, "beginnings have received less attention from theorists than endings" (97). Phelan restricts his presentation to works that deal with fiction, but his remark is even more relevant to the type of narrative that Gérard Genette calls "factual" (67): texts such as histories, biographies, and newspaper reports, that is, texts that recount real events and claim to recount them as they actually occurred. Indeed, with a few exceptions (to which I will return later), theorists have not investigated beginnings in factual narratives. Like Hayden White, they have examined how those narratives are organized, but mostly they have scrutinized endings, arguing that even when a story is made of real events and situations, the way it closes is especially significant; for it is the last stage in the plot that confers meaning upon that story, making it—to use White's categories—into a tragedy, a comedy, a romance, or a satire.

My purpose is to fill part of this void by looking at the way factual narratives get started. Limiting my inquiry to historical studies, I will review three of the questions that such studies are raising, namely: On what strategies do historians rely in order to launch their accounts? Are beginnings especially arbitrary in historical writing? And do historians reflect on that arbitrariness, as novelists occasionally do? I take my examples from histories of World War II, more precisely, in histories of that war that are structured as narratives. For not all historical studies tell stories. In this instance, some works about World War II follow specific themes (e.g., Marc Ferro's *Questions sur la IIe Guerre mondiale*) or develop an argument (e.g., Richard Overy's *Why the Allies Won*). They, as a result, do not unfold along temporal lines, posing problems that are different from the ones I plan to take up here.

Literary theorists disagree as to what constitutes a novel's actual "beginning." Some (e.g., Verrier) locate this unit in the paratext; others (e.g., Gollut and Zufferey), in the first sentence of the text; others still (e.g., Sternberg), in an "exposition" that can be delayed or distributed throughout the work. By "beginning" I mean here the first lines or paragraphs of the text itself. However, because historical studies often include a paratext that cannot be ignored, I will mention the presence of such entities as the preface, the foreword, and the introduction when they play a role in the narrative the historian is conducting.

The Modalities of Historical Beginnings

The distinction story-discourse, under this form or another (e.g., *fabula-syuzhet*), has been standard in narratology. Theorists have recently challenged its value, arguing that the dichotomy between the chronological order of the events and the actual disposition of those events in the narrative does not account for the specificity of many modern and postmodern texts, which are characterized by their "fuzzy temporality" (Herman 212). My assumption is that the opposition story-discourse is still useful to describe historical narratives but that it must be supplemented with a third component, which Dorrit Cohn calls "reference" (112): the documentary apparatus that constitutes the base for such narratives, warranting their claim to represent a real past. From the standpoint of narrative theory, "reference" differs from "story" in that it lies outside the text. The Treaty of Versailles and the people who signed it, for example, are constituents in studies of World War I; but they also exist in the archives, where the treaty can be consulted and the identity of the politicians who were involved in the negotiations can also be verified. The love letters sent by Emma Bovary, on the other hand, figure only in the narrative devised by Flaubert; they are not reproductions of documents, and Emma herself has a textual, rather than a referential, existence. (While Flaubert supposedly based his narrative on an actual case, he never made the historian's claim to recount that case "as it actually occurred.") As far as time is concerned, the documentary apparatus of historiography provides stable chronologies, in which events have been ordered according to the available evidence. To return to the Treaty of Versailles: records establish that it was signed after the end of the war, a sequence that historians are not free to modify, although they may elect to organize their discourse differently (e.g., by opening their study of World War I with the signing of the treaty). Looking at a piece of historiography, it is thus possible to assess not just the relations between story time and discourse time (as it is in fiction, where the story can only be reconstructed from the discourse) but also the relations between those two entities and the "reference time" of authorized chronologies. In other words, it is possible to investigate how historians arrange the events they report in relation to the way those events actually unfolded, or, more exactly, in relation to the way the evidence shows that those events unfolded—taking for granted that some episodes cannot be dated with certainty and that the exact time when others occurred is often the subject of controversies among scholars.

Focusing on the beginnings of studies about World War II provides a convenient way of measuring the relations among story time, discourse time, and reference time in historical narrative. Indeed, the chronology of important historical events (e.g., the Holocaust) has been difficult to establish, and specialists still disagree on such crucial points as "the exact timing of Hitler's decision for total destruction of Europe's Jews" (Bergen 40). World War II, by contrast, has a legal, precise "reference beginning": early September 1939, between September 1, when German troops crossed the Polish border, and September 3, when France and England "declared war" on Germany (a performative speech act if there ever was one). By "reference beginning" I thus mean here "the days when the war broke out," or, more specifically, "the days when documents establish that acts of war were committed and the war was officially declared." Scholars, to my knowledge, have not challenged this chronology (e.g., to claim that France "actually" declared war on September 4), although they have conferred different meanings upon this critical period. Leaving issues of interpretation to specialists, and looking at the way historians articulate the relations among the beginning of their discourse, the beginning of their story, and the "reference" beginning of the war, we can observe that histories of the conflict start in accordance with three main models.

In the first model, the study opens ab ovo with a description of the events and situations in which the historian sees the origins of the war. The beginning of the discourse, in this instance, coincides by and large with the beginning of the story, though not with the early September 1939 "reference beginning." That initial description can be found in the paratext. Roger Céré's introduction, for example, recounts briefly the period of the German attempt at "hegemony" (6), which, according to the historian, extended from 1871 to 1945. But the account of the war's origins can also be located at the beginning of the text proper. Winston Churchill's *The Second World War* thus opens with a detailed, 315-page narrative of the period 1919–39, conspicuously titled "From War to War." Similarly, the first volume of the nine-volume study *Das Deutsche Reich und der Zweite Weltkrieg* is devoted to an examination of the "origins and pre-conditions of the German war politics"; over more than seven hundred pages, it dissects such subjects as German ideological struggles, economic crises, and rearmament strategies from the end of the Weimar Republic to the summer of 1939. As these examples show, beginnings ab ovo in histories of World War II can include from a few to several hundred pages and can take us back in time to dates as different as 1871, 1919, and 1932. These large variations point to a problem that is not specific to historiography but which poses itself with special acuteness in this type of narrative: where to start the story? In the case of a period as complex as World War II, how much information should the historian provide in order to explain the far and immediate causes of the conflict? Answers to these questions depend on the nature and scope of the endeavor. In this instance, Céré is limited to 128 pages by the format of a series ("Que sais-je?") that aims at popularization. Churchill and the authors of *Das Deutsche Reich und der Zweite Weltkrieg*, on the other hand, do not have similar restrictions; they can also assume an audience that is more specialized, or at least one that is not looking for quick information. On a different plane, the fact that beginnings ab ovo can take us to various points from 1871 to 1932 shows that "reference" does not have a narrative structure. In other words, the documentary apparatus on which scholars depend reveals what happened and when. But that apparatus does not provide a plot; it is the historian who orders the events he or she has selected, in this instance, who decides at what point in time the story should begin.

In the second model, the study opens in medias res with a narrative of the events of early September 1939. The beginning of the discourse, in this model, does not coincide with the beginning of the story as described above, but with the "reference beginning." The text starts with an account of the invasion of Poland, then of England's and France's declaration of war on Germany. That account can take the form of a summary:

> At the dawn of September 1st 1939, the first units of a powerful German army crossed Germany's Eastern border and entered Poland. Two days later, the governments of Great Britain and France . . . declared themselves to be in a state of war with Germany. (Wright 9)

But the beginning of the narrative can also be "scenic," that is, focused on the activities of a few individuals at a specific time and place:

> August 31, 1939. The night is falling on the woods of Ratibor, in Lower Silesia. . . . Eight men busy themselves near the two trucks that have brought them to this discreet place. Nervous, they get dressed. Their head, Alfred Naujocks, has given them the Polish soldier uniforms that they put on in a hurry. (Montagnon 13)

The historian goes on to tell how the eight men seized the radio station in the German town of Gleiwitz, then, claiming to be Polish, read a proclamation stating that Danzig was a Polish city and Germany was plunging Europe into war. The German press reported the incident on September 1, and Hitler, in a speech that same day, explained that an "intolerable series of border violations" had obliged him to "meet force with force" (14). Whether they take the form of a summary or a scene, these openings in medias res are usually followed by an analepsis that supplies (some of) the antecedents of the conflict.

Thus, Wright's narrative of the German invasion only takes the first five lines in chapter 1 of his study; the rest of that chapter is devoted to an account of the "ten days of intense diplomatic activities" that preceded the outbreak of the war (9). Similarly, Montagnon's report of the staged border incident in Gleiwitz occupies the first page and a half of his work; it is followed by an overview of the military situation in late summer 1939, then—the narrative jumping over time again—by a description of the German attack. Obviously, historians beginning their narrative of the war with an examination of the events of early September 1939 cannot presume that readers know about the background; they must at some point go back in time, though how far they go back and how much information they provide varies depending on the nature of their enterprise.

In the third model, the study opens in medias res with the narrative of an event that preceded the outbreak of the war. In this case, the beginning of the discourse coincides neither with the beginning of the story nor with the "reference beginning." The episode that the text singles out occurred before the outset of the hostilities, during the first months of 1939 or even earlier:

> On April 1, 1939, the world's Press carried the news that Mr Neville Chamberlain's Cabinet, reversing its policy of appeasement and detachment, had pledged Britain to defend Poland against any threats from Germany, with the aim of ensuring peace in Europe. (Liddell Hart 3)

> On January 1, 1939, the apostologic nuncio, as the Dean of the diplomatic Corps, presented his and his colleagues' wishes to the President of the French Republic. In his speech, Mgr Valerio Valeri expressed the hope that the new year would see peace to keep shining over Europe. (Bauer 17)

> During the summer of 1936, thousands of Nazi militants met on the grounds of the Nuremberg stadium, especially built for this ceremony; they cheered a triumphalist speech of their *Führer*, Adolf Hitler, and attended a grandiose parade of the German army. (Kemp 13)

These openings are part of beginnings ab ovo, in which the historian reports an event that he or she regards as significant (the Chamberlain cabinet's policy change) or revealing (the nuncio's speech, of a certain type of wishful thinking; the Nazi parade, of Germany's bellicose attitudes). After this initial anecdote, however, the texts continues with a description that falls under "background"; it does not afford more details about the political turn in London nor the New Year reception in Paris, but contributes data about the Allies' goals when they entered the war (Liddell Hart), the situation in Europe after the Munich agreements (Bauer), and the growth of the dictatorships in the 1930s (Kemp).

Considering these starts from the standpoint of the typologies that literary theorists have worked out to describe beginnings in fictional narrative, a few empty slots are immediately noticeable. Some, of course, could be assumed. Thus, no competent reader would really expect a scholarly study of World War II to begin *in media verba*, with the "emergence of an unknown voice" (Del Lungo 122), as the text does in experimental pieces of fiction such as Robert Pinget's *L'Inquisitoire* or Nathalie Sarraute's *Le Planétarium*. Such beginnings would be incompatible with the epistemological and stylistic requirements of historiography, because the data they supply could not be supported by evidence and the language they use would not conform to the conventions of the "plain style." On the other hand, it is more surprising to observe that no text, in my corpus at least, begins in medias res literally speaking: with a narrative not of the first days of the war but of a subsequent episode, such as the German army's attack on Holland, Belgium, and France, or its surrender in Stalingrad. Similarly, no study (again, in my corpus) begins "with the end," for instance, with the signature of the German capitulation in Berlin, the bombing of Hiroshima, or any other event announcing that the conflict has come (or is coming) to a term. The beginnings that most resemble this model are situated in the paratext. They consist of introductions or forewords in which the historian does not furnish a background to the conflict but rather reflects on the conflict's nature on the basis of information and insights that were not available before 1945 and even later. Yves Durand, Henri Michel, and Jean Quellien, for example, all insist on the fact that World War II (unlike World War I) really deserves the qualifier "World," because it involved so many geographic areas (Quellien 9). They also stress that it could genuinely be called "total," as it had military, economic, and ideological aspects and drew millions of people into it (Durand 21; Michel 5). To be sure, such general considerations do not constitute beginning "with the end," as the discovery of a dead body does in many detective novels. Nevertheless, they launch the discourse with the conclusion of the story, programming a particular type of reception. In this instance, readers are urged to ask not exactly "who done it" (studies in my corpus posit Germany's guilt from the onset) but rather how the war, initially limited to Europe and to a confrontation of a military kind, became "world" and "total."

But What Actually Existed Here before the Big Bang?

The literary theorists who have investigated beginnings have often pointed to their arbitrariness in fictional narrative. Hillis Miller, for example, working from the assumptions of deconstruction, insists that every beginning is grounded in a paradox: a new story must be based on "something solidly present and preexistent, some generative source of authority," but that antecedent foundation "needs in turn some prior foundation, in an infinite regress" (57). The novelist Amos Oz argues along the same lines, though he poses the problem in more concrete terms:

> If we wish to begin a story with the sentence "Gilbert was born in Gedera the day after the storm that uprooted the chinaberry tree and destroyed the fence," we may have to tell about the falling of the chinaberry tree, perhaps about its planting, or we might have to go back to when, from where, and why Gilbert's parents came to Gedera, of all places, and why Gedera was settled, and where the fallen fence was. . . . In short, if the story is to live up to its ideal duty, it must go back at least all the way to the Big Bang. . . . And by the way, what actually existed here before the Big Bang? (9–10)

For both Miller and Oz, therefore, fictional beginnings are most discretionary; cutting in the continuum of time, they open gaps that the most detailed analepses can never entirely fill. Yet the two critics do not draw the same conclusions from this observation, and they assign different tasks to the analysis of literary beginnings. For Miller, always anxious to identify new aporia, the goal of the investigation can only be to expose "the impossibility of beginning," or the way any beginning "occurs over the chasm of its impossibility" (59). For Oz, who as a practicing novelist tends to think in terms of craftsmanship, it is to examine how the author has negotiated the difficulties that come with writing the first lines of a story, what kind of opening "contract" he or she has established with the reader (7).

The problems that characterize beginnings in fictional narrative arguably are compounded in historiography. Indeed, in most cases, historians have to deal with preexisting stories—stories that already have a beginning, or even several alternative beginnings. The arbitrariness of the "cut" they make in order to launch their narrative is thus more obvious than it is in fiction. To return to Oz's example: the author who starts his tale as Oz does ("Gilbert was born in Gedera the day after the storm") is free to provide or not to provide information about the events that preceded Gilbert's birth; he or she is bound only by conventions of coherence, which will dictate whether or not analepses are needed for a correct understanding of the story, and how far back in time such analepses have to take. Historians reporting those same events, however, would have to reckon with the available evidence, and more often than not with already published versions of Gilbert's story. Thus, their decision to begin their narrative where they do and to supply or leave out additional data would not fall under "coherence" exclusively; it could also be measured against documents related to Gedera's history as well as against other scholars' accounts of Gilbert's life that start at a different point in time.

The arbitrariness of historical beginnings is particularly noticeable in narratives of large events such as World War II. Indeed, the war and the period that preceded it have been abundantly documented and have generated numerous studies. The cut that an historian makes to open his or her account of the conflict can thus be assessed with respect to the record and to other cuts made by other scholars, prompting Miller-Oz types of questions. Those questions could first bear on the beginning of the discourse, especially, on the event(s) selected to open the narrative in medias res. To return to some of my examples: If the first units of the German army crossed the Polish border "at the dawn" of September 1, what were these units doing the night before? If the radio station in Gleiwitz was seized by Germans dressed in Polish uniforms, who had devised this operation, and when? And if the apostologic nuncio in Paris expressed wishes for peace on January 1, 1939, was this gesture part of a policy of the Church that had earlier manifestations? But arbitrariness is even more conspicuous in the beginnings that studies of World War II assign to the story, whether through openings ab ovo or through the analepses that generally follow openings in medias res. If, for example, the period of German attempt at hegemony started in 1871, what were German (i.e., Prussian, Bavarian, etc.) politics before that date? If the era 1919–39 must be described in order to account for World War II, how about earlier phases of the clash between Germany and its neighbors? If the ten days that preceded the outbreak of the war were characterized by intensive diplomatic activities, was anything undertaken during the summer of 1939 in order to prevent the conflict? Finally, expecting such questions, have the historians I am considering made their decisions explicit? That is, have they explained or justified why they begin their accounts of the war where they do and not at an earlier (or later) moment?

Arbitrariness and Self-Reflexivity

Historians interested in theory have often deplored their colleagues' lack of self-consciousness—the fact that if those colleagues are usually ready to elaborate about their methods, they seem reluctant to discuss matters of epistemology and especially writing. One of the only scholars to take up the issue of beginnings in historical narratives, Sande Cohen, has thus indicted the first sentence in Peter Gay's study "A Short Political History of the Weimar Republic":

"The Weimar Republic was proclaimed on November 9, 1918, by the Social Democrat Philip Scheidemann." According to Cohen, the problem in this sentence lies with a typical feature of history writing, namely, the pretense to objectivity. The historian proceeds as though he were absent from his report, erasing his "performance" (he does not say "as I hope to prove, the Weimar Republic"); and he posits the existence of the entity "Weimar Republic," ignoring the mediation of language (he does not write "what was *called* the Weimar Republic") (112–13). One could add that Gay makes his narrative begin on the day the new state was born, but that his standpoint is retrospective: Scheidemann proclaimed the "German Republic" on November 9, 1918, but the label "Weimar Republic" was coined later, after the Assembly elected in January 1919 decided to meet in Weimar rather than in Berlin, because conditions in the capital had become too "unpredictable" (Eyck 45, 64). Gay's first sentence, therefore, combines an opening in medias res with a piece of information that was not available when the events occurred; and it includes no comment on that opening, whether on the date chosen (its importance is taken for granted) or on the anachronism of making Scheidemann proclaim a state that had yet to be named.

The historians in my corpus hardly show more self-consciousness than Gay does. Thus, none of the beginnings in medias res I have quoted admits a self-reflexive component, in which the author indicates why the events he or she has selected deserve what Edward Said calls the "status" that their very location confers upon them (50). The only remarks of this type I could identify are found in beginnings ab ovo, for instance, in the opening of Peter Calvocoressi, Guy Wint, and John Pritchard's *Total War:*

> There are two extreme views about the European origins of the Second World War. One is that it was all Hitler's fault. The other is that it was a war in which Hitler, along with a lot of other people, and for much of the same reasons, got involved. Both views stand condemned by their very simplicity. This book supports neither but it has to start somewhere, and it starts with Hitler and the Nazis. (17)

To be sure, the authors do not bother to theorize their position the way Cohen wishes historians would. Instead, they flaunt the arbitrariness of their beginning: since a book "has to start somewhere," their study may start where it does without providing further explanations. The arbitrariness concerns here the beginning of the discourse—the fact that the first section of chapter 1 in the book is titled "Hitler" (and not, say, "Chamberlain")—but it also bears on the beginning of the story, on the fact that the first chronological step in the narrative consists of an analysis of the Nazis' rise to power in the 1930s (and not, say, of the Allies' policies in the 1920s). In this respect, the scholars' offhanded comments could also be taken as bearing on the vexed issue of "origins." For what they show is that historians, when they provide the background they deem to be the necessary for the understanding of the conflict, are not searching for an ultimate foundation, for a beginning in Aristotle's sense of "that which does not itself follow anything by causal necessity, but after which something naturally is or comes to be" (qtd. in Richardson 249). Rather, their goal is to find the best way of "plotting and patterning" their data, of shaping them as an "overall story," as Robert Berkhofer puts it in his analysis of beginnings in histories of the United States (122).

Other scholars are more reluctant than the authors of *Total War* to acknowledge the arbitrariness of their beginnings, and they strive to justify the way they start their accounts. Gerhard Weinberg, for example, opens the introduction to his *A World in Arms* with the following statement:

> Although this book contains a chapter on the background of World War II, it defines the war as beginning in 1939 in Europe. While some have argued that the war was merely a continuation of World War I after a temporary interruption created by the armistice of 1918 . . . such a perspective ignores not only the different origins and nature of the prior conflict but obscures instead of illuminating the special character of the second one. (1)

Weinberg also reflects on the label "World War II" as Cohen does on the label "Weimar Republic." In the first sentence of chapter 1 he writes that when German troops attacked Poland "a terrible conflict began that was quickly called 'The Second World War'" (6). Yet Weinberg does not follow up to ask an interesting historiographic question, namely: when, where, and by whom was the term "World War II" initially coined? Indeed, to state that "World War II" began in September 1939 would constitute the same anachronism as to assert that Scheidemann proclaimed "the Weimar Republic" in November 1918. Or, more precisely, such a statement would inscribe the historian's retrospective standpoint, as it does Gay's in the sentence quoted by Cohen. For the information was not available in 1939, as neither the Germans when they entered Poland, nor the French and the British when they declared war on Germany, were aware that the conflict that had started was to become "World War II."

The historians of the war who take the trouble of clarifying why their story begins where it does, however, often disagree as to the point in time when the conflict initially started. For instance, while Weinberg defines the war as "beginning in 1939 in Europe," Bradley Smith contends that, viewed from the long time span and a global perspective, the war began in the early 1930s in the East. Chapter 1 in his *The War's Long Shadow* is thus titled "China's War," and the first sentence reads:

> Although Westerners tend to think of the start of World War II in terms of 1939 or 1941, China and the world had their first brush with the Second Great War in 1931, when Japanese military forces "peacefully" occupied the north Chinese border province of Manchuria. (21)

True, Smith is careful not to claim that "World War II" started in 1931. He uses the term "the Second Great War," a play on the phrase that was available in the early 1930s: "the Great War." Yet Smith's thesis remains clear: the conflict, however we might call it, cannot be restricted to events that occurred between 1939 and 1945, as it extends upstream to the war in Asia, as well as downstream to the cold war. The specificity of Smith's study, in relation to the works on the war I have quoted so far, thus resides in a displacement that is both temporal *and* spatial. For other historians of the war make their story begin in the 1930s; but Smith is the only one, in my corpus at least, to eschew Eurocentrism by making his story start not just earlier in time than 1939, but (much) farther in space than the Polish border.

This observation brings me to a brief, final remark. The theorists who have concerned themselves with historiography have emphasized that accounts of the past are always open-ended. That is, their endings can always be rewritten, because new evidence will emerge, new questions will be asked, or, more fundamentally, because "earlier events will continue to receive differing descriptions through the relations in which they stand to events later in time than themselves" (Danto 340). But it could also be argued that histories are necessarily, so to speak, open-begun. Indeed, as a result of work in the archives, of a different problematization of the topic under scrutiny, or of a change of lens, events that were described as having started at moment X can be shown to have started earlier, at moment Y, or later, at moment Z. As the preceding analyses should have shown, World War II is a case in point. For some dates, like those referring to the declaration of war, cannot be changed unless research demonstrates that they are wrong; but our vantage point toward such materials is always moving, and our descriptions of the past will have to change accordingly. In this respect, historical beginnings of course differ deeply from fictional beginnings. For anyone, obviously, can rewrite the opening lines of *Madame Bovary*. But one will never have to rewrite them because newly uncovered documents force us to; and, more basically, one will never have to rewrite them because time has elapsed, providing a better understanding of the characters, their actions, and the overall context.

Works Cited

The books about World War II were selected among the studies available at the library of the University of Lausanne, Switzerland, under the Dewey call number 940.53. For the sake of homogeneity, the sample was limited to studies written by Western historians.

Bauer, Eddy. *Histoire controversée de la Deuxième Guerre mondiale*. Monaco: Rombaldi, 1966.

Bergen, Doris L. "The Barbarity of Footnotes: History and the Holocaust." *Teaching the Representation of the Holocaust*. Ed. Marianne Hirsch and Irene Kacandes. New York: MLA, 2004. 37–51.

Berkhofer, Robert F. *Beyond the Great Story: History as Text and Discourse.* Cambridge: Harvard University Press, 1995.
Calvocoressi, Peter, Guy Wint, and John Pritchard. *Total War: The Causes and Courses of the Second World War.* New York: Viking, 1989.
Céré, Roger. *La Seconde Guerre mondiale.* Paris: Presses Universitaires de France, 1947.
Churchill, Winston S. *The Second World War.* Vol. 1, *The Gathering Storm.* London: Cassell, 1948.
Cohen, Sande. *Historical Culture: On the Recoding of an Academic Discipline.* Berkeley: University of California Press, 1986.
Cohn, Dorrit. *The Distinction of Fiction.* Cambridge: Harvard University Press, 1999.
Danto, Arthur. *Narration and Knowledge.* New York: Columbia University Press, 1985.
Deist, Wilhelm, Manfred Messerschmidt, Hans-Erich Volkmann, and Wolfram Wette. *Das Deutsche Reich und der Zweite Weltkrieg.* Stuttgart: Deutsche Verlags-Anstalt, 1979.
Del Lungo, Andrea. *L'Incipit romanesque.* Paris: Seuil, 2003.
Durand, Yves. *Histoire générale de la Deuxième Guerre mondiale.* Paris: Complexe, 1997.
Eyck, Erich. *A History of the Weimar Republic.* Trans. Harlan P. Hanson and Robert G. L. Waite. Cambridge: Harvard University Press, 1962.
Ferro, Marc. *Questions sur la IIe Guerre mondiale.* Paris: Castermann, 1993.
Genette, Gérard. *Fiction et diction.* Paris: Seuil, 1991.
Gollut, Jean-Daniel, and Joël Zufferey. *Construire un monde: Les Phrases initiales de "La Comédie humaine."* Lausanne: Delachaux et Niestlé, 2000.
Herman, David. *Story Logic: Problems and Possibilities of Narrative.* Lincoln: University of Nebraska Press, 2002.
Kemp, Anthony. *1939–1945: Le Monde en guerre.* Trans. Pierre-M. Reyss. Paris: Gallimard, 1995.
Liddell Hart, Basil George. *History of the Second World War.* London: Cassell, 1970.
Michel, Henri. *La Seconde Guerre mondiale.* Paris: Presses Universitaires de France, 1972.
Miller, Hillis J. *Reading Narrative.* Norman: University of Oklahoma Press, 1998.
Montagnon, Pierre. *La grande histoire de la Seconde Guerre mondiale.* Paris: Pygmalion, 1999.

Overy, Richard. *Why the Allies Won*. New York: Norton, 1995.
Oz, Amos. *The Story Begins: Essays on Literature*. Trans. Maggie Bar-Tura. New York: Harcourt Brace, 1998.
Phelan, James. "Beginnings and Endings: Theories and Typologies of How Novels Open and Close." *Encyclopedia of the Novel*. Ed. Paul Schellinger. Chicago: Fitzroy Dearborn, 1998. 96–99.
Quellien, Jean. *Histoire de la Seconde Guerre mondiale*. Rennes: Editions Ouest-France, 1995.
Richardson, Brian. "Beginnings and Ends. Introduction: Openings and Closure." *Narrative Dynamics: Essays on Time, Plot, Closure, and Frames*. Ed. Brian Richardson. Columbus: Ohio State University Press, 2002. 249–55.
Said, Edward W. *Beginnings: Intention and Method*. New York: Basic Books, 1975.
Smith, Bradley F. *The War's Long Shadow: The Second World War and Its Aftermath*. New York: Simon and Schuster, 1986.
Sternberg, Meir. *Expositional Modes and Temporal Ordering in Fiction*. Baltimore: Johns Hopkins University Press, 1978.
Verrier, Jean. *Les Débuts de roman*. Paris: Bertrand-Lacoste, 1988.
Weinberg, Gerhard L. *A World at Arms: A Global History of World War II*. Cambridge: Cambridge University Press, 1994.
White, Hayden. *Metahistory: The Historical Imagination in Nineteenth-Century Europe*. Baltimore: Johns Hopkins University Press, 1973.
Wright, Gordon. *L'Europe en guerre: 1939–1945*. Trans. Marthe Blinoff. Paris: Armand Colin, 1971.

PART TWO

Beginnings in Narrative Literature

In the modern era, theorists of beginnings have generally gravitated toward one of three positions: first, the attempt to establish a fixed point where the sequence of events commences; second, the identification of two opposed trajectories that writers must navigate between; and third, the hypothesis that all beginnings are somehow arbitrary, fabricated, or illusory.

In the first category, Vladimir Propp imagined folktales as discrete entities with unambiguous starting points ("The king sends Ivan after the princess"). The subsequent structuralist tradition would continue to articulate story beginnings in a similar fashion. Todorov would formalize Propp's analysis into the general claim that an initial state of equilibrium is disturbed by the introduction of a serious disequilibrium; the narrative then attempts to reestablish a new equilibrium that is similar to but not identical with the original state (50–52). Other structuralists (Bremond, Prince) would employ comparable formulations, as would Peter Brooks in his study of plot. This general stance would also inform cognitive approaches as well as work in the social sciences, for example, the positions of J. M. Mandler and Nancy Stein, both of whom stress the establishment of the setting and the initiating event (see Stein and Policastro 113–27 for an overview of these and related positions). Meir Sternberg, in his seminal account of narrative exposition, gives signal importance to the first scene represented in a narrative: this establishes the work's "fictive present"; all temporally prior material belongs to the exposition, regardless of where it appears in the text. "The exposition always constitutes the beginning of the fabula, the first part of the chronologically ordered sequence of motifs as reconstructed by the reader," he writes, "but it is not necessarily located at the beginning of the sujet" (13–14). Using the example of Henry James's *The Ambassadors*, Sternberg states that "the beginning of the fabula is the earliest event in Strether's history that we learn about in the course of the novel (namely, his marriage); while the beginning of the sujet coincides, of course, with the beginning of the first chapter" (9–10).

The most comprehensive work that delineates a number of distinct starting points is that of Phelan, who, as will be seen in the final section of this volume, outlines four different starting points in narrative: the exposition or setting; the launch or opening instability that sets the plot in motion; the initiation or commencement of engagement between author or narrator and audience; and the entrance, which initiates the reader's entrance into the narrative proper. In her essay in this section, Catherine Romagnolo offers an equally thorough modeling of the various types of beginnings and also includes a category for thematic beginnings, since works that foreground formal beginning strategies regularly interweave thematic discussions of origins into their texts. This daring move helps push narrative theory toward a constructivist perspective that refuses to separate strategies of narrative composition from the larger conceptual issues that inspire those techniques.

In the second category, Edward Said distinguishes between the more active individual establishment of a beginning with the more passive acceptance of a communal or official origin. He points to the seemingly contradictory nature of beginnings, which seem to be always already predetermined and yet, at the same time, to effect a break from that which precedes them. In this section, Gaura Shankar Narayan traces the struggle within Salman Rushdie's *Midnight's Children* to contest originary narratives while establishing an ironic starting point for his stories of the birth and growth of an individual and a nation. In a similar vein, Carlos Riobo's essay, "*Heartbreak Tango*: Manuel Puig's Counter-Archive," identifies the common desire among many Latin American "boom" novelists to establish an origin in a Spanish colonial archive with which to ground their fictions and shows how Puig's work disrupts this project.

Stephen Kellman, in his study of opening lines of a work, has posited a different opposition, noting that opening lines generally do one of two things: either "thrust us immediately into the text or . . . retard our encounter until we are prepared for it" (146). In *Openings: Narrative Beginnings from the Epic to the Novel*, A. D. Nuttall outlines a comparable though rather more cosmic dichotomy, the "artificial" versus the "natural" beginning, and focuses on "the various tensions which exist between the formal freedom to begin a work where one likes and an opposite sense that all good openings are somehow naturally rooted, are echoes, more or less remote, of an original creative act: in medias res, as against 'In the beginning'" (vii–viii). By the end of his analysis he finds both terms of this dichotomy to be problematic.

In the third category, J. Hillis Miller, building on the work of Said and Derrida, suggests that "the paradox of beginnings is that one must have something solidly present and pre-existent, some generative source or authority, on which the development of a new story may be based. That antecedent foundation needs in turn some prior foundation, in an infinite regress" (57). In the first essay in this section, Tita Chico takes up this position and applies it to *Tristram Shandy*, examining that work's infinite recess of implicit beginnings. In the next essay, Melba Cuddy-Keane, looking at modernist narratives (especially those by Woolf), likewise takes up the question of the foundations or grounding that beginnings seem to imply; her essay draws important attention to beginning's "ragged edge," starting points that always turn out to be provisional or arbitrary and point back to still earlier (though no more definitive) beginnings, suggesting the possibility of what might be called an endless "writing before the beginning." My own essay continues in this direction, pointing out unresolvable problems in the establishment of definitive beginnings in a work's story (*fabula*), discourse (*syuzhet*), and preliminary epitext, using Joyce's "The Dead" and Beckett's *Molloy* as examples to illustrate this position. Finally, Ryan Claycomb points out the various ways that beginnings in dramas can be deferred, disguised, or deconstructed, while Jessica Laccetti elucidates the multiple (and ingenious) possible beginning points of feminist hypertext fiction.

Works Cited

Kellman, Steven G. "Grand Openings and Plain: On the Poetics of Opening Lines" *Sub-Stance* 17 (1977): 139–47.

Miller, J. Hillis. "Beginnings." *Reading Narrative*. Norman: University of Oklahoma Press, 1998. 57–60.

Nuttall, A. D. *Openings: Narrative Beginnings from the Epic to the Novel*. Oxford: Oxford University Press, 1992.

Stein, Nancy L., and Margaret Policastro. "The Concept of a Story: A Comparison between Children's and Teacher's Viewpoints." *Learning and Comprehension of Text*. Ed. Heinz Mandl, Nancy L. Stein, and Tom Trabasso. Hillsdale NJ: Erlbaum, 1984. 113–55.

Sternberg, Meir. *Expositional Modes and Temporal Ordering in Fiction*. Baltimore: Johns Hopkins University Press, 1978.

Todorov, Tzvetan. *Poetics of Prose*. Trans. Richard Howard. Minneapolis: University of Minnesota Press, 1981.

5

"The More I Write, the More I Shall Have to Write" The Many Beginnings of *Tristram Shandy*

TITA CHICO

When Laurence Sterne's wide-eyed Tristram Shandy eagerly takes up the project of writing his bildungsroman, "the history of myself," he expresses a fervent desire to begin at the beginning: he promises "to go on tracing every thing in it, as *Horace* says, *ab Ovo*" (1: 5). With his faulty allusion to Horace (who, of course, praises Homer for beginning in the middle, not at the beginning), our narrator opens *The Life and Opinions of Tristram Shandy, Gentleman* (1759–67) in his parents' bed and in one sense imagines the beginning of a story as the moment of conception. The conception of Tristram can be located in a time and a place, but it is *not* a narrative beginning, or at least not one that Sterne will define as a narrative beginning. So Tristram tries to begin again. In volume 3, Tristram-as-author announces, almost breathlessly, that everyone is offstage, which now finally gives him time to produce the book's preface: "All my heroes are off my hands;—'tis the first time I have had a moment to spare,—and I'll make use of it, and write my preface" (1: 226). As a subject he is born over the course of several chapters, most of which are occupied with narrating everything but his birth. The *syuzhet* of the novel, experienced when we read from beginning to end, takes us from the moment of Tristram's conception to—by volume 9—a time *before* his birth, when the Widow Wadman woos his uncle Toby. By the end of the novel we are back not at the beginning but to an episode that takes place before Tristram is conceived. And, perhaps not surprisingly, there are even chapters in which Tristram the author gets "lost" and promises to "begin" that part of the story again (2: 557–61).

Tristram Shandy is a novel that never seems to get going, always sliding back to tell us more. What is remarkable is that we witness Tristram forever straining to say enough so that he can *begin* his story. In volume 1, chapter 14, Tristram confesses that "I have been at it these six weeks, making all the speed I possibly could,—and am not yet born." He goes on to qualify himself and points to a distinction that comes to shape the novel: "I have just been able, and that's all, to tell you *when* it [his birth] happen'd, but not *how*;—so that you see the thing is yet far from being accomplished" (1: 42). Beginning in time—whether his parents' bed or his own birth—does not satisfy Tristram's requirements for narrative. It is this "how" that remains elusive throughout *Tristram Shandy*, the reader's need to know *everything* to be able to understand *anything*, and the simultaneous glimmer of hope that this can happen. Tristram resolves this problem—at least momentarily—with the promise that he will continue to write, though he also acknowledges that writing produces the need for *more* writing: he admits that "I had no conception of" the need to write the "how," "but which, I am convinced now, will rather increase than diminish as I advance" (1: 42).

Why?

Since the novel's publication, readers have struggled to explain this phenomenon. Some have borrowed Sterne's own vocabulary to argue that the narrative is both obsessed with progression and daunted by the impossibility of adhering to it (Moglen, *Irony* 147–62; González 55–64), sometimes calling the work dialogic (Tadié 1–3) or arguing that it is variously doubled (Lamb, *Fiction* 23–30, 73–76).[1] Tristram, in one of his many moments of apparent (if fleeting) conviction, gives critics the language for this model of interpretation: "In a word, my work is digressive, and it is progressive too,—and at the same time" (1: 81). It is the kind of reading Horace Walpole took from the text in 1760 when he observed that *Tristram Shandy*'s "great humour . . . consists in the whole narration always going backwards" (4: 369). For Walpole, this is also the novel's great liability: "I can conceive a man saying that it would be droll to write a book in that manner, but have no notion of his persevering in executing it. It makes one smile two or three times at the beginning, but in recompense makes one yawn for two hours" (369).

But Tristram seems to be preoccupied with the epistemology of writing, and so for my purposes here, Wolfgang Iser's and J. Hillis Miller's readings are most suggestive.[2] Iser has famously questioned Tristram's sense of beginning, claiming that the text exposes "beginning as a retroactive patterning in accordance with the result intended"; in other words, Tristram's inability to begin reflects the constructed nature of narrative patterns (9). Moreover, Iser argues that Sterne's text points to—in Iser's words, "stages"—the elusive nature of lived experience. Similarly, Miller contends that *Tristram Shandy*'s inability to begin embodies the principle of "infinite regress"; and considering the novel's "middle," he argues that Sterne's novel offers "a hilarious parody and undoing of the idea of a continuous and complete life story" (58, 71). Reading the chapter on "lines" in volume 6, which Sterne comically presents as bathetic metaphors for narrative structure, Miller notes for us that the ideal brought under satiric pressure is the "straight" line, which Sterne takes literally—and draws and then breaks. The straight line in *Tristram Shandy*, Miller contends, both gives shape to the idea of a linear narrative and exposes its absurdity. Miller concludes that "the interest of narrative lies in its digressions, in episodes that might be diagrammed as loops, knots, interruptions, or detours making a visible figure" (68). Most revealing is Miller's suggestion that the line itself—when it carries "more information"—becomes increasingly curved, knotted, or hieroglyphic (70). It has become a critical commonplace to describe the novel as having a "non-linear narration" (Blackwell 115).

I agree with these readings for the ways they illuminate the play in Sterne's text with what Gérard Genette calls the "temporal *order* of the events that are being told and the pseudo-temporal order of the narrative" (25). But to focus on Sterne's narrative "line" as such runs the risk of obscuring what this "undoing" accomplishes, beyond a kind of claim for indeterminacy, and what rises in its place; this is always the case when critics read Sterne primarily as parody.[3] To view Sterne's text as solely organized around the dialectic of progression-as-time and digression-as-opinion, or even to characterize Sterne's narrative as being made up of plot and digression, too neatly characterizes the specifically epistemological implications of *Tristram Shandy*, namely, the status of those things that seem to disrupt the prospect of temporal order: narrative details. If we only think of Sterne's narrative as either progressive or digressive, we miss the ways in which Sterne's text is both fixated on details as simultaneously necessary to narrating a life and the fundamental impediment to doing so. Implicit in Iser's and Miller's interpretations of *Tristram Shandy*, and of all narrative, is that narrative is constituted by "information" and that information—those novelistic details that make up narrative—is itself a kind of stable entity that produces an unstable narrative line. But there is more to the detail itself than this manner of reading acknowledges.

The difficulty that Tristram finds "beginning" reveals the novel's engagement with eighteenth-century discourses of the "detail."[4] Tristram's text is characterized by an amplitude of detail—not the non-narrative details of description, but *narrative* details (Ronen 275–80)—and a desire for even more of them, never specifying what might be "enough." By volume 1, chapter 14, six weeks have passed in the life of Tristram-the-author, while not a day in the life of Tristram-the-subject has been "lived" in print. This is a sharp reminder of the dissonance between the passing of time in one's life and in narrative, between the clock ticking and a *sense* of time (Sherman 1998). But it is also an indication of the nature of the detail itself. Tristram's fixation on the details of his story—what others label "digressions" or what Miller calls "information"—is a means of displacing narrative order with a narrative of details. Naomi Schor has shown us that the "detail" in late-eighteenth-century aesthetics was feminized and subordinated by the likes of Joshua Reynolds, who saw the detail as a vehicle for "pollution" and favored instead notions of sublimity (16, 11–22). In Schor's formulation, the masculine sublime emerges in order to keep the feminized detail in check.[5] The primacy of the detail as ornamental—key to Schor's argument—has been discussed more recently by Cynthia Wall, who offers a rich archaeology of the emergence of spatial and visual description in the eighteenth century (7–40).[6] As valuable as these studies are, however, they account for one facet of the detail's history and do not address the central question of the narrative detail.

Where, then, did novelists turn to develop the language of detailed observation in the eighteenth century? One source can be found in empiricism, which promulgates a method of and language for detailed observation. Details for experimental philosophers, particularly microscopists—a science, of course, that depends upon defining and understanding details—are everyday observations, diurnal by nature. In support of microscopy and its popularization, Robert Hooke (author of the ground-breaking *Micrographia; Or, Some Physiological Descriptions of Minute Bodies*) and his followers throughout the eighteenth century urged readers to take up the microscope to observe their natural—and domestic—settings, contending that these views produce aesthetically admirable objects of contemplation.[7] Hooke's rhetorical innovation resulted, in part, from the language of familiarity that he used, for the objects under view are described through analogy to everyday objects (Wall 72). But as I argue elsewhere, Hooke defines the microscopic detail as simultaneously an observed particular *and* a theoretical construct (Chico 148–52). Minute particulars become minute particulars because they are chosen by the viewer—those are the details that *matter*. Hooke argues for a methodology that acknowledges the theoretical nature of observed particulars: any demarcation of "small" things is a "scrupulous choice, and a strict examination, of the reality, constancy and centrality of the Particulars that we admit" (3). Moreover, he introduces the possibility that details themselves have the potential to deviate from the particular and become, instead, an axiom or general principle (xiii). Details for Hooke are several things. They are observed particulars, the things the microscopist sees under the microscope. But they are likewise the sum of the multiple choices the microscopist makes, and they take on the potential to displace abstraction altogether, producing their own kind of theory.

How do the discourses of microscopy help us to understand *Tristram Shandy*? If Hooke's revelation was to see in the detail the potential for theory, then Sterne's was to see in the detail the potential for narrative.[8] In Sterne's world, details not only constitute the "information" of narrative but also imply and beget narrative—they even have narrative *within* them. Details disrupt the temporal order of the narrative through their accumulation and require (even embody) their own narrative, thus deferring the very possibility of a "singular" beginning, or at least exposing the very artificiality of constructing one. Tristram Shandy discovers that for every detail he utters, there is one that precedes it, one that must be articulated for clarification. In the midst of telling the story of Widow Wadman and Uncle Toby, Tristram interrupts himself to promise that he will give full details at the right time, a promise that implies a naturalized order to detailed narration that itself is never evident in the novel: "After a series of attacks and repulses in a course of nine months on my uncle *Toby*'s quarter, a most minute account of every particular of which shall be given in its proper place, my uncle *Toby*, honest man! found it necessary to draw off his forces, and raise the siege somewhat indignantly" (1: 246). The detail is an isolated piece of information, but it also conveys a sense of order and sequence: thus, there is enacted in the very detail itself a sense of a larger structure, a sense of its relation to other details, and an implied order—"every particular" "given in its proper place." And so we have the pseudo-temporal order of narrative, with a beginning, a middle, and an end, constituted by the right detail provided at the right time. Sterne's novel exploits the idea that every detail contains this potential and has its own story that clamors to be told.

Tristram Shandy is therefore constituted by the narrative potential of details, not by digressions. Tristram himself uses the language of advancement and being "thrown so many volumes back" to describe his method, but he also indicates that the metaphor of a narrative line, no matter its shape or direction, is misleading (1: 341). He is not merely narrating "backwards," as Walpole sees it, or presenting curves, knots, and hieroglyphs, as Miller sees it. Tristram is acknowledging that every detail begets narrative; he announces that he is not a "common writer" but rather one who attends to the details of lived experience, in all of their potential and contingency: "And why not?—and the transactions and opinions of it take up as much description—And for what reason should they be cut short? as at this rate I should just live 364 times faster than I should write—It must follow, an' please your worships, that the more I write, the more I shall have to write"

(1: 342). The predominant narrative structure of *Tristram Shandy* is therefore shaped by this simultaneous celebration of and frustration with detailed observation, underscored by an exploitation of the narrative of the detail per se. Tristram promises at various points to give the reader all the details necessary for the "story," but he is just as likely to rail that there are so many more details necessary for that story even to be told. No wonder, then, that he opens one chapter in volume 3 by "go[ing] back to the ******—in the last chapter" (1: 217). Or that Uncle Toby's unremarkable sentence, "I think, replied he,—it would not be amiss, brother, if we rung the bell," begins in volume 1, chapter 21, only to conclude in volume 2, chapter 6 (1: 114). As soon as Uncle Toby utters the words "I think," Tristram-as-narrator interrupts: "But to enter rightly into my uncle *Toby*'s sentiments upon this matter, you must be made to enter first a little into his character, the out-lines of which I shall just give you, and then the dialogue between him and my father will go on as well again" (1: 70–71). Tristram cannot let Uncle Toby finish speaking until Tristram has given the reader the story of Toby himself. Uncle Toby's "I think" requires what Tristram calls "description"; the very fact that these words come from the mouth of Tristram's Uncle Toby requires that the speaker be described, that the reader enter into the relationship between Uncle Toby and Tristram's father, Walter Shandy.

The brilliance of Tristram's narration resides in the fact that Uncle Toby continues to exist in the life of Tristram-as-subject, even while Tristram-as-narrator labors to produce the right details that will make Uncle Toby's speech meaningful. Tristram pauses in one sense (in the temporal order of the narrative but not in the time of the writing) to produce the story of Uncle Toby, but he also notes that Uncle Toby himself does not cease to exist, much less stay stationary, as in a modern-day cinematic freeze-frame: "But I forget my uncle *Toby*," Tristram says as he catches himself, "whom all this while we have left knocking the ashes out of his tobacco pipe" (1: 72). Here Tristram famously uses the language of "digressions," a term that readers too often replicate without interrogating. He reminds his reader that these "digressions" do not actually move the narrative backward, for the events of the story, the *fabula*, continue apace.

Remember—Uncle Toby continues to knock the ashes out of his tobacco pipe:

> For in this long digression which I was accidentally led into, as in all my digressions (one only excepted) there is a master-stroke of digressive skill, the merit of which has all along, I fear, been overlooked by my reader,—not for want of penetration in him,—but because 'tis an excellence seldom looked for, or expected indeed, in a digression;—and it is this: That tho' my digressions are all fair, as you observe,—and that I fly off from what I am about, as far and as often too as any writer in *Great-Britain*; yet I constantly take care to order affairs so, that my main business does not stand still in my absence. (1: 80)

Rereading Sterne's language allows us to see that what constitutes *Tristram Shandy* is not a principle of infinite regression, a novelistic zigzagging between advancement and retreat, but a structure of amplitude, what Tristram calls "a master-stroke of digressive skill." Telling in this passage is Tristram's emphasis on order: he insists that what some might interpret as flying off is a misreading. To call these narrative amplifications "digressions" mislabels them, for the term "digression" does not allow for the element that Tristram prizes here. A "digression" implies something off the point, whereas these bits of text are as central as anything else to Tristram's narrative.

Tristram's homage to his master-stroke likewise implicates the reader. Not only does Tristram introduce a possible (and ultimately prevalent) misreading, but he also articulates the readerly obligation that his novel requires. If details institute their own kind of narrative sequence, even if it is one that is open to revision, then it is incumbent upon the reader to note each and every one of those details. Sterne's construction of the potentially distracted reader is of particular note. At one point (of many), Tristram rebukes the reader: "If the reader has not a clear conception of the rood and the half of ground which lay at the bottom of my uncle Toby's kitchen-garden, and which was the scene of so many of his delicious hours,—the fault is not in me,—but in his imagination;—for I am sure I gave him so minute a description, I was almost ashamed of it" (2: 534).

These minute accounts, Tristram insists, are helpful to the reader, and if the novel fails to make sense, then the fault lies in the reader's imagination; later Tristram explains that the narrative of details is designed to "keep all tight together in the reader's fancy" (2: 557–58). Tristram demands the reader's focused attention, even though Tristram himself acknowledges the impossibility of attending to *every* detail and underscores that some are more important than others. Even so, he still reprimands the reader for *missing* a detail about his mother and tells "Madam" to go back and reread the previous chapter; in the meantime, he continues to address his "other" readers, thus giving "Madam" enough time to reread and catch up (1: 64–65). Though Tristram flails in his attempt to record every detail, he demands that his readers attend to every detail. His petulance and his accommodation introduce a key and insurmountable deferral—can "Madam" ever catch up? Can a reader ever have enough details to understand a narrative? By even posing these questions, *Tristram Shandy* illustrates the centrality of details in this text's theory of narrative, suggesting that what Tristram calls the "deviations from a straight line" (1: 41) of a story's plot ultimately come to stand for the action of plot and the idea of a character's development over time.

But even within the confines of this essay, I have implied a linearity to the detail's narrative potential that the novel does not fully endorse. To begin something new is not only to leave something old: it is also to leave *several* things old and untold. The novel dramatizes that any beginning necessarily evokes all that is before it, so that when Tristram announces that "we are now going to enter upon a new scene of events," he proceeds to list all that "we" shall leave:

> Leave we then the breeches in the taylor's hands, with my father standing over him with his cane, reading him as he sat at work a lecture upon the *latus clavus*, and pointing to the precise part of the waistband, where he was determined to have it sewed on.—
>
> Leave we my mother—(truest of all the *Poco-curante*'s of her sex!)—careless about it, as about every thing else in the world which concerned her;—that is,—indifferent whether it was all done this way or that,—provided it was but done at all.—

> Leave we *Slop* likewise to the full profits of all my dishonours.—
>
> Leave we poor *Le Fever* to recover, and get home from *Marseilles* as he can.—And last of all,—because the hardest of all—
>
> Let us leave, if possible, *myself*:—But 'tis impossible,—I must go along with you to the end of the work. (2: 533–34)

Sterne's novel shows us that there are a host of other stories that not only demand their own narrative amplification and detailing but that are also forsaken when we choose another direction. Tristram's refusal just to "begin" with the new scene—to begin at all—suggests a narrative theory that acknowledges and is ultimately driven by the markedly exponential narrative potential of the detail.

While Sterne tempts us by drawing various narrative lines, even to make fun of them, to take them too seriously threatens to keep us from seeing the narrative model that the novel ultimately endorses. In *Tristram Shandy* there is always the hope that everything can be properly told in its appropriate order, but nothing seems to be. We should read the novel's play with temporal order, thematized so fully by the inability to begin despite various efforts, as a vehicle for a larger epistemological point: the basic units of representation through which a life gets written convey amplitude and multiplicity and a range of narratives. Though the novel seemingly presents self-subverting narratives, *Tristram Shandy* should be read as Sterne's great admission that plots of development are ultimately dependent upon the very unit of the detail, a category of representation that encompasses and produces its own narratives. Therefore, while Sterne's text sets out to narrate a life story, it results in a theory of narrative that subordinates a master plot such as the bildungsroman to the *implied* narrative of a detail.

Perhaps not surprisingly, *Tristram Shandy*'s ambivalently expressed "beginning" is not the first of its kind in the eighteenth century, but harks back to Swift's *A Tale of a Tub* (1704), a prose narrative text whose title means "a cock and bull story"—just the phrase that constitutes *Tristram Shandy*'s abrupt end. *A Tale of a Tub* begins with an almost endless string of beginnings itself: a title page, an anonymous "Apology,"

"The More I Write, the More I Shall Have to Write" 93

the bookseller's dedication to Lord Somers, the bookseller's dedication to the reader, the hack's dedication to Prince Posterity, a preface, the introduction, which is labeled section 1, and then the "beginning" of the *Tale* in section 2. *A Tale of a Tub* likewise includes chapters of "digressions"—even one in praise of digressions—that eventually overtake the tale, turning out to be anything but digressions. Edward W. Said briefly links the two texts when he cites both *Tristram Shandy* and *A Tale of a Tub* as examples of a hysterical beginning (44), but to tell the story of *this* beginning is perhaps wisely saved for later.

Notes

1. For example, Moglen argues that *Tristram Shandy* reflects the anxiety of subjectivity in the face of eighteenth-century patriarchy; the novel's "urge to indeterminacy," expressed as a "nostalgic desire for return," not only serves to represent an internally divided subjectivity, but also the doomed failure that masculinity faces. Thus we can extrapolate that not being able to begin is a reflection of the self's inability to assimilate, though this is not integral to Moglen's argument (*Trauma* 104, 88–89).
2. See Markley for a related critique of Miller's reading.
3. Keymer likewise argues that Sterne does not merely parody Richardson and Fielding but reworks their novelistic legacies (25).
4. The unit of the "detail" has been central to understanding the English novel ever since Ian Watt's *The Rise of the Novel* hinged its definition of "formal realism" on details and particularity, without defining, in turn, what is meant by those designations. Watt argues that formal realism obliges novels "to satisfy its reader with such details of the story as the individuality of the actors concerned, the particulars of the times and places of their actions, details which are presented through a more largely referential use of language than is common in other literary forms" (32). Of course, Watt famously avoids Sterne.
5. Notably, Schor's first "novelistic" example is Jane Austen, a writer whom I see as inheriting the vexed history of detailed observation from a variety of eighteenth-century sources and models, including Sterne.
6. In a similarly suggestive vein, Lamb has identified the "minute particular" in late-eighteenth-century travel narratives to the South Seas, particularly Captain Cook's voyages, as mechanisms of colonial discourse ("Particulars" 281–94; also *Preserving* 76–113).
7. The following passage from Adams's *Essays on the Microscope* is typi-

cal: "It leads, to use the words of an ingenious writer, to the discovery of a thousand wonders in the works of his hand, who created ourselves, as well as the objects of our admiration; it improves the faculties, exalts the comprehension, and multiplies the inlets to happiness; is a new source of praise to him, to whom all we pay is nothing of what we owe; and while it pleases the imagination with the unbounded treasures it offers to the view, it tends to make the whole life one continued act of admiration" (2).

8. Others, notably Landa and New, have turned to microscopy to read *Tristram Shandy*, though their interpretations are focused on Sterne's allusions to the popular microscopical textbook, Henry Baker's *The Microscope Made Easy* (1743), and the image of the homunculus.

Works Cited

Adams, George. *Essays on the Microscope*. London, 1787.

Blackwell, Bonnie. "*Tristram Shandy* and the Theater of the Mechanical Mother." ELH 68.1 (2001): 81–133.

Chico, Tita. "Minute Particulars: Microscopy and Eighteenth-Century Narrative." *Mosaic: A Journal for the Interdisciplinary Study of Literature* 39.2 (2006): 143–61.

Genette, Gérard. "Order, Duration, and Frequency." *Narrative Dynamics: Essays on Time, Plot, Closure, and Frames*. Ed. Brian Richardson. Columbus: Ohio State University Press, 2002. 25–34.

González, Antonio Ballesteros. "Digression and Intertextual Parody in Nashe, Sterne and Joyce." *Laurence Sterne in Modernism and Postmodernism*. Ed. David Pierce and Peter de Voogd. Amsterdam: Rodopi, 1996. 55–64.

Hooke, Robert. *Micrographia; Or, Some Physiological Descriptions of Minute Bodies*. London, 1665.

Iser, Wolfgang. *Lawrence Sterne*: Tristram Shandy. Cambridge: Cambridge University Press, 1988.

Keymer, Thomas. *Sterne, the Moderns, and the Novel*. Oxford: Oxford University Press, 2002.

Lamb, Jonathan. "Minute Particulars and the Representation of South Pacific Discovery." *Eighteenth-Century Studies* 28.3 (1995): 281–94.

———. *Preserving the Self in the South Seas, 1680–1840*. Chicago: University of Chicago Press, 2001.

———. *Sterne's Fiction and the Double Principle*. Cambridge: Cambridge University Press, 1989.

Landa, Louis A. "The Shandean Homunculus: The Background of Sterne's 'Little Gentleman.'" *Restoration and Eighteenth-Century Literature: Essays in Honor of Alan Dugald McKillop*. Ed. Carroll Camden. Chicago: University of Chicago Press, 1963. 49–68.

Markley, Robert M. "*Tristram Shandy* and 'Narrative Middles': J. Hillis Miller and the Style of Deconstructive Criticism." *Genre* 17 (1984): 179–90.

Miller, J. Hillis. *Reading Narrative*. Norman: University of Oklahoma Press, 1998.

Moglen, Helene. *The Philosophical Irony of Laurence Sterne*. Gainesville: University Presses of Florida, 1975.

———. *The Trauma of Gender: A Feminist Theory of the English Novel*. Berkeley: University of California Press, 2001.

New, Melvyn. "Laurence Sterne and Henry Baker's *The Microscope Made Easy*." *Studies in English Literature, 1500–1900* 10.3 (1970): 591–604.

Ronen, Ruth. "Description, Narrative and Representation." *Narrative* 5.3 (1997): 274–86.

Said, Edward W. *Beginnings: Intention and Method*. New York: Basic Books, 1975.

Schor, Naomi. *Reading in Detail: Aesthetics and the Feminine*. New York: Methuen, 1987.

Sherman, Stuart. *Telling Time: Clocks, Diaries, and English Diurnal Form, 1660–1785*. Chicago: University of Chicago Press, 1996.

Sterne, Laurence. *The Life and Opinions of Tristram Shandy, Gentleman*. Ed. Melvyn New and Joan New. 3 vols. Gainesville: University Presses of Florida, 1978.

Tadié, Alexis. *Sterne's Whimsical Theatres of Language: Orality, Gesture, Literacy*. Hants, UK: Ashgate, 2003.

Wall, Cynthia. *The Prose of Things: Transformations of Description in the Eighteenth Century*. Chicago: University of Chicago Press, 2006.

Walpole, Horace. *The Letters of Horace Walpole, Fourth Earl of Oxford*. Ed. Paget Toynbee. 16 vols. Oxford: Oxford University Press, 1903.

Watt, Ian. *The Rise of the Novel: Studies in Defoe, Richardson, and Fielding*. Berkeley: University of California Press, 1957.

6

Virginia Woolf and Beginning's Ragged Edge

MELBA CUDDY-KEANE

Pick up a book and feel in your hands its compact, three-dimensional, sturdy shape. Open the book and run your eye down the clean edge of its left-hand page. For readers, beginning a book means entering into an unknown, alien space, and most studies of narrative beginnings consequently focus on techniques for providing an introduction or initiating the reader (immediately or gradually) into both story and discourse in the text's first words. Conceptually, beginning inevitably suggests something different and new, just as the material book implies a separate object with an integrity of its own. Continuous front and back covers define a self-contained and distinctive unit; the title page stands like a gateway; even the straight edge of the margin insinuates a boundary line around the text. We open to what is inside the book as if to a new world.

Yet even the physical book semiotically signs the impossibility of impermeable borders: books crowd together on our shelves, rubbing covers, the printed pages themselves transposed from other media—electronic files, typescript, or manuscript. Both literally and conceptually, as Virginia Woolf wrote, "Books descend from books as families descend from families" ("Leaning Tower" 163). Furthermore, as she more famously wrote in *A Room of One's Own*, "masterpieces are not single and solitary births; they are the outcome of many years of thinking in common, of thinking by the body of the people, so that the experience of the mass is behind the single voice" (71). Beginning, in a book, is both an initiatory gesture and a drawing upon and drawing out of what has gone before.

The paradoxical nature of beginnings is itself a familiar story, and one clearly implicit in studies of allusion, intertextuality, and adaptation. What narratology needs to investigate further is the way certain texts overtly engage this paradox by overwriting their narrative beginnings with evocations of ghostly pre-texts and by deploying such pre-texts to subvert the conventional assumptions that stories originate in instigating incidents and are shaped by causally determining pasts. To initiate but also to frustrate the reader's expectations of entering a new world; to invoke prior thoughts and prior voices but to forestall any attribution of originary words or deeds—the text that performs such complex rhetorical acts manifests the intricate nature of beginning not as a clean cut, but as a ragged edge.[1]

I am positing here a category of narrative marked by self-problematizing or even self-canceling beginnings, whether such beginnings are figured in the present narrative or implicit in the narrative's past. Textual energy, in these works, pushes against the clean-cut edge of the paper, reconstructing the opening page as if it were a bit of torn cloth. A ragged beginning exposes dangling threads, those on the present cloth and those, by implication, on the larger cloth from which the piece was torn. Most narratives, of course, gesture to prior events, but in self-problematizing beginnings the skein of the past is infinitely unrollable, while the present is both severed *and* connected by ghostly threads. The truly revolutionary nature of this practice is indicated by the absence of terms to discuss it. Narrative theory generally assumes that a fixed beginning point emerges somewhere in the story and that it supplies the motivating force for the action that proceeds; Gerald Prince's *A Dictionary of Narratology*, for example, defines *beginning* as "The incident initiating the process of change in a PLOT or ACTION" (10). Our task now is to account for the shift, in the language of William Faulkner's *Absalom, Absalom!*, from the ex nihilo creationist mimicry of Thomas Sutpen's "*Be Sutpen's Hundred* like the olden time *Be Light*" (3) to a continuous but ever-changing stream of narrative voices, imaged, like the Mississippi, as a communal umbilical cord (269), or as a series of connecting ponds, with the ripple of one person's speech inevitably washing over and through the words of the next, so that "happen is never once" (273).[2]

However, to invoke *Absalom, Absalom!* raises the potential confusion of the ragged edge with another, admittedly similar, paradigm—in medias res. Faulkner's first chapter opens with intimations of past narrative, and these will, in later narrative time, be variously fleshed out to reveal the origins of the Sutpen story. The Homeric opening in the "middle" of an action inscribes a clear beginning, although one disclosed through flashback, or even multiple flashbacks, in the later pages of the book. The ragged edge, by contrast, harkens back to voices and experiences never to be explained or articulated in the narrative to come. The ghostly presence of voices always prior and outside the text means that narrative is never ultimately traceable to a point of origin, for there is no single, absolute point of origin to which narrative could be traced. No godlike creationist act informs the narrative as an a priori trope; and, pace Stephen Dedalus, the artist's creation is not figured in godlike terms. As opposed to a tale with beginning and ending, narrative is an always ongoing process to which the reader, as it were, tunes in.

Although self-problematizing beginnings may not be exclusive to modernist writing, the modernist period arguably intensified the ambiguity that the ragged edge implies.[3] As revolutionaries, modernists challenged the teleological modeling of time that underpinned Victorian ideas of progress, complicated constructions of individual identity with theories of multiple and unconscious motivation, and turned their attention to what Leonard Woolf calls the "backstairs of history"—the voices of ordinary people—not as subsidiary to the literary work or historical event but as indispensable to its existence (141). These and other new modes of thinking demanded a discourse that self-consciously modeled itself as a break with the past: "in or about December, 1910," the old conventions, as Virginia Woolf asserts, would no longer do ("Mr. Bennett" 320). But even revolution carries its burden of history. Pound's "Make it new!" recycles the words of a Chinese emperor (Dettmar 2), and Stephen Dedalus's visionary project of giving form to "the uncreated conscience of [his] race" must still be "forged" (its originality faked?) from Irish ore (Joyce 276). Even in revolutionary modernism, the sedimentary past complicates the constructs of the autonomous work of art and creation as an autonomous act. Human consciousness confronts conditions unlike any it has known before, yet it simultaneously comprehends the impossibility of describing those conditions with absolute novelty. Narratives, as we will see in the works of Virginia Woolf, are compelled both to begin and to enact the impossibility of beginnings.

Forms of Anti-beginning

In the works of Virginia Woolf, beginnings are replete with strategies of anti-beginning. Rather than initiating action, her openings plunge us into actions in process, in three instances with first lines that articulate a response to or a continuation of something previously written or said: "'So of course,' wrote Betty Flanders" (*Jacob's Room* 3); "'Yes, of course. . . . But,'" says Mrs. Ramsay (*To the Lighthouse* 9); and the Fernham speaker opens with "But, you may say" (*A Room of One's Own* 1). Although readers subsequently gain enough information to hypothesize a generalized situation, the words anterior to the first line are never explicitly revealed. No flashback situates the opening in medias res; we do not, as in epic, stand outside a story whose ordered structure we ultimately reconstruct. As a result, beginning is situated not in the narrative (or "story") but in the process of reading (inscribed by the "discourse"), and it is *we* who begin by "listening in" to a story that is already well under way. For the opening words effect a slight hesitation in our attentive processes. As parts of speech that are, in the linguistic sentence, grammatically dependent, "but," "so," and "yes" signal an anterior pre-text that we have missed.

Opening to the word "so" in *Jacob's Room*, we find ourselves well advanced in a narrative (with a prior history), written in a letter (with a previously written but not cited salutation), to an addressee (who may or may not have sent correspondence to which the present letter is a response). From Mrs. Flanders's subsequent reference to an "accident," readers can imaginatively sketch in a plausible story: one of her sons (Jacob?) presumably broke something (what?) at a boardinghouse where they were staying, causing the family to relocate to other lodgings. When we later grasp how Mrs. Flanders, a widow, serves as a flattering looking glass for Captain Barfoot's grandiose self-portraits, we can guess his reciprocal function as the sympathetic recipient of her own self-dramatization. But the retrospective reading initiated by our opening questions is never so satisfied with its conclusions that it stops. If "so" precipitates, in the letter, the forward momentum of Mrs. Flanders's hand, it initiates, in the reader, the consciousness of a missing antecedent clause. Lacking a frame, we seek it in multiple places, casting our lines further and further back in time. Where in the larger narrative do we locate the beginnings of Mrs. Flanders's distress? In the accident that precipitated the family's move? In the fatality of her being widowed two years before? In the still vaster realm of "the eternal conspiracy of hush and clean bottles" (14) and the ages-old burden of maternal care in a threatening world? Or, in the less anthropocentric, more universal rhythm of the weakly crab (caught by Jacob) climbing and falling back into its bucket, climbing and falling back? And what could fill in the missing exposition for Jacob's own story? In what sentence is the narrative of Jacob's life the clause that follows "so"? In "A Sketch of the Past," Woolf wrote, "I see myself as a fish in a stream; deflected; held in place; but cannot describe the stream" (80). The "beginnings" of Jacob's life cannot be fixed or determined, or it would cease to be a stream. Strategies of anti-beginning insert the individual into life's continuum and define the act of reading as stepping into the flux.

While the "so" of *Jacob's Room* signals a larger trajectory of time and experience flowing before and around the individual life, "But, you may say" and "Yes, of course. . . . But" situate the individual utterance within a conversational stream. Both *A Room of One's Own* and *To the Lighthouse* open in the dialogic mode, and numerous critics have explored the implications for the ensuing text: the undercutting of hegemonic, monologic authority, the initiation of a feminist discourse informed by polyvocality and chiasmic turns and shifts. But the opening words have the further function of giving shape to a narrative "before." While each work opens on a female speaker pitted against and challenging a dominant patriarchal discourse, her actual words are directed to complicit, not oppositional, ears: an audience of women students in the essay-lecture, and Mrs. Ramsay's son James in the novel. And both speakers' words evidently respond to a previous but unrecorded utterance: the lecturer anticipates her audience's objection (But, you *may* say) on the basis of their prior (but not textually stated) request (an invitation to talk about women and fiction); the mother responds to her son's similarly unsounded, unwritten question (*will* he be able to go to the lighthouse the next day?). It is not the speaker who interrupts, but the reader, intruding into a conversation in which a certain discursive contract has already been assumed.

In these works, as in *Jacob's Room*, the reader soon has enough information to sketch in the situation, but my interest here is in rhetorical effect. "Once upon a time" gets us all ready and nicely settled in our chairs. "But" and "Yes" signal our late arrival on the scene, prompting inevitable anxieties about our ability ever fully to know the life that has been in process in a hypothesized prior time. Such retrospective speculation is further prompted, in each book, by gestures to an unconscious life anterior to the first words: the desire to which Mrs. Ramsay responds is sensed by James (who is six years old) as an emotion he has experienced for "years and years"; the lecturer at Fernham warns that she will be probing for prejudices and assumptions that lie too deep for articulation and can only be fished up, in miniature, from the depths of the stream. But it is also the reader's late arrival that produces the sense of an inarticulate prehistory, not only of the present narrative but of perception itself. In a diary entry written between *To the Lighthouse* and *A Room of One's Own*, Woolf wrote: "What I like, or one of the things I like, about motoring is the sense it gives one of lighting accidentally, like a voyager who touches another planet with the tip of his toe, upon scenes which would have gone on, have always gone on, will go on, unrecorded, save for this chance glimpse" (3: 153). Beginning's ragged edge is the ghostly echo of things that "have gone on, have always gone on, will go on, unrecorded"; listening in, like alighting on a foreign planet, situates the life within the book in the larger stream of unrecorded time.

A slightly different strategy of anti-beginning is a pattern of infinite regression, signaled, in the opening of *Mrs. Dalloway*, by the conjunction "for." Of all Woolf's novels, *Mrs. Dalloway* might seem to make the clearest straight-edge start, with its definitive announcement of determination and act: "Mrs. Dalloway said she would buy the flowers herself" (3). Immediately following this sentence, however, the logic of "for" reveals the previously occurring "ground" or "reason" motivating Clarissa's announced intent:[4] "For Lucy had her work cut out for her." Like "so" and "but," "for" in this usage is a coordinating conjunction; unlike "since" or "because," which subordinate motivation to act, "for" places the prior event on an equal footing with the present. Then, as the passage continues, repetitions of "for" refer us to various other possible beginnings, none subordinate to any other, but each subsequently less definite as narrative scene. Clarissa experiences the first whiff of fresh, early morning air as a plunge into a lake: "For so it had always seemed"; the scene wobbles through a lifetime of memory before alighting on a moment when she was eighteen. In the next paragraph, a moment of suspension—Clarissa's experience of indefinite time before the definitive hour struck by Big Ben—is similarly informed by an indeterminate "before": "For having lived in Westminster—how many years now? over twenty" (4). The single day of Mrs. Dalloway's present acquires density through the ever-expanding traces of the past, just as the narrative, in its larger frame, acquires density through the prior, though largely unnarrated and hence uncontainable, experiences of war. And since the pattern of infinite regression here does not mean receding further and further back but receding over and over again, it makes untenable any posited resting place of a single beginning, even in hypothetical time.

Perhaps most radically, strategies of anti-beginning serve as narrative filter for Woolf's most extended allusion to the biblical myth of creation: the echo of Genesis in the first section of *The Waves*. Opening in darkness, in a world of no distinguishable forms, the italicized prelude might seem to replicate a scene of ex nihilo creation (the beginning of day imitating the beginning of consciousness and initiating the beginning of form). Yet the informing paradigm wobbles between tropes of creation and tropes of disclosure or discovery, ambiguously mixing metaphors of birth and revelation. If the sun is the eye, then the movement from dark to light, from undifferentiated mass ("the sea was indistinguishable from the sky") to articulated forms ("the sun sharpened the walls of the house"), suggests the separation of matter from chaos as a generative visual act (7, 8). If, however, the sun *strikes* the eye, then a slowly emerging landscape is recorded, notated, and doubled in the mind, the refraction of light instilling the retinal image. Perception in this guise apprehends what has preceded, in its existence, the sensory act. Furthermore, while external reality is creatively and generatively constructed through mental images, the images themselves encode the previously observed: a wrinkled cloth, a breathing sleeper, sediment clearing in wine, or the arm of a woman raising a lamp. Seven times in the first three paragraphs, the words "as if" and "like" signal the dependency of perception on associations that antedate the immediate scene. Two different kinds of pre-text are thus invoked: a reservoir of mental images in communal memory and an objective reality existing independently of any memory narrative in our minds. The implications are accordingly doubly transformative. Unlike the creative fiat of "*Be Light*," here the artist, as the partially obscured figure of the woman whose arm raises the lamp, is creative and creating *without* being a single and authoritative point of origin. And for the reader, beginning means entering a process whose very multiplicity prevents any reduction of the previous or the ensuing text into a single narrative line.

Beginnings and Novelty

In various ways, Woolf's opening words thus creep out from their place between the printer's covers to link with what has been said or thought before. And the implications again reveal the fallacy of earlier assumptions about modernist thought. Far from being ahistorical autonomous formalism, Woolf's writing is permeated with historical consciousness; and instead of plunging us into subjective individualism, the adumbrated, pluralistic "source text" grounds the narrative in an indeterminate, heterogeneous, communal past. However, such potentially positive expansions of narrative bring attendant threats. The negation of a single origin frees us from confinement in a totalizing monolinear narrative, but the ever-proliferating accumulation of prehistories threatens to confine the future to endless reenactments of the past. The question—and one crucial to Woolf's revolutionary feminist thinking—is whether one can engage the wholeness of continuum and the intermediary, rather than originating, role of the artist and still allow a space for radical freedom to occur.

This problem is dispelled, however, precisely because the shift from monism to pluralism makes it possible to conceive the radically new. By abandoning the construct of a single, unitary origin in one fixed point in time, Woolf's narratives recast beginnings as both multiple and always pervasively potential. If antecedents of present experience have come into existence in different forms at different times, then the phenomenon of beginning can occur at any future point as well. A new eddy can flow into the stream, a new thread be woven into the cloth, to enter and transform the holistic continuum of ongoing life. Such perception resembles T. S. Eliot's belief that each new poem both adds to and alters the literary tradition, and his assertion that "every hundred years or so" a critic will emerge to "set the poets and the poems in a new order" (*Use* 108). In Woolf's writing, however, reformations of the past are everyday and continuous, not occasional and monumental. In addition, and particularly in her later works, Woolf's plural and reiterated beginnings pave the way for new forms of being, radically other than what has existed before.

This construct of time as continuous and yet ever changing, repetitive yet never the same, recalls the correspondences, frequently noted, between Woolf's narrative structures and Henri Bergson's concept of duration, or *durée*. For a narratological understanding of the integral tie between narrative pluralism and an open future, however, we can more usefully turn to the late work of William James. James increasingly recognized similarities between his thought and Bergson's as connections not of influence but affinity. In similar fashion, what James expresses in one register, Woolf does in another, and their affinities illuminate the philosophical implications that Woolf's unconventional beginnings encode.

In his posthumous *Some Problems in Philosophy*, William James investigates the philosophical ramifications of positing one "supreme purpose and inclusive story"—a conjecture of monism—as opposed to numerous stories that "run alongside each other"—the pluralist hypothesis (131). However, converting that oppositional relation into one of paradox, James argues that the physical world manifests "neither absolute oneness nor absolute manyness," nor does one mode achieve primacy over the other; rather, "an infinite hetereogeneity among things exists alongside of whatever likeness of kind we discover" (127, 128). The problem James then identifies is with the monistic thesis, which, in reducing reality to the single attribute of oneness, additionally circumscribes the future as always "co-implicated with the past" (139). Pluralism, in contrast, conceives an "additive world" in which disparate realities coexist in loose relations, as if connected by "the bare conjunctions 'with' and 'and'" (136). Additive relations, moreover, make it possible for genuine novelty to "leak in" (132).

Woolf's juxtaposed fragments, lateral associative movements, and multiple simultaneous plots have been well recognized, but we can now link these structural features to the way beginning is represented and conceived. Woolf's disjunctive narrative acts signal a continuous "leaking in" of novelty, dispersing beginning gestures throughout her text and stimulating a forward-moving momentum into an increasingly rich, increasingly heterogeneous world. Again James's explanations connect such pluralistic, disjunctive structures with interventions of the radically new. The "classic obstacle to pluralism" and hence to novelty, he argues, is the "principle of causality" (189). For if all effects proceed from causes, effect is always inherent in the cause. What is created is always created out of what already exists; nothing can come into existence that is not some manifestation of the old. Against such limiting causality, James posits a different perceptual experience, one responsive to infinite variety: "Time keeps budding into new moments, every one of which presents a content which in its individuality never was before and will never be again" (148). Our conceptual understandings, which explain by "deducing the identical from the identical," can name new forms, but only in the terms of the already known, so that "if the world is to be conceptually rationalized no novelty can really come" (152). But our own experience, James argues, tells us otherwise: "the perceptual flux is the authentic stuff of each of our biographies, and yields a perfect effervescence of novelty all the time" (151). Transposing James's words to a different medium, Woolf's false starts, multiple starts, radical breaks, and sudden narrative leaps challenge fixed concepts with the shocks of perceptual novelty, making beginning a perpetual possibility, to and beyond the end.

Beginnings beyond the End

If the openings of Woolf's novels adumbrate ghostly and multiple pre-texts, the ensuing narratives function as prologue, framing and shaping the proleptic gestures on the final page. Even *Jacob's Room*, the novel that seems most to end in loss, creates its final impact through the elided presence of beginnings. In the social sphere, Jacob's fate is driven by strong elements of classic causality: the gendered pathways that regulate his life just as much as Florinda's and Fanny's, the forces that send him to his privileged education in Cambridge and, as an ironic result of that privilege, off to fight in the war. But Woolf's pluralistic narrative structure defies the hegemony of causality, opening itself to the intrusion of multiple pathways through the inscription of broken links.[5] The blank spaces separating textual fragments leave literal gaps on the page, which are widened perceptually by sudden shifts in perspective, abrupt relocations in space, and precipitous leaps forward in time. The passage of time is motion, but it is a motion whose car frequently jumps the rails. And it is this interrupted, zigzag movement—the course, we might say, of repeatedly halting and newly beginning—that brings a genuinely pluralist subject into view. As Woolf wrote in "The Leaning Tower," "A writer has to keep his eye upon a model that moves, that changes, upon an object that is not one object but innumerable objects" (162). Jacob moves, changes, appears in innumerable guises: both the multiplicity of Jacobs, which our outsider's perspective can only intuit in fragmented glimpses, and the adumbrated potentiality of Jacob's becoming, in the future, something other or more than his past. The antiwar protest of this novel is directed not only at the termination of a rich and vibrant life that once existed but, in addition, at the preclusion of the unborn selves that unpredictably could have shaped Jacob's life to come. While Jacob's death may logically, though tragically, end the plotted causality, his abandoned and empty shoes—for where would he have walked in them?—recast the novel as prologue to a movement that *might* have been. The beginning projected at the end of this novel is predicative, even in its erasure, of both onward flow and the possibilities of radical change.

Even so cursorily outlined, *Jacob's Room* draws together the central themes in this study so far: beginning is all about motion, and self-problematizing beginnings extend that motion both before the first and after the final words. Furthermore, in pluralistic narrative, beginnings are multiple, recurring, and additive: they happen severally and frequently, and they join rather than break with the past. Yet the ragged edge of beginning manifests a double nature as continuance and change. In Woolf's writing, beginning both happens over and over again (hence the repetitive patterns) and simultaneously interjects something new (hence the spaces and gaps). Finally, if openings sound echoes of ghostly pre-texts, so closings prefigure ghostly post-texts; in *Jacob's Room*, even the finality of death fades perceptibly into ongoing life.[6]

While beginnings are reconfigured and relocated throughout Woolf's fiction,[7] post-textual beginnings are most overtly signaled in her last two novels, as erupting war gave questions about the future an increasingly urgent ring. Both *The Years* and *Between the Acts* end on the brink of beginnings projected beyond narrative time, perhaps even beyond the language or discourse that has constituted the textual world. Dialogue in *The Years* halts on Eleanor's interrogative, "And now?" (435).[8] In *Between the Acts*, the closing lines recast the entire narrative as prologue to the text about to play: "Then the curtain rose. They spoke" (219). Furthermore, both structurally and thematically, these narratives are fissured with cracks of possibility for novelty to leak in.[9] At the Pargiters' final party, Peggy's reiterated phrase "living . . . living differently, differently" opens up an ever-increasing space, with the punctuation between the repeated "differently"s progressing from a comma (391) to a dash (422) to an ellipsis (423). Then, into this opening, discursive difference erupts with the entrance of the caretaker's children and their strangely captivating, incomprehensible song. *Between the Acts* similarly underscores its trope of "scraps, orts and fragments" (188) with anticipations of a differently configured world: "Let's break the rhythm and forget the rhyme" (187), for "it was time someone invented a new plot" (215).

But pluralistic narratives are prognostic of possibilities, not of outcomes, and the clash of contradictory impulses has left critics divided about these novels' intended aims. Apart from controversies over optimistic and pessimistic readings, interpretations differ in emphasizing either the freedom offered by disjunction or the determinism implicit in a reiterating past. For the dawn that ends the Pargiters' party begins a new yet *another* day; the rising curtain in *Between the Acts* locates the narrated text as intermission, to be followed by a new yet *another* act. The ragged edge, however, negotiates between reenactment and revolution; for Woolf, it is the combination of continuity and novelty that offers hope.

This double motion explains the otherwise puzzling note that makes, not an ending, but a point of arrest in many of Woolf's longer works: a trope of reconciliation, or détente, or confrontation between the sexes. Such narrative conventionality may strike us as odd in a writer who so opposed her culture's gendered plots, in both life and fiction. For Woolf, however, the polarization of entrenched gender identifications was inseparable from the most significant conflicts of her generation, so that her hoverings around the traditional sexual plot suggest a constant return to the site where the rip of cloth must take place. Thus echoing the end of *A Room of One's Own*, Eleanor Pargiter looks out a window to see an unknown man and woman in a taxi, although this couple moves out of the taxi and into a house, not—as in the earlier work—into the taxi and down the street. In the final scene of *Between the Acts*, Isa and Giles transform from audience members to figures in a play, recalling Mrs. Swithin's observation that the Chinese "put a dagger on the table and that's a battle" (142). Functioning at a supra-character level, these emblematic figures encapsulate both the hostilities between the sexes and the larger hostilities of warring civilizations, all placed within repetitive cycles of destruction and rebuilding. But each novel also configures space where newness can intrude. In *The Years*, the couple emerging from the taxi is glossed first with the love between Nicholas, a Polish and possibly Jewish homosexual, and Sara, a sexually ambiguous and decidedly unconventional woman, and then by Eleanor's holding out her hands to her brother Morris. The house is still a shell for human community, but the home of the Victorian paterfamilias has been shed, making, with respect to the fate of the larger human family, a radically open question of Eleanor's last words, "And now?" *Between the Acts* halts on a yet more radical node of beginning: the mind at the point "*before* roads were made, or houses" (219; emphasis added). Like James, Woolf gestures beyond the limitations of entrenched concepts to the limitation of concepts themselves, just as Lily cries out, in *To the Lighthouse*, for "the thing itself before it has been made anything," in order to "start afresh" (287). Thus, in *Between the Acts,* the grammar of the future moves through repetition to possibility: "they *must* fight," "they *would* embrace," "another life *might* be born" (219; emphasis added).[10] We are impelled by the past, but freedom from teleological narrative makes new interventions (positive or negative) possible in the post-textual world.

New Beginnings, New Wholes

Pluralism in narrative casts beginnings as anti-beginnings, and endings as polyvalent beginnings.[11] Finally, in redefining the edges of narrative, pluralism reconfigures wholes. As we have seen, embracing the unknown and difference does not exclude repetition and recurrence; admitting discontinuity does not deny or negate continuities. In a similar pluralistic paradox, allowing for the "yet to be" does not preclude conception of the "all." But apprehended within the flux, James explains, totality no longer appears as "a sum harvested and gathered in"; instead, totality becomes the experience of "all that is there" (163). In turning from "static to growing forms of being" (170), we replace "the wholly irrelevant notion of a bounded total" (169) with the holistic perception of nothing excluded, "an entirely different demand" (162). In similar fashion, Woolf offers a fluid modeling of the whole community, emergent from a heterogeneous past and with potentials for additive new voices in the future. Whereas Eliot, in *Four Quartets*, reconciles paradoxical reversals of beginnings and ends by moving to a mystical still point outside time, Woolf situates endless beginnings in the flows of time. In her hands, beginning's ragged edge slips us in between multiple histories and possible futures, immersing us in a stream of pluralistic voices sounding before and after the covers of the book.

Notes

1. Using a similar metaphor, Woolf wrote of her abandoned draft of "The Hour": "oh the cold raw edges of one's relinquished pages" (*Diary* 2: 289).
2. Although "umbilical" suggests "mother" and hence "birth," Faulkner's Mississippi is both river and "Environment itself" (269), just as the umbilical is both the Mississippi and talk. Faulkner's emphasis is not on parturition and separation but on imbricated coexistence.
3. In a nonmodernist correlate, Thomas King similarly opposes the structure of aboriginal stories to the paradigm of biblical creation. While creation myths abound in Native stories, the multiple variants wrought by changes in storytellers and audiences, the reliance on collaboration and performance, and the play with notions of infinite regression and multiple retellings—each of King's chapters begins with (almost but not quite) the same story—produce effects much akin to beginning's ragged edge.
4. *OED*, definition B.2.a.
5. While rejecting totalizing narratives of causality, James nevertheless recognizes "perceptual experience of the kind of thing we mean by causation" (219), although he posits that the feeling that "successive states continue each other" (213) may be a product of human activity itself, the action of "sustaining a felt purpose against felt obstacles, and overcoming or being overcome" (212). Narrative desire, situating readers like moths buzzing around the flame of Jacob, may well supply this felt causality in *Jacob's Room*.
6. We find a similarly unorthodox "beginning" in the dispersal of Rachel's self into the conscious and unconscious minds of others in the last chapter of *The Voyage Out*.
7. In addition to recasting the creation myth, *The Waves*, for example, enacts at least three narrative beginnings: in the imagistic interludes, in the internalized monologues, and in Bernard's retelling and summing up.
8. The additive implications of the words are clear.
9. Employing an image that resonates with the present essay, J. Hillis Miller comments that "*Between the Acts* remains projective, hypothetical, incomplete. It possesses unknown gaps or frayed edges" (218).
10. With similar attention to verb form, Pamela Caughie notes the significance of Lily's claim, at the end of *To the Lighthouse*. With the words "I *have had* my vision," Lily consigns her artwork to the flux (486; emphasis in Caughie).

11. In a different version of this essay, I expand my consideration of Woolf's ragged ends. I would like to thank Clemson University Digital Press for permission to republish parts of my article "Afterword: Inside and Outside the Covers: Beginnings, Endings, and Woolf's Non-coercive Ethical Texts," *Woolfian Boundaries: Selected Papers from the Sixteenth Annual International Conference on Virginia Woolf*, ed. Anna Burrells, Steve Ellis, Deborah Parsons, and Kathryn Simpson. Clemson SC: Clemson University Digital Press, 2007. 172–80.

Works Cited

Caughie, Pamela. "Virginia Woolf: *To the Lighthouse*." *A Companion to Modernist Literature and Culture*. Ed. David Bradshaw and Kevin J. H. Dettmar. Oxford: Blackwell, 2006. 486–98.

Dettmar, Kevin J. H. 2006. Introduction. *A Companion to Modernist Literature and Culture*. Ed. David Bradshaw and Kevin J. H. Dettmar. Oxford: Blackwell, 2006. 1–5.

Eliot, T. S. *Four Quartets*. 1943. London: Faber and Faber, 1944.

———. *The Use of Poetry and the Use of Criticism*. 1933. London: Faber and Faber, 1964.

Faulkner, William. *Absalom, Absalom! The Corrected Text*. 1936. New York: Modern Library, 1993.

James, William. *Some Problems of Philosophy: A Beginning of an Introduction to Philosophy*. New York: Longmans, Green, 1911.

Joyce, James. *A Portrait of the Artist as a Young Man*. Ed. Seamus Deane. 1915. Harmondsworth: Penguin, 1992.

King, Thomas. *The Truth about Stories: A Native Narrative*. Minneapolis: University of Minnesota Press, 2005.

Miller, J. Hillis. *Fiction and Repetition*. Cambridge: Harvard University Press, 1982.

Prince, Gerald. *A Dictionary of Narratology*. Lincoln: University of Nebraska Press, 1989.

Woolf, Leonard S. "The Pageant of History." *Essays on Literature, History, Politics, etc*. Freeport NY: Books for Libraries, 1970. 125–48.

Woolf, Virginia. *Between the Acts*. New York: Harcourt Brace, 1941.

———. *The Diary of Virginia Woolf*. Ed. Anne Olivier Bell. 5 vols. New York: Harcourt, 1977–84.

———. *Jacob's Room*. 1922. New York: Harcourt Brace, 1923.

———. "The Leaning Tower" (1940). *Collected Essays*. Ed. Leonard Woolf. New York: Harcourt Brace, 1967. 2: 162–81.

———. "Mr. Bennett and Mrs. Brown" (1924). *Collected Essays*. Ed. Leonard Woolf. New York: Harcourt Brace, 1967. 1: 319–37.

———. *Mrs. Dalloway.* New York: Harcourt Brace, 1925.
———. *A Room of One's Own.* New York: Harcourt Brace, 1929.
———. "A Sketch of the Past" (1976). *Moments of Being.* Ed. Jeanne Schulkind. 2nd ed. San Diego: Harcourt Brace Jovanovich, 1985. 61–159.
———. *To the Lighthouse.* New York: Harcourt Brace, 1927.
———. *The Waves.* New York: Harcourt Brace, 1931.
———. *The Years.* New York: Harcourt Brace, 1937.

7

A Theory of Narrative Beginnings and the Beginnings of "The Dead" and *Molloy*

BRIAN RICHARDSON

The central theoretical question surrounding this topic is precisely what constitutes the beginning of a narrative. I argue in this essay that there are three distinct kinds of beginnings: one in the narrative text (*syuzhet*), one in the story as reconstructed from the text (*fabula*), and one in the prefatory and framing material provided by the author that circumscribes the narrative proper (authorial antetext). There is also what may be called an "institutional antetext" that frames (or attempts to frame) the book before it is read.

In nearly all cases, there is no ambiguity concerning the beginning of the *syuzhet*: it is the first page of the narrative proper. It is perhaps the very fixity of the *syuzhet* that is the ground for play with beginnings in the other two areas. It should be noted, however, that recently several new kinds of narrative have appeared that dislodge this stability. There is the "novel in the box" by Marc Saporta (*Composition #1*, 1962), a series of unnumbered autonomous pages which the reader is invited to shuffle before reading. Ana Castillo's epistolary novel *The Mixquiahuala Letters* extends the compositional technique of Cortàzar's *Hopscotch* and offers different points of entry for different readers: cynics are advised to begin with the second letter, while the quixotic are told to begin with the third. Many hypertext novels have several possible points of entry, as Jessica Laccetti demonstrates later in this volume.

The question of exactly where the *fabula* begins is, by contrast, a difficult one to determine with precision. Is it the chronologically first dramatized scene, narrated incident, mentioned act, or inferable event? Each possible answer is problematic. Meir Sternberg states that the beginning of the *fabula* of *The Ambassadors* is the first narrated event in the history of Lambert Strether. He does not indicate the criterion he uses for this determination, nor does he consider other possibilities of establishing the origin of the *fabula*, such as the earliest disclosed event in the history of Strether's family, or those surrounding the other families involved in this story. Neither does he mention the difficulties that would be posed by more ambiguous, recessive, or unretrievable beginnings of the *fabula* in more elusive texts.

Even a seemingly straightforward example can reveal how hard it is to come up with a definitive beginning that does not require several interpretive decisions that are unlikely to be agreed on by most readers. Let us start with a text that contains several references to the past, Joyce's "The Dead," and ask where its story begins. If our definition is that of dramatized scenes, as Romagnolo claims in her essay in this volume, then it begins as the guests are arriving at the party at the Morkans': with one partial exception at the beginning of the text, there are no analepses; the entire narrative is told in a completely linear manner, as any reference to the past comes from memory or a conversation in the "narrative present tense." But this response is clearly inadequate, since the point of the story is the revelation of a significant past event, the death of Michael Furey, and its powerful transformation of the protagonist, Gabriel Conroy. This centerpiece of the story, narrated by Gretta, would have to be part of the *fabula*, I believe. Otherwise, to take another example, all the past events of Oedipus's life would not be part of the *fabula* of Sophocles' *Oedipus Rex*; this is clearly an unsatisfactory conclusion, since the story has to stretch at least as far back as the prophecy which stated that Oedipus would kill his father and marry his mother. Mieke Bal is one of the few theorists to discuss this possibility; she calls it an "embedded fabula that explains and determines the primary fabula" (144). However, I suspect this ingenious delineation will seem inadequate to most theorists: to refer to the cause of the central story as an embedded fabula would seem to imply that it might not be the same story simply because it is disclosed by a character's speech rather than through stage enactment or authorial narration. And in the case of *Oedipus Rex*, Sandor Goodhart has shown that the backstory that everyone ends up believing has some interesting discrepancies and might not be entirely true. This should warn us against uncritically including uncorroborated episodes derived from characters' narratives as a fixed part of the *fabula*. Sometimes they are, and sometimes they aren't.

But if we allow narrated events into the *fabula*, and it seems we must, where do we stop? Are not any other anterior events discussed or alluded to by the characters equally part of the story proper? Through conversations and free indirect discourse we learn of Lily's leaving school, last year's party, Freddy Malin's penchant for borrowing, Gabriel's attending the university with Molly Ivors, his mother's disapproval of Gretta when they married, virtues of long-deceased tenors, and, in what may be the oldest recalled event, the story of Gabriel's grandfather's horse (an episode, it might be noted, that is unconnected to the main story line but which acts as a *mise en abyme* of Gabriel's situation). Is this the beginning of the *fabula*? There are of course many other earlier events implicitly alluded to as well: the statue of Daniel O'Connell, the Wellington monument, and even the picture of the two princes murdered in the Tower of London attest to distant historical events. For that matter, the references to Christmas presume the birth of Jesus, while the allusions to ancient Greek divinities and an enemy hero (Paris) take us further back to the time of the Trojan War—we have now virtually arrived at the literal *ovo* that Horace had admonished us about.

One can push this line of argumentation even further. The opening sentence of Beckett's *Murphy*, "The sun shone, having no alternative, on the nothing new" (1), both invokes the phrase from Ecclesiastes and presumably implies an earlier time before the sun could be said to shine. Amos Oz takes this argument even further: "Isn't there always, without exception, a latent beginning-before-the-beginning? A foreword to the introduction to the prologue?" (8–9). He goes on to suggest that any story, "if it is to live up to its ideal duty, must go back at least all the way to the Big Bang, that cosmic orgasm with which, presumably, all the smaller bangs began" (10). Not only is there a definite logic in Oz's playful statement, but the fact of the matter is that such an infinite regress of antecedents not only can be but actually has been put in practice. It is not unusual for Native American autobiographers to begin with the story of their ancestors, their nation, or to go even further back: Geronimo's story of his life begins, "In the beginning the world was covered with darkness. There was no sun, no day" (59); only after several creation myths and a brief account of the various Apache groups does he arrive at the moment when he is born (69). In the realm of popular fiction, one may similarly point to the epic sagas of James A. Michener, which often begin with the geological origins of the setting of the work, followed by accounts of the earliest human habitation, and then stories of wave after wave of immigration over the centuries. *Hawaii*, for example, starts with the words "Millions upon millions of years ago, when the continents were already formed" (1) and goes on to narrate the first appearance of the Hawaiian islands.

So where then does the story really begin? I don't think there is an easy solution to this dilemma. One other obvious solution is to take the first incident that is causally connected to those that follow. Such a choice would correspond well to a number of different accounts, including Aristotle's definition of "that which does not itself follow anything by causal necessity, but after which something naturally is or comes to be" (§ 7.3) as well as the following statement in Gerald Prince's *Dictionary of Narratology*: "the incident initiating the process of change in a plot or action. This incident does not necessarily follow but is necessarily followed by other incidents" (10). Also consonant with this approach are Brooks's identification of the beginning as the initiation of narrative desire, Phelan's notion of "Launch," and the theoreticians who, drawing on story grammars, identify the beginning as the first item in the sequence of connected significant events (Tomashevsky's bound motifs, Barthes's cardinal functions [93–97], Chatman's kernels [53–56]).

But if the idea of the first event referred to by the text is far too inclusive, the idea of the first function is much too restrictive. Most of the events narrated in the early portions of "The Dead" (and many of the subsequent ones until the party is almost over) are not directly connected to the events that follow; they are rather what Tomashevsky would call "free motifs," Barthes "indices," and Chatman "satellites." As in so many seemingly "plotless" modernist works, many events are included for their thematic, symbolic, or analogical relation to the main events of the text, not because they partake in an unbroken chain of causally determined events such as that found in a novel by Jane Austen. The sequence of the bound motifs must thus be reduced to a subset of the story, and determining the first instance of the former will not help us establish the beginning of the latter. Bound motifs, those "which may not be omitted without disturbing the coherence of the narrative" (Tomashevsky 166), are useful concepts for the analysis of many tightly plotted works, and we may understand why theorists like Propp, Brooks, Phelan ("Launch") and Romagnolo ("Causal Beginnings") wish to employ this as a central category of analysis, even as some (like Romagnolo) note how difficult it can be to find the precise origin of this elusive thread. In between the bound motifs and the free motifs there often exists a hazy realm of ambiguous motifs that are neither entirely bound nor exactly free. Thus, Gabriel's brief encounter with Lily near the beginning of the text almost certainly has no consequences for the chain of events that later unfolds: it anticipates rather than precipitates them. The same is largely true of his later encounter with Molly Ivors; both episodes could be omitted without affecting the final, climactic third of the text.

I conclude from this investigation that there is no ready formula for ascertaining the actual beginning of a story; instead, we must select a principle that will lead us in the direction we want to go. We need to critically sift through the various possibilities, whether dramatized, narrated by a character, or otherwise alluded to, until we arrive at the first significant event of the story. Our most accurate concept will thus be a avowedly shifting one, and one that thereby points to the elusive and often arbitrary nature of beginnings. The consequence for our reading of "The Dead" is thus a seemingly paradoxical one: building on recent postcolonial criticism of the text, I would argue that the first essential event of the story is an unnarrated one that colors all the subsequent material, informs every major scene, is implicit in Gabriel's three encounters with women who symbolize Ireland, and is embodied by the stunning presence of the dead Michael Furey that is the culmination of the novella's plot: that is, the English occupation of Ireland (see Cheng 128–47). This occupation, it might be added, is one which itself lacks a fixed beginning but can be fairly accurately said to have taken place in stages over the course of several centuries.

What I call the authorial antetext is the totality of authorial material that precedes the first words of the narrative. In most cases this includes the title, dedication, epigraph, table of contents, author's note or preface, and other related material. Though independent of the story proper, these are often integral components of the work: to take the standard example, imagine how differently we would read Joyce's novel if it were not entitled *Ulysses*. Likewise, the familiar list of "other works by the same author" helps identify the work and its appropriate reception, especially when the author is using a pen name and is not revealing all the other books actually written by the same author. Caroline Heilbrun negotiates this issue by listing "Other Books by Amanda Cross" inside the cover of the pseudonymous mysteries she has penned. The prefatory material to Nabokov's *Look at the Harlequins!* includes a list of "Books by the Narrator," a list of volumes that parodies the one usually found inside Nabokov's books (e.g., Nabokov's *Laughter in the Dark* becomes the narrator's *Slaughter in the Light*). Even the copyright notice can disclose an interesting story, as in the case of suppressed works like Lawrence's *Lady Chatterly's Lover*, as John Sutherland has explained in his discussion of beginnings (65–71). The antetextual designation of the work as fiction or nonfiction is as important as any other component; its significance becomes obvious when it is absent or incorrect, as happened when James Weldon Johnson's *Autobiography of an Ex-Colored Man* was published without the name of its author or the information that it was a work of fiction. Readers naturally assumed that the book was an autobiography and that the fictional narrator was its actual author (see Rohy).

Each type of beginning contains the seeds of its own violation; these too must be reckoned with and included in a comprehensive theoretical account. We have already seen how the beginning of the *syuzhet* can be subverted by the rare texts that refuse to present themselves in any fixed order; this includes the more playful kinds of hypertext fictions. As we also noted, the beginning of the *fabula* can be problematized by the proliferation of minor anterior events or digressions that are not necessary to the unfolding of the plot. There are also red herrings, which promise to produce conflicts that do not in fact appear: these constitute a series of visible pistols that, despite Chekhov's dictum, are never fired. The main drama at the beginning of "The Dead" is the fear that Freddy Malins will, once again, drink too much and spoil the party. This never happens; Freddy turns out to be just fine. This is instead an example of what one might designate, adapting Phelan's term, a "false launch." More transgressive are the recent experimental texts like the nouveaux romans that use alternative means such as verbal or conceptual generators to set in motion the events that ensue in a manner independent of traditional emplotment (see Richardson). And perhaps the most thorough violation of a story's beginning is represented by the kind of text that circles back to its starting point, like *Finnegans Wake*, where the last sentence is also the first sentence.

There are two common ways of violating the conventions of the antetext. The first is to include all the appropriate introductory units but to situate them in all the wrong places, a familiar practice since Sterne's *Tristram Shandy*, where the preface is placed in the middle of the third book and a dedication does not appear until the fifth volume. The other is to introduce fictional elements into the conventionally nonfictional apparatus such as the author's preface. Hawthorne's "The Custom House," which precedes and introduces *The Scarlet Letter*, is one such document. The fictional elements in it are subtly situated and gradually developed; they are easily missed by casual readers (see Pearson).

We also need to include what may be called the "institutional antetext" (the subject of exhaustive analysis by Genette), that includes variable and nonauthorial framing elements. The status of the authorial antetext is fairly clear in most recent works, as we have just seen; it includes all the authorial material in the book that frames the narrative proper. We need to distinguish this authorized antetext from that provided by other sources (particularly, the publisher), such as the cover design, frontispiece, lettering, illustrations, the collection of favorable critical notices the book has received, and even the book's binding. Insofar as these entities conform to the tenor of the text they may be seen as extensions of the authorial antetext; insofar as they contradict or are irrelevant to the work they may be dismissed as temporary devices to satisfy economic, ideological, or private demands.

In the rest of this essay I will briefly examine the problematics of beginnings in the work of Samuel Beckett. The first sentences of most of Beckett's texts are generally quite unusual: "Finished, it's finished, nearly finished, it must be nearly finished" (*Endgame* 1); "I shall soon be quite dead at last in spite of all" (*Malone Dies, Three Novels* 179); "I gave up before birth, it's not possible otherwise" (Fizzle 4, *Prose* 234; "For to end yet again" (Fizzle 8, *Prose* 243); "I don't know when I died" ("The Calmative," *Prose* 61); "All that goes before forget" ("Enough," *Prose* 186); and "Try again. Fail again. Better again. Or better worse" (*Worstward Ho, Nohow On* 89). These opening sentences repeatedly problematize the act of beginning, as textual openings often fail to begin properly or refuse to point to any plausible subject of narrative interest and instead announce conclusions or endings. As each text continues, however, the act of beginning irrupts into the text at repeated and unlikely moments. The beginning, it would seem, is arbitrary, inessential, or useless, yet it cannot be dismissed and keeps returning in the text: the first sentence of Fizzle 8, just quoted ("For to end yet again"), is followed by these words: "skull alone in a dark place pent bowed on a board to begin" (243). Thus, the ending announced at the outset immediately (and paradoxically) yields to an originary scene and declaration of an intent to begin. Below I will trace out this curious dynamic of non-, pseudo-, and repeated beginnings and show how Beckett negates and inverts conventional notions of plot and progression.

One of the more intriguing and illustrative beginnings is that of *Molloy*, which can help illuminate the issues involved in the theory of narrative beginnings as well as the difference between modernist and postmodern kinds of openings. *Molloy* is composed of two ambiguously related narratives: a first-person account by a man who claims to be Molloy, and an account by Jacques Moran, who describes his quest for a man who seems to be named Molloy. In Beckett's trilogy this text is followed by *Malone Dies*, a novel that seems like another version of the first half of *Molloy* and is itself followed by *The Unnamable*, a narration about the impossibility of narration.

The first words of the *syuzhet* of *Molloy* and the trilogy are, "I am in my mother's room. It's I who live there now. I don't know how I got there" (7). This is a typical Beckettian beginning that defies the basic rules of the narratable and seems to lead to no narrative tension, insufficiency, or lack. It precedes, appropriately, the retrospectively narrated story of a failed quest, a wayward journey with a most dubious goal. Unlike in a modernist text, where the narrative tension might center on his discovering how he came to be where he is (as Proust's novel ultimately reveals how Marcel became a writer), Molloy will never learn how he got to his mother's room, and he doesn't especially care to find out. After additional discussion of the setting of the writing, the narrator gives a confused account of two figures he seems to have observed walking toward each other, unless he is mistaken, which could easily be the case. After several pages of rumination on the possible encounter of this pair, he decides to go to visit his mother. An account ensues of the wayward and often futile journey, during which he forgets the reasons that impelled him toward her. In the end of his narrative, he collapses in a forest after hearing a voice call to him. Every causal progression is dubious or adventitious, and all forms of teleology are vain; the beginnings of the action of the novel, like all the other actions, seem to lead nowhere.

The discourse about beginnings and the status of the various texts in play are equally inconclusive. On the second page of the text we are given a confusing statement about beginnings. We are told that a man comes every Sunday to take away the papers that Molloy writes. The narrator continues: "It was he told me I'd begun all wrong, that I should have begun all differently. He might be right. I began at the beginning, like an old bollocks, can you imagine that? Here's my beginning. Because they're keeping it apparently. I took a lot of trouble with it. Here it is. It gave me a lot of trouble. It was the beginning, do you understand? Whereas now it's nearly the end. . . . Here's my beginning. It must mean something or they wouldn't keep it. Here it is" (8). A possible gloss on these ambiguous words might give us the following: "In an earlier draft, I had told my story chronologically, beginning at the beginning. But they [*pace* Horace] rejected that method. Now I begin my text retrospectively, describing the scene of writing after all the events have taken place. This other method seems to be the one they want, since they seem to be retaining this version." (It should be noted that, in a typical Beckettian paradox, Molloy cannot know that the pages he is currently writing are the ones that will be retained by "them.") Since the "Moran" section of *Molloy* does more or less start at the beginning, there is a good chance that it may be the earlier draft being referred to here.

The prefatory account is rapidly followed in the English translation by the promise of still more beginnings: "This time, then once more I think, then perhaps a last time, then I think it'll be over, with that world too" (8). It is not clear whether the same story will be begun again and again or whether new stories will be produced (or retrieved), and it is precisely this question of narrative identity that in numerous forms suffuses the ensuing texts. The overarching sense is that beginnings constitute nothing new and that endings likewise resolve nothing. Or in the words of Malone, "I knew that all was about to end, or to begin again, it little mattered which, and it little mattered how" (161). The basic frames of beginning and ending are eviscerated, just as the notion of any teleological progression is exploded. Beckett will only give us one damned thing after another, with an arbitrary beginning and an inconclusive ending. In doing so he resists (or parodies) the entire logic of plot in traditional narrative. He does not even allow one to posit that the same events are beginning again, since he so problematizes the concepts of identity and difference. There is in the end only the constant repetition of the ineffectual act of starting yet again.

The theoretical categories outlined above are likewise tampered with by this author. The beginning of the *syuzhet*, normally the first page of the narrative proper, threatens to become unfixed by the fact of the book's two disjointed parts and the suggestion that the version placed second, Moran's narrative, might just be the prior one and that one could therefore begin equally well with it. Finally, we may ask which text is to be considered primary? The original French version differs from the English translation at points; most significantly for our purposes, the early line "This time, then once more I think, then perhaps a last time, then I think it'll be over, with that world too" (8) expands significantly on the French edition by adding one more time: "Cette fois-ci, puis encore une je pense, puis c'en sera fini je pense, de ce monde-là aussi" (9). *L'innommable* does not seem to have been imagined as part of the original sequence.

The status of the beginning of the *fabula* of *Molloy* is still more elusive. Playing with the trope of birth as beginning, the narrator claims to remember his entry into the world. But since he "remembers" emerging from his mother's rectum rather than her womb ("first taste of the shit"), we may safely conclude that this origin is literally false, however resonant it may be as metaphor or metafiction (excretion is regularly equated with writing in Beckett). In fact, every recollected past event is qualified, doubted, or denied ("I say that now, but after all what do I know now about then" [31]); major narrated events are subsequently "denarrated" ("I went back into the house and wrote, It is midnight. The rain is beating on the windows. It was not midnight. It was not raining" [176]). There is no solid set of facts we might assemble together into a *fabula*; we are left with only the ambiguous discourse of the text.

Even the work's minimal antetext is somewhat unclear. When John Calder was preparing to publish the three novels together, he asked Beckett whether he could call them a trilogy. Beckett refused, and later he refused the word "trinity." After another request for "trilogy" from his American publisher, Barney Rosset of Grove Press, Beckett responded, "Delighted you are doing the 3 in 1 soon. Simply can't think, as I told Calder, of a general title and can't bear the thought of [the] word trilogy appearing anywhere. . . . If it's possible to present the thing without either I'd be grateful" (qtd. in Gontarski xii). Though he promised to "cudgel his fused" synapses to come up with a word or two to describe the relation of the three texts, no such word ever emerged. The three books remain in a partially indeterminate relation to each other, unexplained by any antetextual indicator.

For Beckett, every beginning is false, a clumsy artifice, or a deliberate lie. The unbroken plenum of his characters' experience does not allow for the crisp, distinct segregation of events into a framework that permits beginnings or endings to arise. And in this insistence Beckett may well be representing human experience better than those who, following Aristotle, would bracket off one segment as "that which itself does not follow anything by causal necessity"; Beckett's works (and, I suggest, human existence) are much better modeled by Henry James's opposite affirmation that "really, universally, relations stop nowhere, and the exquisite problem of the artist is eternally but to draw, by a geometry of his own, the circle within which they may happily *appear* to do so" (171–72).

Beckett affirms the continuity of relations, but he refuses to provide the illusion of a "natural" starting or stopping point. This perception is widely shared by modernist authors. As one of André Gide's characters states: "I consider that life never presents us with anything which may not be looked upon as a fresh starting point, no less than as a termination. 'Might be continued' these are the words with which I should like to finish my *Counterfeiters*" (335). Insofar as a work is mimetic and has a significant scope—that is, insofar as it describes a social world—every beginning will be provisional or arbitrary, just as Hogan and Carrard have shown all beginnings of historical narratives to commence with an ultimately fabricated (and invariably debatable) starting point. Forster once said that if not for death and marriage, he could not imagine how most novelists would conclude their stories. But death and marriage end nothing but a thread of events woven within a thicker skein, as probate, divorce, and child support amply illustrate.

As we may deduce from the examples of the ancient cycle of Trojan epics (of which only Homer's are extant), the fictional worlds of Balzac or Faulkner, or the latest additions to the "Star Wars" films, there is always the possibility of a prequel to explain how events had arrived at the beginning point of the chronologically later narrative. As Sartre's Roquetin states, "The scenery changes, people come in and go out. That's all. There are no beginnings" (39). And as for nonmimetic or antimimetic fiction, an author may always create an anterior beginning to any such narrative, as Beckett so insistently demonstrates. Even an origin myth can be reframed by an earlier origin tale from before the beginning. At every level, then, beginnings are provisional concepts, inherently unstable, typically elusive, and always capable of being rewritten.

Works Cited

Aristotle. *Poetics. Critical Theory since Plato.* Ed. Hazard Adams. New York: Harcourt Brace Jovanovich, 1971. 48–66.
Bal, Mieke. *Narratology.* Trans. Christine van Boheemen. Toronto: University of Toronto Press, 1985.
Barthes, Roland. "Introduction to the Structural Study of Narrative." *Image Music Text.* Trans. Stephen Heath. New York: Hill and Wang, 1977. 79–124.
Beckett, Samuel. *The Complete Short Prose, 1929–1989.* New York: Grove, 1995.
———. *Endgame and Act Without Words.* New York: Grove, 1958.
———. *Molloy.* Paris: Editions de Minuit, 1951.
———. *Nohow On: Company, Ill Seen Ill Said, Worstward Ho.* New York: Grove, 1996.
———. *Three Novels: Molloy, Malone Dies, The Unnamable.* New York: Grove, 1958.
Chatman, Seymour. *Story and Discourse: Narrative Structure in Fiction and Film.* Ithaca: Cornell University Press, 1978.
Cheng, Vincent. *Joyce, Race, and Empire.* Cambridge: Cambridge University Press, 1995.
Geronimo. *Geronimo: His Own Story.* Ed. S. M. Barrett. New York: Ballantine, 1971.
Gide, André. *The Counterfeiters.* Trans. Dorothy Bussy. New York: Random, 1973.
Gontarski, S. E. "Introduction: The Conjuring of Something Out of Nothing: Samuel Beckett's 'Closed Space' Novels." Beckett, *Nohow On.* vii–xxvii.
Goodhart, Sandor. "Oedipus and Laius' Many Murderers." *Diacritics* 7 (1978): 55–71.
James, Henry. *Theory of Fiction.* Ed. James E. Miller Jr. Lincoln: University of Nebraska Press, 1972.
Joyce, James. *Dubliners.* New York: Viking, 1961.
Michener, James A. *Hawaii.* New York: Fawcett Crest, 1959.
Oz, Amos. *The Story Begins: Essays on Literature.* Trans. Maggie Bar-Tura. New York: Harcourt Brace, 1999.

Pearson, John H. "The Politics of Framing in the Late Nineteenth Century." *Mosaic* 23 (1990): 15–30.

Prince, Gerald. *Dictionary of Narratology*. 2nd ed. Lincoln: University of Nebraska Press, 2003.

Richardson, Brian. "Beyond the Poetics of Plot: Alternative Forms of Narrative Progression and the Multiple Trajectories of *Ulysses*." *A Companion to Narrative Theory*. Ed. James Phelan and Peter J. Rabinowitz. Malden MA: Blackwell, 2005. 167–80.

Rohy, Valerie, "The Insistence of the Letter: James Weldon Johnson's *Autobiography*." Forthcoming.

Sartre, Jean-Paul. *Nausea*. Trans. Lloyd Alexander. New York: New Directions, 1964.

Sutherland, John. *How to Read a Novel: A User's Guide*. New York: St. Martin's, 2006.

Sternberg, Meir. *Expositional Modes and Temporal Ordering in Fiction*. Baltimore: Johns Hopkins University Press, 1978.

Tomashevsky, Boris. "Thematics." *Russian Formalist Criticism: Four Essays*. Ed. and trans. Lee T. Lemon and Marion J. Reis. Lincoln: University of Nebraska Press, 1965. 61–95.

8

Heartbreak Tango

Manuel Puig's Counter-Archive

CARLOS RIOBÓ

Scholars have identified the figure of the "archive" as the origin of Latin American narrative. This repository of colonial letters, chronicles, and contracts is the crucible for a literary tradition that speaks in a patriarchal, authoritative voice. Latin American writers of the latter part of the twentieth century look for the beginning of a literary identity in the archive to which they can trace their own legitimate lineages. Many writers of that period (known as the "Boom") are preoccupied with an outright search for their own literary origins. They are interested in finding a traditional model for their narratives. Manuel Puig, not a Boom writer, reexamines the beginnings of this tradition, however, in his pseudo-serial novel *Heartbreak Tango* (*Boquitas pintadas*). The beginning and end of this novel reveal and challenge the patriarchal discourse present at Latin American narrative's putative beginning. Puig's novel uncovers the patriarchal disguise that discourse must wear in order to be ensconced within the archive. The traditional view of the archive excludes or hides the illiterate and subliterary cultural variants in Latin America, which, for Puig, also contribute to a narrative tradition.

Beginnings, above all, are very important in the Latin American literary tradition. The so-called Boom writers, the most representative of whom is Gabriel García Márquez, established their own literary origins and legitimacy in their novels. They wrote at a time before narrative in Latin America was seen as having a legitimate and transcendental tradition behind it. Boom novels searched for the essence of Latin American identity, fashioning the search for origins and identity itself as the theme of their writing. These novels brought together the major discursive modalities through which Latin America has been narrated throughout its history. Historically at the margins of Western culture and traditionally the object of study and not the subject, Latin America has been described through legal, scientific, and anthropological discourses.[1] Boom writers include in their novels these different forms of storytelling through which the novelty of Latin America and Latin American identity have been defined and narrated from the beginning. Writers "adopted the avant-garde strategy of proclaiming a new beginning and declaring most of the traditional masters obsolete" (Pope 229). The first stories of Latin America were told through legal discourse: "The Archive goes back to the origins of Latin American narrative because it returns to the language of the law" (González Echevarría 18).

As González Echevarría asserts, "the law figures prominently in the first of the masterstories the novel tells. . . . When the Latin American novel returns to that origin, it does so through the figure of the Archive, the legal repository of knowledge and power from which it sprung" (8). Alejo Carpentier's *Lost Steps* tries to take us back to that putative beginning of writing. What he takes us to "instead is a variety of beginnings at the origin, the most powerful being the language of the law" (González Echevarría 4). In *One Hundred Years of Solitude*, García Márquez also takes his reader through the several narrative modalities through which Latin America has been written about. Although the scientific discourse of nineteenth-century travel books has a marked presence in the novel (Alexander von Humboldt is expressly mentioned), "the most tenuous presence [in the novel] is that of the legal text, but one can infer it from the allusions to the chronicles that were in fact *relaciones*, and particularly in the founding of Macondo" (González Echevarría 22).[2] In Augusto Roa Bastos's *I, the Supreme*, Patiño supervises documents that are contained in the Paraguayan Archives of State. These Boom writers therefore rehearsed the previous Latin American narrative vehicles in their own novels as part of an effort both to subsume and to surpass them.

Among the Boom writers who embed the trope of the archive at the heart of their novels are Gabriel García Márquez, Carlos Fuentes,

Alejo Carpentier, and Roa Bastos. In *One Hundred Years of Solitude*, for example, Melquíades's room holds the parchment in which he has encoded the history of Macondo from its beginnings. Fuentes's *Terra Nostra* harkens back to Charles V and his creation of the Archive at Simancas. In *The Lost Steps*, Carpentier returns to the heart of the Latin American jungle, only to find the foundational colonial city of Santa Mónica de los Venados, the archival city, deserted and empty of its manuscripts. Carpentier's protagonist must write his own documents there, in the jungle, in a gesture that inaugurates Latin American narrative once more. Finally, Roa Bastos's *I, the Supreme* is full of post-independence archives.

The archive has been the object of much consideration and study, particularly since the latter half of the twentieth century. Borges's version of the (fictional) archive, "The Analytical Language of John Wilkins" ("El idioma analitico de John Wilkins," 1952), is inscribed within Michel Foucault's study of the archive in *The Order of Things* (1966). Roberto González Echevarría's *Myth and Archive* propounds a theory of the origins of the novel in 1990, and Jacques Derrida's *Archive Fever: A Freudian Impression* is first delivered as a lecture in 1994 and published in 1995.[3] Because these major writers and critical theorists have nuanced or different views of the archive, I will present my use of the term but only summarize theirs.

Foucault's "archive," as posited in his later book, *The Archaeology of Knowledge*, is a "unified field theory" of sorts. The archive is his nexus for bringing together seemingly distant cultural formations. It is, as Foucault says, "the system that governs the appearance of statements and unique events" (129). He discusses the historical conditions that result from the classification of information and argues that when archives are created they become authoritative institutions. They define what is possible and what is not in terms of what can be spoken. Foucault's archive is a set of relations and institutions that allow discourse to exist. It is not a static collection of texts. In the end, Foucault is concerned with the ways in which culture and knowledge can be performances of power.[4]

González Echevarría's definition of the archive is the most apposite to my study. González Echevarría defines it as the repository containing the legal origins of Latin American narrative and, ultimately, of Latin

America itself. The origins of Latin America, after all, are prefigured in a contract between Columbus and the Spanish Crown prior to October 1492, and then fleshed out in legal and notarial documents between Habsburg Spain and its subjects in the Americas. The vast Spanish bureaucratic machine of the Habsburgs provides a discursive formula, *la relación*, for addressing the Crown. Rhetorical privilege is afforded all those who take part in the archive's scriptural economy, because this economy recognizes those who are able to simulate its discourse. Even the illiterate are able to have letters written on their behalf, using the recognized conventions. The archive is, indeed, kept in a real building, then two major buildings, and then others, where the overwhelming amount of written documents that grow out of the American encounter are housed in Spain.[5]

A tremendous number of contracts and letters crisscrossed the Atlantic in the sixteenth century, many of which are embellished in efforts by explorers and colonists to gain the Crown's favor. These writings may be read as fiction, after all. As a result, the Latin American narrative tradition is born out of this intercourse. In Habsburg Spain and in its colonies, writing is an act of submitting to a prescribed formula of address to authority, the specifics of which are beyond the scope of this study. Those who can write, or who can get someone such as a scribe to write for them, can simulate the discourse of power and can address power itself—the king of Spain or his direct representatives. The Latin American narrative tradition is therefore born out of the derivative relationship between power and writing issuing from this epistolary intercourse and rhetorical disguise.

The twentieth-century Latin American novel is linked to these early American chronicles through its own penchant for discursive simulation. In particular, this simulation manifests itself, as González Echevarría puts it, in "the novel's persistent disclaimer of literary origins and its imitation of other kinds of [non-literary] discourse" (ix). This non-literary discourse that the novel imitates, however, is always one that happens to be invested with truth value, power, or privilege at that moment in time and by that society. For example, in sixteenth-century Spain the discourse of legitimacy is a legal one. Despite such a disavowal of the literary, both the twentieth-century novel and the early chronicles of the "New World" presume a literate subject who may access dominant forms of writing, or high culture. After all, the archive is a repository for the idiom of power or its simulation. The origins of the Latin American literary tradition, and of Latin America itself, are in the archives of Habsburg Spain.

Manuel Puig's second novel, *Heartbreak Tango* (1969), implicitly expands (and even questions) the work of Boom writers, however, which holds the archive as the master frame in which to search for the origin of Latin America's beginnings and historical identity. This search is commonly undertaken by Boom writers in their self-aware tomes of epic scope that treat culture deferentially as something hallowed and apart from the degraded commodities of everyday life. Within the lettered worlds of the Boom novels, culture and origins are contained in manuscripts and archives, which hold out the possibility of interpretation or recognition by authority. Puig's characters do not have access to such enfranchising discursive modes; the archive to which Boom novelists trace their literary lineage does not provide a locus for the intersection of writing and power in the town of Coronel Vallejos of *Heartbreak Tango*. Instead, this world functions through a different cultural economy. The writing of Puig's characters—when they are more than functionally literate, that is—mimics discursive formulas and rhetorical gestures of popular culture and the mass media. Ultimately, writing in *Heartbreak Tango* is beholden to rhetorical models rife with melodramatic sentimentality and social codes of behavior replete with clichés and platitudes. These codes are imitated by disenfranchised members of the larger Argentine society, such as women, as well as men of the lower rungs of the social ladder. A look at both the beginning and ending of Puig's novel will illustrate these insights.

In *Heartbreak Tango*, subgenre and frame are announced in the novel's subtitle, *Folletín (Serial)*. This supposed replication of the generic model of the serial novel suggests a text potentially out of control, a text that might regenerate itself ad infinitum due to the open-ended nature of serial fiction. The "information" in the text is further complicated, since it exists within Chinese boxes, or different levels of embedded narration. The most problematic fragments with regard to level of narration and text insertion are those that reproduce common registers, such as letters, records, and gossip. Through these disenfranchised registers we learn about the missing patriarchal protagonist—the town's Don Juan, Juan Carlos, who is already dead when the work opens. The novel's third episode, for example, begins with a non-narrative, detailed description of a collection of photographs in a picture album. We see old images of Juan Carlos and other townsfolk over a couple of decades. Puig's generically hybrid text negotiates the patriarchy in a fragmentary work, without a continuous first-level narrator responsible for the whole. In the end, all the traditional men in the novel's world are dead or dying, and women hold their memories within marginal genres—letters—in their hands.

Puig gives *Heartbreak Tango* an identity that is counter to the prestige of the serial novel as he continues to reformulate the Latin American cultural canon. As we have seen, a traditional trope of Latin American narrative is the use of a legalistic or a notarial frame—a frame invested with truth value by a patriarchal society's zeitgeist, within which a writer would seek legitimacy for his or her work. *Heartbreak Tango* rearranges the hierarchy such that the novel, in this case a marker of high culture, is now a simulation of a popular, subliterary form. Within, there is a narrative about the unlettered patriarchal male, which seeks enfranchisement, and the story of a woman who transgresses her society's polarized space: she commits an act of violence against the patriarchy but goes unpunished by it.

A rough synopsis of the plot is as follows: the novel opens with a town's local newspaper's notice of the death of Juan Carlos Etchepare, whom we quickly learn is the local Don Juan. The novel ends with the death of Nené, one of Juan Carlos's girlfriends and a local shopgirl, who eventually marries up within her middle-class world. The final scene of the novel is of Nené's collection of her and Juan Carlos's love letters falling down a chute where they are incinerated as fragments of their texts are illuminated in the flames before they burn. In between, the novel basically follows two love triangles: one involves Nené and Juan Carlos, and the other results in the unpunished murder of Pancho by one of his jilted female lovers, Raba.

Heartbreak Tango literally begins with a first installment or episode, "PRIMERA ENTREGA," which starts with a fragment from a tango song lyric. As an epigraph, the musical fragment sets a popular tone and introduces a text that, together with other genres in the chapter and novel, mixes generic forms. Puig thus suggests that the reader need not have any specialized type of formal, traditional learning to read the text—if anything, the reader must have a certain degree of familiarity with popular culture. *Heartbreak Tango* mixes fragments from newspaper articles, letters, gossip, musical lyrics, police blotters, confessions to priests, and telephone conversations. There is scant a trace of the traditional omniscient narrator. These myriad generic forms are generally considered subliterary and not canonical. They convey the voices of marginal figures, such as middle-class women, because they purportedly represent the venues that these marginal figures traditionally use in reality.

The men in *Heartbreak Tango* are at the mercy of the women who articulate them and of the narrative vehicle of which they are a part. The only significant male characters are Juan Carlos Etchepare, Pancho, and Nené's husband. Some of the other men, whom we will not examine, are Nené's emaciated and dying father and Juan Carlos's nonexistent (but alluded to) father. The narrative proper opens with an obituary notice for Juan Carlos, the town's heartthrob and womanizer: "The untimely passing of Juan Carlos Etchepare on the 18th of April last, at the early age of 29" (9). Although we get to know a bit about him throughout the novel, Juan Carlos is really only an aura of a traditional male figure: we know of his ultimate demise in the first page of the novel, and we know that he suffers from tuberculosis throughout most of the work. We learn about him mostly through the voices and letters of women. The first such series of letters or voices is from Nené, and it makes up the first and second installments (episodes) of the novel. In expressing her condolences to Juan Carlos's mother, Nené invokes and reanimates the memory of Juan Carlos. This is how the reader perceives him after reading the opening obituary notice. We hardly hear directly from Juan Carlos himself, but in the first and eighth episodes we do get letters he writes Nené. *Heartbreak Tango* translates the traditional male through this nonpatriarchal, epistolary genre, through which he cannot adequately communicate. He must use generic passages in the letters, which he has someone else write to his various women friends: "I've put this same little paragraph in every letter" (91). Moreover, the voice of the traditional male is reduced to idle threats: "just take care because I left my sentinels posted back there, no dirty tricks because I'll find out, you don't think so? . . . I'll know about it in no time. I can't forgive a dirty turn, don't you ever forget it" (92). The man of action is reduced to clichés and a less-than-authoritative voice within the conventions of the serial novel.

Puig, therefore, is reformulating the Latin American narrative tradition by having one of the most prestigious narrative types—the novel—pretend to be a disenfranchised popular form—the serial. In this way, his women's voices do not seek legitimacy from a patriarchal frame; instead, his men's voices (or their echoes) seek to be communicated through the marginal venues and have thus become marginalized within the larger tradition of Latin American literature. Recall that the theory of the archive evoked at the beginning of this essay holds that the novel pretends to be a nonliterary text, but one invested with legitimacy and authority. The serial novel does not fall under this description. Although Puig uses mass-cultural forms traditionally addressed to women, and the traditional serial usually relies on the audience's passive reception of the narrative, his virtual serial requires the reader's active participation in order to piece together the complex narrative jumps. Moreover, in ending with death, *Heartbreak Tango* breaks with the typical happy ending of the Latin American serial.

The image of the archive is clearest in *Heartbreak Tango*'s final moment, when Nené's husband throws her and Juan Carlos's love letters, which Nené collected decades before, down an incinerator's chute, to be destroyed, after Nené's funeral. These letters are kept by Nené's lawyer—the figure of the law and a reference to the law's role in the traditional view of the archive—to whom she entrusted them in the latter part of her life. In these letters, Juan Carlos tries to speak with the patriarchal male's most unctuous and manipulative rhetorical privilege and authority. At some point earlier in the novel we learn that Juan Carlos is functionally illiterate and actually has a professor, whom he meets in the hospital, write the love letters for him. Juan Carlos has to resort to the simulation of clichés and the style of popular culture, which is reproduced by a higher-ranking member of society. In the end, the novel is devoid of the discourse of power. The ephemeral love letters can easily be discarded. Nené keeps the letters tied together in two separate bundles, using pink ribbon for hers and blue ribbon for those belonging to Juan Carlos. These sentimental and essentialized gender conventions reveal the rules, as it were, that may govern the archive in Puig's novel. The burning of the letters indicates that, in Puig's world, the archive is finite; it is not a transcendental institution or metanarrative. At the very end of the novel we are left with random words and phrases that we read in flashes of light from the fire as they burn: "no dirty tricks because I'll find out," "Kisses till you say stop, Juan Carlos," "Doll, I'm running out of paper" (224).

The rules of the archive in Puig's *Heartbreak Tango* are not allied with power; instead, they are the conventions of bourgeois popular culture, a culture very much a part of Latin America and, certainly, of Puig's own world. *Heartbreak Tango* begins by announcing the absence of the traditional voice of power and ends by emptying its archive of power's simulated discourse. Puig constructs a counter-archive of popular and unsanctioned materials, thereby tracing his legitimate literary origins to the ephemeral voices of popular culture and the mass media.

Notes

1. Esteban Echeverría's *El matadero* and Sarmiento's *Facundo* are texts in which scientific discourse makes an appearance, while the regionalist novel (*novela de la tierra*), such as *Doña Bárbara*, *La vorágine* (*The Whirlpool*), and *Don Segundo Sombra*, unfolds through anthropological discourse, as many critics, but especially Carlos J. Alonso in his *The Spanish American Regional Novel: Modernity and Autochthony*, have demonstrated.
2. González Echevarría's *Myth and Archive* describes the *relación*, a type of report, legal deposition, and letter, which provides the formulaic basis for addressing power in colonial Spanish America.
3. Other studies that use the figure of the archive, albeit in a different sense from my own, are John Guillory's *Cultural Capital: The Problem of Literary Canon Formation* (1993) and Wadda C. Ríos-Font's *The Canon and the Archive: Configuring Literature in Modern Spain* (2004). Foucault also engages issues regarding the archive in *The Order of Things* (1966).

4. Derrida, on the other hand, sees those very collections as the basis for his term. His notion of the modern archive is born of his study of Freud's work, specifically *Civilization and Its Discontents*, *Beyond the Pleasure Principle*, and his writings on the death drive. Derrida's work seeks to naturalize the human being's impulse to collect within the archive. *Archive Fever* begins with an etymological investigation of the word *archive*, isolating its two variants, *arkhe* and *arkheion*. These etyma reveal the principles derived from his study of the archive: a locus where things are instituted and where social order and law are exercised, as well as a house or residence of the *archons*, or chief magistrates. Thus, the archive is housed with those with the power to interpret it and to impose it as law. Ultimately, Derrida, like Foucault, is concerned with culture and knowledge as performances of power.
5. The three major Spanish archives are El Archivo General de Simancas, in Valladolid; the Escorial, just outside Madrid; and El Archivo General de Indias, in Seville. The archives at Simancas, begun by Charles V and finished by Philip II, are considered the first and vastest European storehouses.

Works Cited

Borges, Jorge Luis. *The Library of Babel*. Trans. Andrew Hurley. 1941. Boston: David R. Godine, 2000.

Derrida, Jacques. *Archive Fever: A Freudian Impression*. Trans. Eric Prenowitz. 1995. Chicago: University of Chicago Press, 1996.

Foucault, Michel. *The Archaeology of Knowledge and the Discourse on Language*. Trans. A. M. Sheridan Smith. 1969. New York: Pantheon Books, 1972.

González Echevarría, Roberto. *Myth and Archive: Toward a Theory of Latin American Narrative*. New York: Cambridge University Press, 1990.

Pope, Randolph D. "The Spanish American Novel from 1950 to 1975." *The Cambridge History of Latin American Literature*. Vol. 2, *The Twentieth Century*. Ed. Roberto González Echevarría and Enrique Pupo-Walker. 1996. New York: Cambridge University Press, 2004. 226–78.

Puig, Manuel. *Heartbreak Tango: A Serial*. Trans. Suzanne Jill Levine. 1969. New York: Vintage Books, 1981.

9

Lost Beginnings in Salman Rushdie's *Midnight's Children*

GAURA SHANKAR NARAYAN

Salman Rushdie's *Midnight's Children* opens with a classic statement announcing autobiographical origins: "I was born in the city of Bombay . . . once upon a time" (3). The Dickensian echo signifying the origin of personal identity is joined with a phrase that elides specific temporal origin and thereby confounds and complicates the notion of beginnings. As the opening paragraph proceeds, Rushdie insists on specifying the moment of Saleem's birth, which coincides with "the precise instant of India's arrival at independence" (3). By this act of clarification the text strives to establish a clear trajectory for the child who has been "mysteriously handcuffed to history" (3). The textual desire for specificity is somewhat modified by the pluralism that spills out of the penultimate sentence of the paragraph: "I, Saleem Sinai, later variously called Snotnose, Stainface, Baldy, Sniffer, Buddha and even Piece-of-the-Moon, had become heavily embroiled in Fate—at the best of times a dangerous sort of involvement" (3). The dangerous involvement of Saleem and India sets Rushdie's emblematic hero the task of mirroring his nation and finding a specular identity. Both participants in this reflective dyad recount history in search of clarifying origins as a way of fixing identity; the twinned projects are subject to parallel confusions on account of fabricated origins.

Let us briefly consider the central accident that befalls Saleem and consigns him to a life unmoored from its beginnings. This is the event in which Mary Pereira exchanges the babies and initiates a narrative whereby Saleem both becomes and resists Shiva. Mary performs her private, revolutionary act of baby exchange in homage to her partner, Joseph, who is tragically seeking national coherence and unity. By exchanging the affluent Muslim baby for the poor Hindu baby who has been conceived in an illegitimate encounter between the street performer Vanita and the departing Englishman, William Methwold, Mary farcically realizes the fantasy of Joseph's desire for a unified nation in which all children are potentially equal. Her act complicates a coherent account of personal identity for Saleem, and the complication spills over in the telling of national history. The exchange dislocates Saleem and overwrites his illegitimate origins with an acquired, middle-class legitimacy. It also inserts him into a chronicle of unknown origins, imbuing him with a compulsive need to construct his legitimate story. When Padma, Saleem's narratee, discovers his biological parentage, she says, "What are you telling me? You are an Anglo-Indian? Your name is not your own?" (131). In response we can say to her, "Yes, it is his own. It did not come to him from the beginning, but he has earned it and made it his own." His progress through his life-story has ensured him that limited certitude. When his family finally discovers that the bloodlines connecting them all are discontinuous, they also find that "it *made no difference*! I was still their son: they remained my parents. In a kind of collective failure of imagination, we learned that we simply could not think our way out of our pasts" (131). The overt historical parallel had been drawn a few pages earlier when we were told that "the city was poised, with a new myth glinting in the corners of its eyes . . . a new myth to celebrate, because a nation which had never previously existed was about to win its freedom" (124).

Midnight's Children invites readerly focus on the newness of Saleem and India by eliminating certain continuities and by complicating the narrative of ethnic identity through a master discourse of national identity.[1] By making Saleem the misplaced baby fathered by the departing Englishman rather than the biologically "real" baby of his parents and, simultaneously, by making India a nation that would only exist "by the efforts of a phenomenal collective will," the novel limits the scope of originary narratives both personal and political. By choosing to tell certain stories and eliminate others, the novelistic narratives of both autobiography and history emphatically assert the centrality of a constructed present that is predicated on the narratological and ideological erasure of moments of the past. In the passages quoted above, Rushdie clearly demarcates a fabricated origin for the reality termed "India." Even as he acknowledges the historical existence of India in antiquity, he insistently posits the violent origin of India in modernity. Modern India, in his telling, is "a mass fantasy" shared by "Bengali and Punjabi, Madrasi and Jat." It demands the burial of one set of beginnings in the service of another. The force of this demand is evident in the minor identity crisis of Adam Aziz, who does "not know whether he was Kashmiri or Indian . . . Indian or Kashmiri" (119). In the course of this novel, Rushdie consistently prefers the term "India" to the terms of regional or ethnic identity. Furthermore, the novel constructs India as an eclectic entity with impure origins. In his telling, the narrative of modern, secular, and anglophone India finds validation and sanction as a result of the partial suppression of the possible narrative of ethnic—in some views, "original"—India. This is inevitable, because Rushdie, quite justifiably in view of the recent emergence of politicized Hindu nationalism, equates the desire for ethnic and indigenous identity with a threat to secular democracy.

Rushdie's positing of a fabricated origin for modern India, concomitant with his tacit denial of a so-called originary indigenous nationhood, is an ideologically and linguistically saturated strategy. This strategy embodies the insistently secular ideology of the novel and also reveals every beginning to be a fabrication in the service of a governing ideology. Rushdie's location of the originating points of the identity-seeking narratives of Saleem and India in their imperial—rather than their indigenous—pasts forces a bracketing away of other pasts, which, if narrativized, would unsettle the British legacy and undo the politics of secularism. The British legacy is resoundingly evident in the novel's much-celebrated literary hybridity, which may well be metonymic of the textual construction of secular India, which can only exist through a discontinuous narration of its indigenous regional history. Saleem's personal dislocation amply reflects the imperial rupture in national history and calls attention to the newly independent nation's narrativizing of its new origins in public nation-building documents.

Saleem's birth is announced through phrases borrowed from the

"Tryst with Destiny" speech that Nehru gave during the transfer-of-power ceremonies: "On the stroke of midnight, Sinai brother, your Begum Sahiba gave birth to a large, healthy child: a son!" (129). Nehru's speech, which echoes throughout this novel, celebrates the historical duality of the moment of Indian independence. The moment of independence from imperial control is a moment of fresh beginnings, a moment of awakening to freedom; it is also, in Nehru's terms, a moment of rebirth, when the soul of a nation long suppressed finds utterance. The dual possibilities are starkly visible in the birth of the two children.

Shiva is the wholly Indian child who represents a contrastive narrative possibility to the one represented by Saleem. The novel consistently constructs him as a grim possibility. Shiva finds his place on the national landscape when he joins the All-India Congress just before the 1957 election in which democratic electoral process is betrayed so that the Congress Party can defeat the Communist Party at the polls (254). It is worth noting that in the 1957 elections the Congress Party found political success as a result of its dual policy of Hindu traditionalism at the local level, especially in the Hindi belt, and Nehruvian anglophone secularism at the national level (Jaffrelot 158–69). Implicitly, though not explicitly, it is clear that Shiva has worked at the local level to enforce the covert traditionalist agenda of the Congress Party. Not surprisingly, Shiva and Parvati's child is born during the darkest hour of Indian democracy: "at the precise instant of India's arrival at Emergency, he emerged. . . . Unprophesied, uncelebrated he came . . . just the same, as my time of connection neared its end, his began" (482). The birth of this child complicates clear bloodlines, just as the interventions of William Methwold and Mary Pereira had done. Saleem, "trapped in the web of these interweaving genealogies," wonders "what was beginning, what was ending" (477). As the second Aadam is born, the British blood that flows in Saleem's veins is flushed out of the family, and Shiva's birthright is implicitly restored to him. Tragically for Rushdie's India, Shiva's child, with pure Indian blood, is the "child of a time which damaged reality so badly that nobody ever managed to put it together again" (482).

On the other hand, Saleem, the biracial hybrid child of an English father and Indian mother, carries the optimistic potentialities of history, as is evident in a letter written to him by Nehru: "You are the newest bearer of that ancient face of India which is also eternally young" (139). The youthfulness of Saleem's face overwrites India's antiquity and positions him as the reflective origin of an anglophone nation's desire for a narrative of modernity. The novel celebrates the impure origins of character and nation by privileging the hybrid, *English*, child. Rushdie's privileging of Englishness in this novel is multivalenced, and it showcases the novel's affiliation with a narrative of national history that places greater trust in the continuity with the colonial legacy than in the apparently dubious continuity with an indigenous origin.

The novel's ambiguating of historical fact in its choice of an imperial moment of national origin is central to its creation of a narrative of secular modernity, and this narrative is intertwined with its choice of English as the language of its narration. This choice is also germane to the novel's creation of a truly postcolonial national history that, in the terms of Bill Ashcroft, Gareth Griffiths, and Helen Tiffin, emerges in its "present form out of the experience of colonization" and asserts itself "by foregrounding the tension with the imperial power" (2). This larger, though related, discussion is outside the scope of the present investigation, so I draw attention to it here only briefly.[2] For the present discussion let us investigate the fabricated point of national origin, metonymically represented by the biracial origin of the central character. It is possible to place this fabricated origin, along with the biracial character, in a causal relationship to the particular nature of the national space that Rushdie's novel privileges. On account of this privileging of a fabricated narrative beginning, the novel emphatically constructs Indianness in an eclectic fashion. Further, it initiates an entirely celebratory departure from the fixity of a pure origin, which it renders merely fantastic rather than historically real.

When Mary Pereira is tormented by her grotesque vision of an invasion by a supernatural past, the narrator says, "the past of India rose up to confound her present; the new-born secular state was being given an awesome reminder of its fabulous antiquity, in which democracy and votes for women were irrelevant . . . so that people were seized by atavistic longings, and forgetting the myth of freedom reverted to their old ways" (281). The term "freedom" is crucial to this statement and is profoundly ironized: the narrator appears to be saying that in order to be free of the colonizer, India must remain its offspring. In Nehru's terms, in order for India to awaken to freedom it must dream an English dream. The dominant novelistic point seems to be that in order to preserve the modern nation-state with its commitment to Western liberal humanist ideologies, India must write its British past into its present. It must police history's borders so that aggressive decolonizing tendencies do not lead the nation into originary moments centralized by sectarian ideologies with dubious ethics that are implicitly represented by Shiva. In a curious reversal of literary reflections, the urgent impetus passes to Saleem, whose parentage must also become that of his nation so that Shiva may not have centrality. Both character and nation must choose a past from a variety of options, and both enter into identity-seeking narratives that construct origins and imagine communities. Both fulfill this mandate by being violently dislocated from mythic pasts in order to be inserted into modern history.

Modernity, in Rushdie's narrative, emerges as a result of his centralizing focus on the biracial Saleem. It poses a clear challenge to essentialist notions of national identity. In a scenario of essentialist nationalism, Saleem would lose history and achieve purity, as he does at the end of book 2 in a grim ode to freedom (392–93). Rushdie holds ambiguated "freedom" at bay by giving Saleem and Ahmed an abundance of legitimate and illegitimate ancestors. Both father and son seek to heal the rupture with the personal and national past by inventing origins and linguistically claiming lost territories. The desire for origins is obvious in Ahmed Sinai's desire for fictional ancestors. He tells William Methwold: "Actually, old chap, ours is a pretty distinguished family too. . . . Mughal blood, as a matter of fact. . . . Wrong side of the blanket, of course; but Mughal, certainly" (122). A more remarkable version of this desire is evident in Saleem's unique gift of giving birth to many mothers: "Child of an unknown union, I have had more mothers than most mothers have children; giving birth to parents has been one of my stranger talents" (278). Ahmed and Saleem undertake strategies of textual fabrication in order to locate effaced origins through acts of speech and writing. These textual strategies effectively obscure the reader's ability to fix a legitimate indigenous moment of origin from which personal identity and national history could be said to devolve.

The gap in this story is the unnarrativized, and perhaps unnarratable, indigenous national origin as understood by Gandhi, who said, "You would make India English . . . that is not the Swaraj that I want" (4: 112). Gandhi's India is dislocated from the narrative of this novel, which effaces self-referential origins, perhaps because of anxieties concerning essentialist notions of regional and ethnic identity that have the potential to unwrite the newborn national narrative. Caught in this anxiety, the novel unwrites precolonial hybridities and ongoing indigenous elite traditions of scholarship and literature.[3] Perhaps this is inevitable, given the privilege accorded the central historical moment in the novel, which significantly is not the moment of writing. The novel's centering of the moment of independence may well account for its demarcation of an origin produced by that center. By not permitting itself the risk of venturing outside the immediately known parameters of history and culture, the novel seeks a unifying vision of nation and hero held precariously together. Having barely survived the trauma of Partition and won a stained independence, the emergent nation of this novel seeks reparation for its trauma in acts of writing that appear to preclude risk. It is, after all, easier to do what the British did with some degree of success than to do what no one else has done before. And so the novel buries the lost origins of its hero and his nation and embarks instead on its stories of enforced connection between the two that thoroughly obscure the notion of beginnings.

By confounding historical beginnings and fabricating a narratological one, Rushdie shapes an account of a character who resolutely evades taxonomic inclusion. Saleem is not "really" Hindu or Muslim, just as he is not "really" Indian or English. He is a bastard child who combines various points of origin and accomplishes a wholly paradoxical relationship to the notion of national legitimacy. In finding himself and his nation in a hybrid language of impure birth, Saleem, as Rushdie's agent, challenges notions of indigenous ethnic purity, insisting instead on secular plurality. The notion of purity in this novel is equated with pure origins and is occulted by Englishness. That purity is resisted in english.[4] The novel subverts the longing for pure origins at personal, national, and linguistic levels by privileging hybridity at every level. Rushdie's linguistic choice is deeply performative of his rejection of singularity. In his novelistic world, linguistic purity would undo heteroglossia, betray literary hybridity, and erase cultural eclecticism. Linguistic purity would situate Saleem within his appropriate indigenous origins and clothe him in a dangerous essentialism as it has done with Shiva in India and the Brass Monkey in Pakistan.

In Pakistan, the Brass Monkey mutates into the "Bulbul-e-Din," or "nightingale-of-the-faith" (359). Her "faultless voice" is filled with "the glorious omnipresence of God" (336). In Karachi, she falls "under the insidious spell of that God-ridden country" (334) and becomes a veiled woman.[5] In this narrative, Pakistan appears to be monolithic and singular. Coincidentally, the name *Pakistan* translates into the phrase "pure land/place." Pakistan's valuation of pure origins, its musical nostalgia for its Persian rather than its colonial heritage, its "submission"-demanding faith, and its culture of acquiescence contrast it to the mess of India variously represented by Saleem and by Bombay in the novel. After saying that he "never forgave Karachi for not being Bombay" (352), Saleem announces his allegiance to the "highly-spiced nonconformity of Bombay" (353). In *Midnight's Children*, Bombay is intensely layered and plural. Rushdie recounts the story of its origins as a fishing village before "Mountbatten's tick-tock" (101). This origin has been overwritten by the continuing presence of Englishness in the form of Methwold's estate, which is not only a little bit of Britain in India but also the reason for the transformation of the native inhabitants into mimic men.[6] The overwhelming evidence of English presence, of course, is in Saleem's bloodline and in the novel's literary and linguistic choices.

Rushdie's text of impure origins locates its literary forefathers in more than one land, and its literary performance enacts an appropriative displacement of value. His Bombay is "Prima in Indis, / Gateway to India, / Star of the East / With her face to the West" (102). Perhaps the turn of the face to the West silences "the glorious omnipresence of God" and mutes the possible sound of a voice that could be "compared to that of Muhammed's muezzin Bilal" (336). In *Midnight's Children*, Rushdie's novelistic allegiance is to an India that is created in the immediate aftermath of colonialism and is shaped by Nehru's nationalist visions. These visions bespeak an India that emerges out of colonial history and is caught in the binarisms of its historical moment. Nehruvian politics and ethics appear to be based on decolonizing gestures, but they are also profoundly implicated in colonial institutions and thought processes making postcoloniality an ironic fantasy. The doubleness of this nationalist celebration acquires sharp contours not only through the parallels with the emblematic hero's life but also as a result of the clarifying contrast with Rushdie's notion of Pakistan, which is written on the margins of the main narrative. Early in Saleem's life, his teacher Mr. Zagallo says, "Remember, stupid boys: Pakistan ees a stain on the face of India!" (265). Rushdie's representation of Pakistan naturally raises the question of why India is different. The partial answer to the question is that India is potentially the same. Difference is a matter of narrative constructions and posited beginnings. Belief in this novel rests with the immediate past as a point of origin rather than with an earlier past that is consigned to "pre-coloniality."

The tendency of the novel severally to write and unwrite origins and, thereby, to refuse to fix beginnings amplifies the focus on the act of storytelling, which is performatively represented through the interactions between Saleem and Padma. Padma is committed to narrative linearity and "what-happened-next[ism]" (37). Reincarnating the patience of Sterne's readers, she patiently submits to three chapters' worth of narrative in the hope of gratifying her desire to find out the beginning of the story. At the close of the third chapter she asks, "Is that him? . . . That fat soft cowardly plumpie? Is he going to be your father?" (52). Her question relocates a past event that narrates origins into the future where its originary potential will be undone. Further, as Saleem does not answer the question, the text defers and repeatedly frustrates her desire to know origins. Padma, and perhaps a number of readers like her, would like nothing better than to chart the beginning, middle, and end and in Aristotelian fashion know the story. Loosely following Sterne's method in *Tristram Shandy*, Rushdie's novel provokes a strong desire for clarifying chronology by intertwining political history and autobiography and retaining traces of linear frameworks germane to both discourses. *Midnight's Children* also actively resists and retards both linearity and its accompanying clarity as much by his celebrated magical realism as by his narrative method of embedded beginnings, lost origins, questionable lineage, narrative repetition, circularity, and deferred closure.

The foretelling of the future by Ramram Seth is emblematic of the novel's method (96). His speech recounts the entire story of the novel in brief, but it completely erases beginnings and ends. The speech is paradigmatic of the novel's method of telling, which deliberately refuses questions about birth and death. On account of this elision, the novel commits itself to fantasies about origins and ends. On the register of national history, the most compelling originary fantasy is in the barely told story of the boatman Tai. This "watery Caliban" (10) has "claim to an antiquity so immense that it defied numbering" (9). Tai's custodial relation with history is clear (11). He seems to know the beginnings of history, but we never find out exactly what Tai really knows and if it makes a difference to how Saleem and India imagine themselves.

As the text puts by questions of who really created Saleem and India, it gives itself the privilege of linguistically producing both entities. Using the enormously generative power of language, Rushdie writes his emblematic hero and mirrored nation into intertwined existence (198–99). By usurping the privilege of so-called truth from a muddled history, Rushdie's novel repeatedly creates characters to showcase the arbitrariness of origins in national history and of coherence in personal identity. This generative narrative is briefly interrupted in the wonderfully named chapter "Alpha and Omega," which tells how Saleem lost his finger. The chapter also tells of the discovery of his true parentage and forces a supplemental narrative of identity in which he is not who he is because he is other than that. His nomenclature remains the same, but his status seems to change. He is still Ahmed and Amina's son, but he is now, also, potentially Shiva, who is not the offspring of the departing William Methwold and who is most emphatically the mirror of the dark potentialities of the new nation. This changed understanding of who Saleem is, based on the knowledge of his displaced origins, necessitates not just an explanatory narrative but also an investigation into the nature of personal and national identity. How have Saleem and India become what they are, and will the positing of a different originary moment alter the course of their characters and their histories? This is a profoundly significant question in our troubled times, when we base our notions of national heritage, history, and identity on politicized acts of privilege granted to segments of national history. In other words, we choose to become agents of national truths that emerge out of principles of selection that conceal their political interest, showcasing instead the disinterested "truth" of history.

Notes

1. In *The Satanic Verses*, Rushdie asks, "How does newness come into the world?" (8) and suggests that newness is imbued with derivativeness.
2. Ashcroft, Griffiths, and Tiffin set up a productive distinction between English and english, investigate the crisis of authentic identity in the colonized subject, and call upon the "English language . . . to develop an 'appropriate' usage in order to" account "for post-colonial experience" (11). In Gorra's view, Rushdie's english, or "Angrezi," is precisely that hybridized vehicle of dual belonging (111–48).
3. See Vanita for a discussion of the intellectual elite's immersion in indigenous hybridity.
4. See Gorra 111–48 for a discussion of Rushdie's use of English/english.
5. Fundamentalist potentialities are also realized in Bombay in *The Moor's Last Sigh* (231) which was written after the Ram Janmabhoomi crisis that crystallized in the destruction of the Babri Masjid on December 6, 1992. Gorra comments on the challenge to the Nehruvian legacy encoded in this event (140). Rushdie's dark representation of communal politics in the Bombay underground mourns the death of this legacy. See Jaffrelot 455 for a discussion of the Ram Janmabhoomi crisis.
6. Bhabha's essay "Of Mimicry and Man" comments on the effect of colonial mimicry, which devolves from Macaulay's "Minute."

Works Cited

Ashcroft, Bill, Gareth Griffiths, and Helen Tiffin. *The Empire Writes Back: Theory and Practice in Post-Colonial Literatures*. New Accents series. London: Routledge, 1989.

Bhabha, Homi. "Of Mimicry and Man: The Ambivalence of Colonial Discourse." *The Location of Culture*. London: Routledge, 1994. 85–92.

Gandhi, M. K. *The Selected Works of Mahatma Gandhi*. Ed. Shriman Narayan. 6 vols. Ahmedabad: Navjivan Publishing House, 1968.

Gorra, Michael. *After Empire: Scott, Naipaul, Rushdie*. Chicago: University of Chicago Press, 1997.

Jaffrelot, Christophe. *The Hindu Nationalist Movement in India*. New York: Columbia University Press, 1996.

Rushdie, Salman. *Midnight's Children: A Novel*. 1980. Harmondsworth: Penguin Books, 1991.

———. *The Moor's Last Sigh*. New York: Vintage Books, 1995.

———. *The Satanic Verses*. London: Viking, 1988.

———. *Shame*. New Delhi: Rupa, 1983.

Vanita, Ruth. "Gandhi's Tiger: Multilingual Elites, the Battle for Minds, and English Romantic Literature in Colonial India." *Postcolonial Studies* 5 (2002): 95–110.

10

Recessive Origins in Julia Alvarez's *Garcia Girls* A Feminist Exploration of Narrative Beginnings

CATHERINE ROMAGNOLO

In his seminal study *Beginnings: Intention and Method*, Edward Said defines beginnings as "the first step in the intentional production of meaning" (5). Implicit in Said's study is an understanding of beginnings as integral to comprehending the ways narratives construct knowledge, experience, subjectivity, and identity. Although this "intentional production of meaning" has been a central concern of feminist literary criticism since feminism was in its first wave, feminist theorists have examined nearly every aspect of narrative—except this first step. Several narrative theorists have established the importance of formal beginnings, but with the sole exception of Said they offer almost exclusively formalist readings of canonical male-authored texts, ignoring the difference that gender and social identity make.[1] These studies consistently overlook the full spectrum of textual functions beginnings can perform, an oversight that contributes to their neglecting the ideological and social valences of narrative beginnings. Recognizing critical lapses in such studies compels us to examine seriously the variables of identity that have been elided in the theorization of narrative beginnings.

Interestingly, these critical elisions persist despite the fact that so many writers thematically foreground beginnings in their narratives. Texts as various as Virginia Woolf's *To the Lighthouse*, Edith Wharton's *Summer*, Amy Tan's *The Joy Luck Club*, Toni Morrison's *Beloved*, and Leslie Marmon Silko's *Ceremony*, to name just a few, center on issues concerning beginnings of all types (cultural, national, familial, artistic, etc.). Furthermore, cultural, nationalist, postcolonial, minority, and feminist discourses have all brought scholarly attention to the problems with and importance of beginnings and origins in relation to any discussion of subjectivity, identity, and nation formation. Of particular interest here are feminist scholars of American studies such as Amy Kaplan, Priscilla Wald, and Toni Morrison, who argue for a reexamination of the role origins play in the construction of "American" culture, literature, and national identity. They point out ways that American originary myths obfuscate the historical dependency of American national identity upon U.S. imperialism and colonialism. As Kaplan argues, U.S. cultural and literary studies need to account for "the multiple histories of continental and overseas expansion, conquest, conflict, and resistance which have shaped the cultures of the United States and the cultures of those it has dominated within and beyond its geopolitical boundaries" (4). Despite their theoretical interest, however, none of these critics examine the interconnections between formal and conceptual beginnings. Extending their critical focus on origins, I suggest that the centrality of the concepts of origins and beginnings in critical as well as literary texts compels us to examine the mutually constitutive signification of conceptual and formal beginnings in narrative fiction.

Julia Alvarez's *How the Garcia Girls Lost Their Accents* displays a rich thematic exploration of the recessive nature of beginnings and a formal complexity that make it an ideal text with which to sketch out an example of this type of examination. Alvarez, like many other feminist writers, makes strategic use of beginnings, perhaps because, as Said has asserted, beginnings "immediately establish relationships with works already existing, relationships of either continuity or antagonism or some mixture of both" (3). Beginnings often evoke authority, tradition, and filiation, all ideas upon which the narratives of patriarchy, racism, and nationalism have heavily relied—ideas that feminist thinkers have historically resisted. But, as Alvarez shows us, they may also evoke innovation and a break from the past. Making use of the suggestive power of beginnings, Alvarez works to destabilize hegemonic connotations of beginnings while embracing their subversive potential.

Exploring relationships among concepts that are integrally connected to beginnings, such as language, authenticity, home, family, and collective identity, Alvarez's narrative suggests the importance of an examination of beginnings to a better understanding of her text. And yet, despite her focus, the extant criticism leaves much to be uncovered. For example, while Julie Barak, William Luis, and Ricardo Castells recognize the importance of beginnings in Alvarez's novel, they seem to lack a vocabulary to discuss her strategic use of formal beginnings. In trying to disentangle the different types of beginnings in *Garcia Girls*, all three writers construct imprecise and confusing descriptions of Alvarez's structure. Language derived from narrative theory and feminist studies of narrative form can be greatly useful in alleviating such confusion and enhancing critical studies of contemporary literary narratives like *Garcia Girls*. Furthermore, attending to connections between different types of beginnings in Alvarez's novel facilitates an understanding of her interrogation of the origins of individual and social subjectivity. It also highlights her use of different kinds of beginnings as a mechanism through which to disrupt traditional narratives of immigration as well as static understandings of racialized and gendered identity.

Analyzing formal and conceptual beginnings in texts like *Garcia Girls* demands first a theoretical framework that would facilitate such an examination. Theorists such as Gerald Prince, A. D. Nuttall, and James Phelan have defined narrative beginnings in various useful ways. Prince, for example, echoing Aristotle's definition, defines beginnings as "the incident[s] initiating the process of change in a plot or action . . . not necessarily follow[ing] but . . . necessarily followed by other incidents" (10). Nuttall, on the other hand, narrowing his discussion to the actual opening lines and pages of a narrative text, works through the "tensions which exist between the formal freedom to begin a work of fiction wherever one likes and an opposite sense that all good openings are somehow naturally rooted, are echoes, more or less remote, of an original creative act" (vii–viii). And Phelan, whose approach is particularly useful to my study, identifies a beginning as "that which generates the progression of the narrative by introducing unstable relationships between characters (instabilities) or between implied author and reader or narrator and reader" (97). Unlike other critics, Phelan points out that "beginnings . . . involve more than igniting the engine that drives the plot. They provide exposition about character and setting, they invite readers to move from the world outside the novel to the world of the novel, and they establish relationships among authors, narrators, and audience" (97). To account for these multiple functions, Phelan breaks his understanding of beginnings into four separate categories: exposition, initiation, launch, and entrance (97). These categories go far beyond other theories in their ability to encompass the functions of beginnings in narrative. And yet, no theory has been able to yield a discussion of the many ideological functions beginnings serve on different levels of narrative.[2]

I would like, then, to identify more fully the many ideological and formal functions beginnings play. For, as Meir Sternberg implies in his study of exposition, it is essential that we maintain an awareness of multiple textual levels when we are examining beginnings. My delineation of beginnings seeks to better facilitate an exploration of the relationships among beginnings, chronology, causality, and theme, and, most importantly, to foster a discussion of the many ideological functions beginnings can serve within narratives. To this end, I first introduce and then through a brief reading of *Garcia Girls* sketch out a set of distinctions intended to serve as a lens for the analysis of formal beginnings (discursive, chronological, and causal) and conceptual beginnings in narrative.[3]

Narrative Beginnings: A Set of Distinctions
Formal Beginnings

My theory identifies three types of formal beginnings—discursive, chronological, and causal. These categories represent literal beginnings on three narrative levels: discourse, story, and plot.

Discursive (The Beginning of the Text, the Beginning of a Chapter)
Discursive beginnings are the first and, perhaps, most easily identified category of formal beginnings.[4] They belong to the discourse level of narrative; therefore, they are determined by *how* the story is presented as opposed to being a part of *the story itself*. The category of discursive beginnings, most often referred to as "openings," encompasses what Sternberg describes as the "beginning of the sujet" and what Phelan calls "exposition"; I am including in this category the opening lines

and pages of a narrative text as well as all paratextual material—what I term the *primary opening* of the text. I am also including all of the *secondary openings*—the opening pages or lines of chapters and section breaks (10).⁵ For example, the primary opening of a narrative like *Jane Eyre* includes the very first lines and pages of the text—the opening of the first chapter, in which Jane and the Reed children return from their walk. The secondary openings of *Jane Eyre* include the beginning lines and pages of all thirty-eight chapters and each of the three volumes.

Chronological (The Beginning of the Story)
Chronological beginnings are the second category of formal beginnings, and unlike discursive beginnings, they exist on the story or *fabula* level of the text (they are part of the *story itself*). Defined as the earliest narrated moments in a text, this type of beginning is most closely aligned with what Sternberg calls the "beginning of the fabula" (10). As he implies, it is important to distinguish this type of beginning from discursive beginnings, as the two most often do not coincide. In *Jane Eyre*, for example, the text opens with Jane as a young child at Gateshead. This is not, however, the chronological beginning of Jane's story. In fact, several chapters later we are told of the marriage and untimely death of Jane's parents, two narrated events that temporally precede Jane's stay at Gateshead. Distinguishing chronological beginnings from other types of beginnings in *Jane Eyre* can facilitate a recognition of the non-coincidence of its primary opening and its chronological beginning. This fact can be seen as quite significant to analyses of both the content and form of *Jane Eyre*, for through it, I would argue, Brontë highlights Jane's lack of awareness about her past and indicates a certain ambivalence about the importance of such origins.

Causal (The Beginning of the Plot)
Causal beginnings, the third category of formal beginnings, are catalytic narrative moments. Like Prince's "beginning" or Gustav Freytag's "exciting force," these beginnings belong to the aspect of narrative most often delineated as *plot*, a term used by Peter Brooks and others to describe a causally connected series of narrative elements linked to

but distinct from *story*, a term that most often implies a purely chronological connection. As theorists have stressed, chronological sequence does not necessarily imply causal sequence; therefore, perhaps obviously, the chronological beginning of a narrative might not coincide with the causal beginning. And it is equally important to stress that a causal beginning might not coincide with the opening pages of the text (primary discursive beginning) either.

As with discursive and chronological beginnings, the identification of a causal beginning is highly subject to reader interpretation.[6] Looking again at the example of *Jane Eyre*, we can easily determine that the marriage of Jane's parents is the earliest narrated event or the chronological beginning of the text. However, a number of textual moments suggest themselves as the causal beginning. We might be tempted, for example, to read the causal beginning as one and the same with the chronological beginning, reasoning that Jane's parents' marriage sets into motion the driving conflict of the plot. Alternatively, a similar argument might be made for interpreting the red-room scene, the death of Jane's parents, or the meeting of Jane and Rochester as the fulcrum of the plot.

One might argue that the slipperiness inherent in this category makes its analytical use-value suspect. This characterization, however, would elide the important role causal beginnings inevitably play in the interpretive process; that is, how one identifies the causal beginning of *Jane Eyre* reflects and perhaps even determines how one reads the entire novel. It is, therefore, precisely the ambiguity of this category that makes its use as a critical tool so productive.

Conceptual Beginnings (Thematic Treatment of Beginnings)

Conceptual beginnings represent the thematic exploration, interrogation, or theorization of the concept of origins and/or beginnings. This broad category belongs to the realm of theme and functions on both the story and discourse level of a narrative.[7] That is, conceptual beginnings may be conveyed equally by the way in which the story is presented and by the story itself. Therefore, formal beginnings, as defined above, very often contribute to conceptual beginnings in a narrative. For example, a major theme of *Jane Eyre* is the conflicted importance of origins (familial, national, class) to individual identity. This theme is primarily explored by the content of the narrative through Jane's relationship with her past, but arguably it is also explored through the form of the novel. The structure of Brontë's narrative (which comprises three volumes and multiple discursive beginnings) and the way in which these discursive beginnings are deployed serve to highlight Jane's geographic origins and their importance to the development of her sense of self.

As the above categories suggest, it is necessary for the facilitation of my discussion to distinguish between different types of beginnings and their functions. For similar reasons, it is necessary to distinguish between beginnings, middles, and endings. It is clear, however, that the boundaries between these categories are in many ways permeable.[8] But, these distinctions serve us best and most compellingly when we utilize them to examine the interconnections among various beginnings in narratives. The example of *Jane Eyre* represents a relatively straightforward exemplification. However, a reading of a text that more explicitly and strategically utilizes narrative beginnings can more fully illustrate the potential of the above categories to help us analyze narrative beginnings and their connections to the ideological implications of a given literary text.

Through the Lens of Beginnings: A Reading of *Garcia Girls*

Narrative beginnings, especially discursive beginnings, evoke a sense of possibility. But as Norman Springer suggests, beginnings seem to be intrinsically bound by a limiting of those possibilities. That is, once a text begins, each narrative step taken necessitates a closing off, an end, to innumerable pathways. As J. Hillis Miller asserts, these possibilities are also limited by that which has come before: "The paradox of beginning is that one must have something solidly present and preexistent, some generative source or authority, on which the development of a new story may be based. That antecedent foundation needs in its turn some prior foundation, in an infinite regress" (57). This recessiveness, Miller implies, is inherent to the notion of beginning in narrative, making it "impossible" for one "to begin" and destabilizing notions of authority often adherent to beginnings (57).

In *Garcia Girls*, Alvarez taps into and exploits this instability. By strategically utilizing the form of her narrative to foreground the recessive nature of beginnings and origins, Alvarez mirrors her central character Yolanda's struggle as a "border woman." Gloria Anzaldúa defines a border woman as one who straddles the "psychological, . . . sexual, . . . and spiritual" space where "two or more cultures edge each other." Yolanda's unstable "border woman" status sparks her desire to recover an originary moment of stability that continually recedes from her grasp. Alvarez's novel, however, does not merely "cover over" the "impossibility of getting started," as Miller asserts all narratives "in one way or another" do. Through both form and content, Alvarez's novel attempts to highlight rather than to "cover" this "gap, [this] absence at the origin" (58). In emphasizing the formal and conceptual instability of beginnings, Alvarez illustrates the specificity of her Dominican character's relation to notions of origin and beginning.

The depiction of Yolanda as a border woman is foregrounded by the primary discursive beginning (the opening pages) of Alvarez's text. The preface, an image of a Garcia family tree, acts as a synecdoche for the conceptual beginnings in the rest of the novel. It is a quintessential symbol of a search for origins. And although it might seem at first an attempt to pin down the definitive lineage of the four Garcia sisters, the tree is punctuated by question marks, a dotted line, and vague references to long-lost relatives. These elements of the family tree begin to destabilize traditional immigration paradigms, which rely on notions of definitive cultural origins and concrete new beginnings. They begin interrogating the concept of an either/or identity, raising questions about how individual identity is constructed, how it is connected to familial and cultural origins, and whether these origins define who we are.

Through the structural positioning of this image, Alvarez begins to emphasize the instability of origins and identity. At the opening of her novel, where we might expect her to begin narrowing the scope of her characters through either/or choices, one finds instead a beginning that, rather than serving to better define her characters, places their histories and identities—their stories—into flux and raises as many questions as it answers. The family tree represents Yolanda's past, which she desperately seeks to recover and understand. But instead of offering a clarification of who she is, it signifies the fragmentary, recessive nature of her origins and the polyvocality of Alvarez's beginnings.

Despite the questions raised by this opening, in order to understand her story Yolanda and the reader must work through her past. Alvarez literalizes this point by asking the reader to work through the family tree before reaching the main narrative. Through her opening pages, then, Alvarez begins to define what it means to be a "border woman" and the frustrating search for home and origins that this entails. Instead of the definitive, pure origins that Yolanda searches for, the family tree identifies an unstable, "corrupted" family history peopled by unspecified ancestors like "The great-great-grandfather who married a Swedish girl." This instability calls attention not only to the way that the traumatic act of immigration has fragmented Yolanda's past but also to the way in which her "self" has always been fragmented. Furthermore, it simultaneously evokes and undermines the patrilineal history of both American and Dominican cultures. The titles illustrate the male lineage of Yolanda's family, but through ironic monikers like "Manuelo Gustavo by una mujer del campo," which highlight the illegitimacy of these male ancestors, Alvarez destabilizes their authority. And finally, as the tree signifies through branches such as "The Conquistadores," Alvarez rejects a simplistic idealization of cultural origins and connects Yolanda's fragmented identity to the imperialism and illegitimacy located in Yolanda's cultural and familial past.

Yolanda's identity as a "border woman" and Alvarez's complex narrative form are further elucidated by the interconnections between beginnings and perspective in *Garcia Girls*. Alvarez divides her novel into three major sections, which she separates into several subsections or chapters, organized in reverse chronology. Each of these textual divisions has its own opening (or secondary discursive beginning), and in an interesting if somewhat disorienting use of these beginning pages, Alvarez begins each section with a new point of view. While most of the text is written in the third person, the focalization alternates throughout the text among the Garcia family members. Each chapter, in presenting a different character's perspective on immigration to the United States, destabilizes the notion of a representative immigrant experience and suggests alternative conceptions of U.S. national identity.

The first chapter begins in the third person and is focalized through Yolanda as an adult. Each successive chapter offers a new focalization until the last four chapters, which the sisters as children narrate entirely in first person. Interestingly, this perspective also shifts in distance; that is, the relationships between the focalizer and the other characters seem to change in intimacy. For example, while the primary opening of the narrative is focalized through an adult Yolanda, she refers to her family as if they were strangers: "The mother," "The father," "the aunts." And as the perspective shifts, so does the distance, so that by the end of the text the narrator refers to the characters by their nicknames.

Because of this structure, perspective and beginnings are, from the outset of the text, formally intertwined; that is, the narrative perspective represents a new beginning constructed by the language of the narrative. Each shift in point of view signifies the beginning of a new truth, a new version of the story, as well as the birth of a new subjectivity. These connections between perspective and questions of identity allow us to read the primary opening, occurring in the temporal present and narrated in a third-person distant focalized narration (Yolanda narrating her own life in third person), as indicative of Yolanda's alienation from herself and her community. Moreover, we may read the end, occurring in her childhood and narrated in a less-distant first person, as signifying a more unified subjectivity. Through these shifting voices Alvarez reveals the fragmentation and isolation experienced by the Garcia sisters as they, literally and figuratively, move further from their childhood home. As the sisters mature in the United States and the Dominican Republic, they become more individuated and more isolated from their communities.

Similar to the way that discursive beginnings help us to understand more fully Alvarez's representation of the tension between individual and collective identities, the novel's chronological and causal beginnings suggest another way that narrative beginnings can destabilize traditional patriarchal understandings of history and immigrant subjectivity. Many critics discuss the ideological implications of chronology; however, the ideological implications of temporal sequence in *Garcia Girls* reside most significantly in its beginnings. As mentioned earlier, Alvarez's narrative is broken into three major sections that are organized in reverse chronology, each opening upon a new period of time: 1989 to 1972, 1970 to 1960, and 1960 to 1956. The text opens with Yolanda's visit to the Dominican Republic after nearly three decades of living in the United States (the chronological ending) and recedes toward the closing, in which the four sisters as children are preparing to immigrate to the United States from the Dominican Republic (the chronological beginning).

By reversing the chronology of her narrative, Alvarez places the chronological beginning of her story at the structural end of her text. This reversal breaks with traditional sequential narrative and undermines any sense of progress adhering to the Garcia's immigration to the United States. Connecting this inversion—a common technique in modern and contemporary narratives—to the novel's concern with individual and collective histories illuminates Alvarez's understanding of the ways these histories, these origins, always escape our grasp, continually receding from the wholeness they are supposed to provide. This recession opens a space for the emergence of a complex understanding of the relationships between events in our histories and the development of individual and cultural identities.

We may also view the fact that the narrative opens and closes at the geographic "origins" of the Garcia family—the Dominican Republic—as illustrative of a certain circularity to the process of immigration. This paradigm revises a narrative of linear progression from Dominican to American, where assimilation to the United States is the presumed goal. It undermines a popular myth surrounding immigration to "America," where the United States necessarily implies individual and cultural progress, and opens the way for the novel to thematize how racialization and class structures in the United States prevent the full inclusion of Latina subjects. Additionally, this circular structure implies an unbreakable, nonhierarchical connection between Yolanda's U.S. identity and her Dominican identity.

While a more linear narrative structure might imply a binary relationship between Yolanda's cultural and national beginnings, *Garcia Girls* depicts a more indeterminate relation from which U.S. imperialism is never absent. Neither nation, therefore, is allowed structurally to stand in as a goal or as an authentic cultural origin to which the characters return in order to reestablish wholeness. In this way, Alvarez reinscribes her critique of U.S. imperialism as well as her interrogation of Dominican class, racial, and gender inequalities in the form of her narrative. As the content of the novel critiques the social conditions of each culture, the form offers an alternative to the binary construction of U.S. and Dominican identities; the circular structure forges an alternative subjectivity with connection to both cultures.

Along with the displacement of the chronological beginning in Alvarez's narrative, the positioning of what I argue is the causal beginning in the center of the text extends Alvarez's critique. Prince, in his discussion of narrative beginnings, states that "students of narrative have emphasized that the beginning, which corresponds to the passage from quiescence, homogeneity, and indifference to irritation, heterogeneity and difference, provides narrative with a forward-looking intention" (10). Prince's sense of narrative beginning, similar to my definition of causal beginning, would suggest that in a conventional immigrant narrative, the act of immigration itself might serve as the causal beginning, that is, the moment in the text when the characters pass into "heterogeneity and difference." Or, according to an alternative convention, the act of immigration might also serve as the resolution—the solution to conflicts experienced in the home country from which the characters immigrate. The Garcia family's move from the Dominican Republic to the United States, however, does not reside "naturally" (to use Sternberg's language) at the opening or even at the closing of the novel; instead, Alvarez places it in the center of her text. Such a "deviation" from the "natural" "logical" presentation of narrative elements, Sternberg asserts, is "clearly an indication of artistic purpose." I would add that in this case it is also clearly an indication of ideological purpose; that is, by displacing the causal beginning of a traditional immigrant narrative, Alvarez complicates typical notions of cultural origins and immigrant identity.

The first paradigm, in which the moment of immigration represents a causal beginning, can be read as a critique of U.S. racism and imperialism and as an idealization of a lost homeland, an origin that may or may not be recovered by the end of the story. The second paradigm, where the moment of immigration serves as conclusion, would likely include a period of hardship and adjustment, after which the characters would assimilate into the "melting pot" of the United States. The first situation offers an idealized vision of the homeland, ignoring colonial and imperial domination as well as the gender, race, and class discrimination that has historically existed. The second is equally problematic, for it promotes an ahistorical view of the United States' imperialist involvement in the Caribbean and ignores the struggle for equality that racialized immigrants face in the United States. The novel addresses these conflicts by displacing the causal beginning of a typical immigrant story and preventing it from, on the one hand, becoming the point at which the text moves into "difference, irritation and heterogeneity," or on the other, the point at which the text resolves these differences and irritations. Alvarez's text asserts that this sense of difference, of alienation, is present not just in the United States but also in the Dominican Republic. It stresses the complex social conditions of both nations and questions the effects of imperial exploitation upon the identities of the characters before and after they immigrate to the United States. Alvarez rejects the idea that an authentic origin is recoverable in the midst of years of imperial and colonial intervention.

The form of Alvarez's text places the Garcia story in a more fluid global framework. The text forces recognition of the fact that, especially for female subjects, the "passage from quiescence, homogeneity, and indifference" is more complex and arduous than traditional paradigms allow. In recognizing the structural ambiguity signified by the location of the causal beginning at the center of the text, we become aware of the way *Garcia Girls* undermines a sense of the Dominican Republic as an idealized origin, of immigration to the United States as the origin of displacement and fragmentation, or of the United States as an idealized new beginning.

This immigration experience, then, instead of standing as a static origin, takes on the effect of simultaneity; that is, it proceeds in two narrative directions simultaneously. It flows from the structural center to the primary discursive beginning, narrating the time period from the family's move to the United States to Yolanda's return to the Dominican Republic. At the same time, it proceeds from the textual center to the end, receding backward in time, narrating the period between the family's U.S. immigration and the sisters' childhood in the Dominican Republic. This Janus-faced narrative mirrors a borderland subjectivity, one that is simultaneously looking toward becoming "American" and yet continually turned away, forced to contemplate the "loss" of the title, the loss that accompanies the cultural transition of Latin American immigration.

At the close of the novel, an ending that is also a beginning, Yolanda revisits a haunting memory of a kitten that she, as a young child, separated from its mother: "There are still times I wake up at three o'clock in the morning and peer into the darkness. At that hour and in that loneliness, I hear her, a black furred thing lurking in the corners of my life, her magenta mouth opening, wailing over some violation that lies at the center of my art" (290). Yolanda dreams throughout the narrative of returning to her origins and integrating her fragmented identity into a *whole*, but what remains instead is a *hole*, like the kitten's magenta mouth wide and wailing. Alvarez has, in a sense, written, a "holey" narrative. Mirroring the "border woman's" fragmented identity and her recessive, unrecoverable origins are the many types of "beginnings" in Alvarez's text. Through the lens of these beginnings, Alvarez explores alternatives to traditional patriarchal conceptions of immigrant narratives; she works through her counterhegemonic conception of individual and collective identity formations. By peering through this lens, we as readers can more fully comprehend this conception as well as its connection to a more fluid, polyvocal notion of narrative. As the above quotation makes clear, Alvarez always wishes to keep her beginnings open, attempting never to close off the possibilities they represent. Yolanda's quest has only just begun at the end of Alvarez's narrative. She does not find the wholeness or the authentic origin for which she searches. What she finds instead is simply a receding memory, signifying her fragmentation, no authentic home or self to which she may return.

I would like to thank Brian Richardson, Peter Rabinowitz, and Jim Phelan, whose detailed comments and suggestions have been invaluable to this essay's current conception. This essay is an abridged version of a chapter in a book project about narrative beginnings on which I am currently working.

Notes

1. Steven Kellman, for example, seems unaware of the masculinist bias embedded in his description of narrative openings as a loss of virginity. Similarly, as Susan Winnett argues, implicit in Peter Brooks's description of narrative beginnings as "awakening[s], . . . arousal[s]" is a textual theory that is "profoundly and vulnerably male in its assumptions" (506).
2. Phelan's conception of narrative beginnings is limited to the material (of varying lengths) that is presented at the opening pages of a narrative, while mine, as will become clear, attempts to more broadly account for beginnings on all levels of a narrative.
3. Although my distinctions might be useful more broadly, certain texts in which conceptual beginnings play an important role better lend themselves to analysis by my set of distinctions.
4. While discursive beginnings are, perhaps, easily identified, their boundaries are undoubtedly subjectively determined. The purpose of this study, however, is not to construct immutable categories. It is less concerned with the boundaries of delineation and more with facilitating discussion of how these types of beginnings are in conversation with one another and signify ideologically within particular texts.
5. Secondary openings might easily be considered "middles" rather than "beginnings." I would argue, however, that the categories of beginnings and middles are not mutually exclusive; that is, a section of a text can be considered both a middle and a type of beginning. I would argue further that examining secondary openings as beginnings can yield a discussion of the ways writers like Alvarez use beginnings to explore notions of identity, which examining them as middles cannot do as well.

6. Sternberg points out that chronology is also subject to what he calls "reader reconstruction"; however, unlike a causal beginning, the chronological beginning of a story lends itself well to a somewhat objective determination.
7. Although it is arguable that all texts thematize beginnings in some manner, in this study I am primarily interested in narratives that foreground conceptual beginnings.
8. These distinctions raise important questions about boundaries, such as where does a particular beginning stop and the middle start? How in a serial novel do we classify an ending that is also a beginning? I would propose that probing this very ambiguity can be productive.

Works Cited

Alvarez, Julia. *How the Garcia Girls Lost Their Accents*. New York: Penguin Group, 1991.

Anzaldúa, Gloria. *Borderlands/La Frontera: The New Mestiza*. San Francisco: Aunt Lute Books, 1987.

Barak, Julie. "'Turning and Turning in the Widening Gyre': A Second Coming into Language in Julia Alvarez's *How the Garcia Girls Lost Their Accents*." MELUS 23.1 (1998): 159–76.

Castells, Ricardo. "The Silence of Exile in *How the Garcia Girls Lost Their Accents*." *Bilingual Review* 26.1 (2001): 34–39.

Freytag, Gustav. *Gustav's Technique of the Drama*. New York: Ayer, 1968.

Kaplan, Amy. "Left Alone with America." *Cultures of United States Imperialism*. Ed. Amy Kaplan and Donald Pease. Durham NC: Duke University Press, 1993. 3–21.

Kellman, Steven G. "Grand Openings and Plain: The Poetics of First Lines." *Sub-Stance* 17 (1977): 139–47.

Luis, William. "A Search for Identity in Julia Alvarez's *How the Garcia Girls Lost Their Accents*." *Callaloo* 23.3 (200): 839–49.

Miller, J. Hillis. *Reading Narrative*. Norman: University of Oklahoma Press, 1998.

Nuttall, A. D. *Openings: Narrative Beginnings from the Epic to the Novel*. Oxford: Clarendon Press, 1992.

Phelan, James "Beginnings and Endings: Theories and Typologies of How Novels Open and Close." *Encyclopedia of the Novel*. Ed. Paul Schellinger. Chicago: Fitzroy Dearborn, 1998. 96–99.

Prince, Gerald. *A Dictionary of Narratology*. Lincoln: University of Nebraska Press, 1987.

Said, Edward W. *Beginnings: Intention and Method.* New York: Basic Books, 1975.

Springer, Norman. "The Language of Literary Openings: Hemingway's 'Cat in the Rain.'" *Papers in Comparative Studies* 5 (1987): 103–13.

Sternberg, Meir. *Expositional Modes and Temporal Ordering in Fiction.* Bloomington: Indiana University Press, 1978.

Winnett, Susan. "Coming Unstrung: Women, Men, Narrative, and Principles of Pleasure." PMLA 105 (1990): 505–18.

11

Curtain Up? Disrupted, Disguised, and Delayed Beginnings in Theater and Drama

RYAN CLAYCOMB

You know that this article has begun because of several clear cues: the title appears above, indicating an article about drama; my name is printed just below; and after a standard number of lines, the text begins in earnest. Your entrance into my text (though it is not a narrative) is highly codified and quite stable, and as a writer I can do little to disrupt that stability. Ultimately, you, the reader, knew precisely when I began. Even the most playful of novelistic beginnings, that of Italo Calvino's *If on a winter's night a traveler*, is bound by the conventions of the printed text. The narrative opens with second-person address: "You are about to start reading Italo Calvino's new novel, *If on a winter's night a traveler*" (3). Such an opening straddles the conventions of both prologue (which it appears to be) and narrative (which it is), and readers are likely to experience some disorientation as to whether the narrative has begun. That effect can disrupt a smooth passage into the narrative world, and it sets up the second-person address that drives the text's formal structure. James Phelan notes, "The use of the second person, the present tense, and the content of the sentence suggest that it is a kind of 'Before the Curtain' address to the flesh-and-blood reader—me and you in all our commonality and idiosyncracy. But . . . the address is actually after the curtain, part of the novel proper" (*Reading* 134). Even here the limitations of the book close off the boundary between the real and the narrative: flesh- and-blood readers know they are reading the narrative itself: it starts on the first page and continues accordingly, there are Arabic (not Roman) page numbers, and the narrated "you" is soon revealed to be someone other than the real you.

That Phelan must use the language of theatrical space to describe the trick of Calvino's opening indicates the degree to which the conventions of the book and its physical markers limit ways of conceiving openings that confuse the reader's entrance into the narrative. With a literal curtain to open (or not) and a whole set of pre-show conventions available to induct the audience into the narrative world, theater and drama offer possible narrative beginnings simply unavailable in prose. As modern theater has eroded the fragile membrane between real and dramatic worlds, playwrights, directors, and performers have begun to play with the conventions of the theatrical paratext to blur the narrative beginnings of the plays they perform. Through narrative frames, interactive environments, theatrical false starts, and dramaturgical interventions, such productions disrupt conventional, passive spectatorial practices by disrupting the expectations surrounding narrative beginnings. When the threshold from real world to narrative world is disguised or disrupted, the audience is asked to perform as if they were in the real world—to regard the narrative world as consequential, and not a site of suspended disbelief.

Of course, theorizing beginnings in drama is already tricky. Performances of dramatic texts, unlike novels, do not have a first page to easily identify a narrative beginning. If we choose the first line of dialogue, we ignore stage directions that indicate action crucial to the plot. The first printed words in the dramatic text rarely appear in the performed narrative, yet expositional cues in the opening of a dramatic performance may begin even before the audience enters the theater. This absence of a clear-cut "opening" for a performed narrative means that "beginning" must be thought of as a process rather than as a single originary moment.

Let us consider a conventional process for how a play begins. The audience enters the lobby, perhaps lingers by theater posters, and discusses the anticipated performance. They are seated while the houselights are up, and the program may provide some initial expositional cues. This period of time might be considered the theatrical paratext, and yet the audience is typically still in the here and now, and has not entered what Keir Elam calls the "spatio-temporal elsewhere" that is conjured up in the narrative world of the drama (99). The stage may be shrouded by a curtain, or perhaps it is open on the interior of an elegant drawing room. In this case, the audience is effectively "reading" exposition and is well into a process of entrance into the narrative that Phelan defines as "cognitive, emotional, ethical": a feature of the audience's experience rather than a formal feature of a text ("Beginnings" 97). Still, we can hardly say that the play has yet begun. Then the real heralds of the beginning arrive: dimming lights, an overture, a parting curtain. Finally, the audience can reliably expect a clear beginning (an action or a line of dialogue) and fully enter the dramatic world of the narrative.

In drama as in fiction such conventional openings mark a new narrative world and the audience's entrance into that world. The best ones, as Steven Kellman identifies, are satisfying for their clarity as markers: "The ice," he says, "must be broken with something sharp, or melted with something warm" (144). For such discrete threshold crossings, the sharper or the hotter, the better. They help the audience establish their suspension of disbelief, and in realist theater in particular, they disengage the audience from their own world and allow them to slip into that spatiotemporal other. Essentially, the beginning provides a border to be crossed.

Take a conventional realist play like George Bernard Shaw's *Pygmalion*. Shaw, known for his novelistic secondary text, opens on a very specific spatiotemporal elsewhere: "London at 11:15 p.m." at a specific portico of St. Paul's (13). He sets a representational scene clearly different from the audience's, with characters stationed appropriately for their first lines. Then, as if literally initiating the action of the narrative, "the church clock strikes the first quarter," and the dialogue begins (13). The investment in a passive spectatorial experience is clear for such realist drama, which asks its audience to watch another narrative world through the invisible fourth wall. The audience of *Pygmalion* is never addressed directly, nor is that wall broken elsewhere in the play. The structural investments of the well-made play (a hallmark of much realist drama and nineteenth-century melodrama before it) or the neoclassical emphasis on dramatic unities demand that a discrete beginning demarcate the real world from the dramatic world and allow the audience to passively view that world through the window of the stage. It is precisely this passive spectatorship that avant-garde theories of the twentieth century sought to undermine, from Bertolt Brecht's intellectually engaged Epic Theatre to Antonin Artaud's passion-infused Theatre of Cruelty.

With a participatory ethic that draws on elements of both Brecht and Artaud, Richard Schechner's environmental theater confronts audiences with a performance transaction that goes beyond a unidirectional communiqué from the performers to the passive audience. "An environmental performance," for Schechner, "is one in which *all the elements or parts* making up the performance are recognized as alive. To 'be alive' is to change, develop, transform; to have needs and desires; even potentially, to acquire, express, and have consciousness" (x). In environmental theater these elements include equally the audience, the performers, the entire space, and the production elements: a totally immersive performance experience, one to be experienced from within rather than observed from the outside. Audience members move through the performance space, come into contact with the performers, even participate in the action. Such performances work to achieve a sense of efficacy, the ripple effect of performance that moves beyond performance space and performance time into the real-life world of the audience—what performance theorist Baz Kershaw defines as "the potential that theatre may have to make the immediate effects of performance influence, however minutely, the general historical evolution of wider political and social realities" (1).

Therefore, Schechner's theater works to abolish the sense of otherness to the beginnings marked off in narrative theater, instead preferring them to be encountered and experienced as real. He explicitly argues that "participation," and the concomitant sense of efficacy that grows from real experience, "is incompatible with the idea of a self-contained, autonomous, beginning-middle-and-end artwork" (40). Therefore, environmental performances that use the theatrical paratext create a sense that the performance matters in the real world by emphasizing the rootedness of the performance in real-world transactions and by exposing these temporal boundaries as interrelated, permeable, and ultimately artificial. For example, an audience entering a theatrical "environment" of Schechner's avant-garde company, The Performance Group, will find that the audience's space and the performance space are not separated. Here, they are literally entering the narrative itself, for the immersion into this space is a form of detailed exposition—the audience is in the living space of the narrative, one that the characters move through, potentially interacting with the audience. While this entrance may not constitute plot, the audience's experience here is synched with performance time, and the transition is fluid: their entrance into the narrative world precedes the beginning of the plot. To be sure, both Phelan and Meir Sternberg account for this in theorizing narrative exposition, suggesting that even the paratext of a novel gives clues about the world of the story. Nonetheless, published titles, maps, or cover art cannot create the radically immersive effect of a performance, its ability to disrupt the clear narrative markers of beginning.

Other environmental performances may have audience members entering a space to find action already taking place, as they did in The Performance Group's 1969 *Makbeth*, when they enter to find Lady Makbeth reading Makbeth's letter (Schechner 4). In such a case, the goal might be to expose the degree to which real life is always in medias res, always happening (even as it underscores a disruption of the familiar source text). Another may have spectators arriving as the actors do, watching or even taking part in their warm-ups and notes. Still others have performers themselves doing the work in the lobby, taking tickets, and explaining the rules of the performance. The result is that "performers are seen not as the magic people *of* the story, but as the people who *play* the story" (35–36). Each of these beginnings disrupts the audience's sense of entrance into the narrative world, and while some may clearly mark off performance time, they all underscore the degree to which everyday life moves through performance time, instead of pausing at the threshold (22). If conventional beginnings draw a discrete boundary between the real and representational worlds, then these beginnings ask the audience to redraw those boundaries or even erase them entirely, a key step in achieving a sense of efficacy for the performance, that the real world continues through and overlaps with the narrative one.

Another approach entirely can be found in Einar Schleef's 1997 Berlin performance of Oscar Wilde's *Salome*, which opened with a ten-minute *tableau vivant* instead of the volleys of dialogue that mark the traditional beginning of Wilde's play, after which the curtain fell and the audience was released to intermission (Fischer-Lichte 59–60). In her analysis of this production, Erika Fischer-Lichte contends that "when the picture of a *tableau vivant* was being presented on stage for viewing, a performance was actually taking place in the auditorium. Whereas some spectators insisted on their new roles as beholders of a picture, others took the part of performers and yet others the part of spectators amusing themselves by observing the attempts of the 'performers' to get a response from the actors" (60). If the audience catcalls, appreciative oohs and ahs, and other responses to this "extra" start were the primary performances of the opening "act," we might say that this *Salome*'s beginning happened after the intermission. Or perhaps this theatrical narrative included more than a production of Wilde's script and bled outward into the theatrical frame. While Fischer-Lichte attributes this reconfiguration of audience roles to an intersection between the visual and performed arts, I also assign the effect to the audience's experience of the disrupted narrative beginning. As in any paratextual situation, Schleef's audience had gathered some expositional information—what play was taking place, the source story of Salome perhaps, and maybe the decadent reputation of Wilde's version—all of which set up expectations for what lay behind the curtain.

Instead, the curtain opened to the theatrical equivalent of the rhetorical aporia: a silence that grows out of the inexplicable. Such an opening presents a conundrum: a non-narrative opening, silent and still, of a performed dramatic narrative; instead of featuring acting, it leaves open a space for the audience to act. And, by Fischer-Lichte's account, they did. Certain behaviors she ascribes to theater tradition—boos, catcalls, applause, and so forth—are not, however, ones we associate with the very beginning of a play. The audience, left in the aporia of the *tableau vivant*, did not know what role to take. Should they sit passively until the play ends, as theatrical tradition asks of its audiences? Or should they attempt to spur the actors into motion, performing as subjects who have not left the world of their own reality, the one in which their actions have consequences? Had actors begun their lines, as Fischer-Lichte notes, these spectators would have returned to their roles as audience members and settled into the narrative world of Herod and Salome.

Given *Salome*'s emphasis on looking and beauty, such a stalled beginning forces the audience to linger upon their own practices of looking, and many spectators seem to have done so in interesting ways. Fischer-Lichte uses this example to discuss the role of aesthetic criticism in theater studies, but her example is also specific to the play itself. The mechanism by which the play's thematic elements are catapulted into the real world of the audience—themselves forced not only to view a beautiful picture but to actively perform viewing a beautiful picture—is a quasi-narrative beginning perched precariously on the threshold between stasis and plot, leaving the audience teetering between roles as active subjects and passive spectators. Because the passage from real world to narrative world is neither clearly marked nor smoothly traversed, the audience is left vulnerable to the impact of the latter upon the former.

While the above examples primarily represent directorial choices that alter the beginnings of what are otherwise conventional dramatic narratives, examples that are accounted for within the text of the plays themselves also abound. Indeed, gimmicks wherein characters move from the audience into the action date back to the earliest secular drama in English and already suggest a permeability between the world of the play and the real world. Henry Medwall's 1497 interlude *Fulgens and Lucrece* opens with two characters, A and B, who begin their conversation as though they were merely two acquaintances who meet at the performance site expecting a play, each denying to the other that he is an actor, despite some knowledge of the argument of the play. Such insistence upon their own real-world existence acknowledges an anxiety about the accountability of actors for the content they represent, but it also provides a way to make explicit the argument of the play such that the audience might be less inclined to write it off as fiction, but rather imagine it as discourse that directly impacts the world of fifteenth-century England. The players do not, however, merely disappear from the stage, but proceed to participate in the plot, a decision based on their perceived ability to affect the outcome of the action, and also on their sense of the rightness of its proceedings. Such a narrative beginning suggests that the real world and narrative world are in fact accessible to one another, and we can place the tactic alongside a host of other boundary-breaking conventions germane to medieval and Renaissance theater: the aside, the dances that ended masque performances, and collections taken up by cast members of morality plays. In this case the efficacy of the play's rhetoric in the world beyond the play's boundaries is literalized by the characters who cross those boundaries and are themselves convinced of its argument. Indeed, this permeability has evoked precisely the anxieties expressed in anti-theatrical literature as early as Tertullian's *De Spectaculis* and staged by plays like Thomas Kyd's *The Spanish Tragedy*, which ends with a play-within-a-play featuring a murder that is deadly both within and beyond its metadramatic boundaries.

Of course, what is expressed as anxiety by Roman church fathers and Renaissance playwrights is figured as a performance ideal for latter-day performance theorists such as Schechner, Kershaw, and a host of twentieth-century playwrights who seek to achieve such efficacy by making the transition into the narrative world seamless. For example, Luigi Pirandello's *Six Characters in Search of an Author* creates a narrative world that overlaps almost entirely with the real world: the setting is the theater itself, and the narrative time is written to coincide with real time. The play pries open the boundary between the narrative world and the real world in large part through the way that it asks the audience to enter the scene, by representing a "non-representational" theater as a window into the narrative world. This seamless entrance into the narrative world leaves the portal between narrative worlds open in such a way that the audience must question the permeability of those boundaries.

Pirandello's opening secondary text explicitly instructs, "The spectators will find the curtain raised and the stage as it usually is during the day time. It will be half dark, and empty, so that from the beginning the public may have the impression of an impromptu performance" (211–12). In this way, Pirandello asks his spectators to believe that this is not a theater in representational mode, the site of illusion, or a portal into that spatiotemporal elsewhere, but rather that this is the theater as it really is. Of course, this *is* an illusion, but one necessary to foreground the relationship between the "real" characters (the actors and the manager) and the six self-identified "characters." That is, if the audience enters into an obviously representational space with a clear narrative beginning, then the "actors" and "characters" will seem to be equally fictional. The audience could not construe the actors and the characters as deriving from different planes, and the play's inquiry into the nature of reality and illusion is rendered harmless. But the moment of entrance into a space that might *not* be representing another space leaves the threshold open just enough that we can imagine the "actors" as real, even as we imagine the "characters" as emerging from some other narrative space. In this way, Pirandello asks us to believe that we haven't left the real world. Once this illusion is established, the play can better interrogate that membrane, asking what makes an action real and what gives it power.

Of course, Pirandello's beginning is otherwise ordinary. Yet Peter Rabinowitz notes that a metarule of narrative configuration is that "the ending will somehow be prefigured in the beginning," and if this is the case, the momentary disorientation of the spectator as to which world we are inhabiting—the narrative or the real—prefigures the disorientation of The Manager at the end of the play (305). When The Son is shot dead in the final moments of the narrative, some actors cry, "No, no, it's only make believe, it's only pretence," to which The Father responds, "Pretence? Reality sir, reality!" The Manager's "Pretence? Reality? To hell with it all!" leaves that boundary uncomfortably open, just as the beginning of the play leaves the portal between the real world of the audience and the make-believe of that drama uncomfortably open. It is through this mechanism that, in the words of French playwright Georges Neveux, Pirandello "took us to the very center of the real world and turned it inside out right in front of us, as a fisherman turns inside out the skin of an octopus to lay bare its viscera" (qtd. in Bishop 136).

While Pirandello disguises his audience's entrance into the narrative world by representing the real, Peter Handke's "Offending the Audience" uses the tropes of the traditional beginning to lure the audience into a narrative (in which they will be the protagonists) without ever crossing the promised threshold. In fact, Handke's prolonged, repeated, and persistent disruption of a beginning disrupts the work's very status as narrative. Handke's *Sprechstück* (translated variously as "speech play," "speech work," "work about speech," "work comprised of speech," and "speak-in") is at best a quasi-narrative, for as the players indicate, "This is no drama. No action that has occurred elsewhere is reenacted here. Only a now and a now and a now exist here. This is no make-believe which re-enacts an action that really happened once upon a time. Time plays no role here. We are not acting out a plot" (15).

However, as a quasi-narrative, "Offending the Audience" is a second-person narrative. Indeed, Brian McHale uses the title of the work as emblematic of many postmodern second-person texts (225). Given that the bulk of the script directs the performers to hurl insults at the audience—the subject of most of the sentences—we might say that the audience is the protagonist and is, in important ways, "narrated" by the performers and the performance text. The opening secondary text mandates that "None of the spectators should call attention to himself or offend the eye by his attire. The men should be dressed in dark jackets, with white shirts and inconspicuous ties. The women should shun bright colors" (5). Similarly, the performers describe the audience before their arrival, declaring, "Before you came here, you made certain preparations. You came here with certain preconceptions. You went to the theater. You prepared yourself to go to the theater. You had certain expectations" (22). The plot, then, is the audience's progression from expectations about the conventions of the theater (which include a passive, observing, unself-conscious spectator) to a sense of awareness of their own stake in the performance event. This is a change precipitated by an event that is itself narrated by the performers: "Because we speak to you, you can become conscious of yourself" (20).

These conventional expectations are first and repeatedly frustrated through the disruption of the hoped-for beginning. Initially, we may identify the beginning as similar to that of *Six Characters*, where the secondary text narrates a real-world setting that the audience has entered without knowing that they, the audience members, are being narrated. Accordingly, the second-person narrative (as it were) begins before the audience even enters the space. From the audience's perspective, this beginning is invisible, while another traditional beginning is amply heralded and then never delivered. The secondary text mandates in meticulous detail that the spectators should be "greeted by the usual pre-performance atmosphere": assiduous ushers, formal program, buzzer signals repeated to announce the beginning to the performance, dimming lights, and so forth (5). In doing so, Handke offers up every available signal that a narrative world is about to be presented. The text even suggests feigning signals of a narrative world that will not appear: "One might let them hear noises from behind the curtain, noises that make believe the scenery is being shifted about" (5). The buildup culminates in a meaningful silence, followed by the solemn parting of the curtain to reveal no dramatic world at all, only four performers who slowly advance on the audience: a narrative beginning that begins with no apparent narrative world.

Finally, we might take the play at its word: that there is no beginning, that, as the performers immediately and repeatedly state, "This piece is a prologue" (7). In this case, the performance is not a narrative with a beginning, a middle, and an end but rather merely what precedes something else; it is "not a prologue to another piece, but the prologue to what you did, what you are doing, and what you will do," a line that comes nearly at the end of the piece, just before the performers begin to narrate the audience's departure from the space (28). All of these moments that we might call beginnings, then, are strewn carefully across the text, keeping the audience suspended at the threshold of a narrative that they only slowly come to realize that they star in.

In this way, we might say that despite the work's disavowal of narrative, it represents a beginning in its entirety (even though it also has a clear end), frustrating expected beginnings while narrating a beginning of "what you will do," an action in the real world of the audience. Stanton B. Garner Jr. notes, "This strategy of disavowal ('Here there is no') works to enable the play's central project: the disclosure, through speech, of actuality eclipsed in the processes of dramatic semiosis—especially the actuality of that most invisible participant in dramatic illusionism, the audience" (154). The construction of a quasi-narrative world that is so congruent with the real world that it might even be called real experience itself works in the opposite direction of Pirandello's tactic. In both cases, the secondary texts in the beginning seek to obscure the nature of the relationship between the narrative world and the real world, but while *Six Characters* asks the audience to believe that they haven't left the real world of experience by presenting theater space as if it were not representing another space, Handke provides every formal cue that the audience is about to enter a narrative world. Yet when they reach the much-anticipated threshold, they find that the narrative world comes charging out at them, into the world of their own experience, not of some other space. The membrane between the narrative and the real is erased: "The stage apron is not a line of demarcation" (Handke 10). In this way, "Handke's 'speech play,'" as W. B. Worthen notes, "offends its audience by acknowledging the audience's fictionality, the ways that its experience—all experience—is a function of the power of language" (615). Here again, by disguising and disrupting the audience's sense of a beginning, Handke not only leaves the audience perched on the threshold between reality and representation but also obliterates the illusion that the threshold ever existed.

Unlike the (literally and conceptually) bound work of fiction, performance appears to us as does real life, and as theorists explore this concept we come to understand that real life itself may be made up largely of performances. As a system of representation, then, dramatic performances are poised to disrupt that boundedness by disrupting the perceptual boundaries that mark off the audience's world from the world of the narrative. When playwrights disguise or even erase the temporal boundaries of a clear beginning, the audience is more likely to miss the cognitive markers that they have entered another world, and less likely to write off the action in the theater space as "other" than to read it as real. Steven Kellman's preferred narrative openings either sharply break the narrative ice or melt it gently away, but for playwrights and directors who want to disguise that passage into the narrative, the ice must be as thin as water itself, or better yet, as the air that we breathe.

Works Cited

Bishop, Tom. *Pirandello and the French Theater*. New York: New York University Press, 1960.

Calvino, Italo. *If on a winter's night a traveler*. Trans. William Weaver. New York: Harcourt Brace, 1981.

Elam, Keir. *The Semiotics of Theater and Drama*. London: Routledge, 1980.

Fischer-Lichte, Erica. "*Quo Vadis?* Theatre Studies at the Crossroads." *Modern Drama: Defining the Field*. Ed. Ric Knowles, Joanne Tompkins, and W. B. Worthen. Toronto: University of Toronto Press, 2003. 48–66.

Garner, Stanton B., Jr. *Bodied Spaces: Phenomenology and Performance in Contemporary Drama*. Ithaca NY: Cornell University Press, 1994.

Handke, Peter. "Offending the Audience." *Kaspar and Other Plays*. New York: Hill and Wang, 1969. 1–32.

Kellman, Steven. "Grand Openings and Plain: The Poetics of First Lines." *Sub-Stance* 17 (1977): 139–47.

Kershaw, Baz. *The Politics of Performance: Radical Theatre as Cultural Intervention*. London: Routledge, 1992.

McHale, Brian. *Postmodernist Fiction*. London: Routledge, 1987.

Phelan, James. "Beginnings and Endings: Theories and Typologies of How Novels Open and Close." *Encyclopedia of the Novel*. Ed. Paul E. Schellinger. Chicago: Fitzroy Dearborn, 1998. 96–99.

———. *Reading People, Reading Plots: Character Progression and the Interpretation of Narrative*. Chicago: University of Chicago Press, 1989.

Pirandello, Luigi. *Six Characters in Search of an Author*. *Naked Masks: Five Plays*. Ed. and trans. Eric Bentley. New York: Dutton, 1952. 211–75.

Rabinowitz, Peter J. "Reading Beginnings and Endings." *Narrative Dynamics: Essays in Time, Closure, and Plot*. Ed. Brian Richardson. Columbus: Ohio State University Press, 2002. 300–313.

Schechner, Richard. *Environmental Theater*. Exp. ed. New York: Applause, 1987.

Shaw, George Bernard. *Pygmalion*. Middlesex UK: Penguin, 1916.

Sternberg, Meir. *Expositional Modes and Temporal Ordering in Fiction*. Baltimore: Johns Hopkins University Press, 1978.

Worthen, W. B. Introduction to "Offending the Audience." By Peter Handke. *Modern Drama*. Ed. W. B. Worthen. Fort Worth: Harcourt Brace, 1995. 614–15.

12

Where to Begin?

Multiple Narrative Paths in Web Fiction

JESSICA LACCETTI

While postmodernism may eschew closure in both history and narrative, it seems that the need to classify narrative beginnings as a single originary juncture remains necessary. On the one hand, Gerald Prince sees narrative beginnings as "the incident initiating the process of change in a plot or action . . . not necessarily follow[ing] but . . . necessarily followed by other incidents" (10). On the other hand, critics like A. D. Nuttall prefer a structurally circumscribed view that situates narrative openings at the textual start which is "naturally rooted . . . [and is] an original creative act" (viii). Although creating a broader interpretation of narrative beginnings, James Phelan's four categories—exposition, initiation, introduction, and entrance—nonetheless signal a single and definitive starting point (97). Whether pointing to beginnings at the level of *discours* or at the level of *histoire*, it seems there is a tendency to establish a clear-cut origin or, indeed, conclusion.

Web fiction narratives are stories that can tangibly thrust against such containment. They are stories that cannot easily be experienced in a single reading session or even a single space. According to Jay Bolter, "the key feature of hypertext is fluid text" (5). Web fictions such as the one I will discuss in this essay are composed of a network of connections, becoming multilinear and offering manifold possibilities through the narrative; "each hypertext is a set of different potential texts awaiting realization" (Bolter 5). They are stories with multiple "contours," as Michael Joyce might put it, which can bring fresh insight to the act(s) of reading and the representation of subjectivity.

The Web and our technologically turned-on culture of Blackberrys, iPods, YouTube, and del.icio.us nurture a sense of connection with others and with texts. Although postmodern fiction—or creators like Sterne and Cortazar—may encourage readers to search for unusual connections, the texts remain recognizable as unities. Plays are usually presented on a stage with an identifiable beginning, middle, and end, and the audience is typically sure of the boundaries that exist among the play, the audience, and real life.[1] Likewise, books are usually clearly delimited by their covers, as cinematic films are by the conventional positions of spectators opposite the screen. Even television employs distinguishable boundaries between channels and shows.[2] Web-based fictions, on the other hand, often do not have definite divisions (at least from readers' perspectives) between chapters or sections, and some Web fictions do not have clear boundaries between the narrative itself and external Web sites that might feature in the story.

Keeping in mind Shelley Jackson's persuasive observation that "hypertext does not provide so much courtly guidance across the intellectual terrain, but catapults you from spot to spot," this essay maps possible starting points (at the level of discourse), sequences, and connections in Caitlin Fisher's Web fiction *These Waves of Girls*. Attempting to piece together narrative segments that at first—at least to the uninitiated reader—seem complex and contradictory (Fisher, "Thoughts") is important, because as narrative sequencing changes, so too must our ways of understanding and reading. Thus what follows is invariably conscious that each "beginning" is partial, provisional, and subject to change.

Backgrounds of Beginnings

For Edward Said, a narrative beginning is either "temporal and transitive" or "intransitive and conceptual"; the point of departure is a moment of "polemic ... [and] discovery ... what Emile Benveniste describes as the 'axial moment which provides the zero point of the computation'" (76). Such a beginning promotes initiation and direction, allowing readers to interrogate, examine, and reflect. On the other hand, for Said, an intransitive beginning is a "bristling paradox" whose "existence cannot be doubted, yet its pertinence is wholly to itself" (77). As a result, Said seems to draw an equation between beginning and "making" certain (78). The specific uncertainty of beginnings, what Said calls "the unknown," seems to "haunt" (78) readers so that they are always already searching for certainty. Understood in these terms, beginnings may look more like constructed and constructing practices.

The inherent significance of "the" beginning, then, is the influence it must have for the narrative that follows it. But the beginning need not be situated or established at the opening or outset of the Web fiction in order to endow meaning or to structure the narrative as someone like Henry James would have it: "Really, universally, relations stop nowhere, and the exquisite problem of the artist is eternally but to draw, by a geometry of his own, the circle within which they shall happily *appear* to do so. . . . [A] young embroiderer of the canvas of life soon began to work in terror, fairly, of the vast expanse of that surface, of the boundless number of its distinct perforations for the needle" (1041).

As James rightly notes, relations are endless, and generally for Web fiction "everything is deeply intertwingled" (Nelson 45). Rather than employing beginnings as a type of geometry that circumscribes "the vast expanse" of narrative, certain Web fictions seek to amplify multiplicity in order to move beyond structural rigidities. Hyperfictions like Fisher's signal a different way of creating relationships among narrative threads, images, and sounds that enables numerous possibilities for beginnings and, therefore, sequentialities. The precise role of a segment of narrative can vary according to the function it is called upon to perform in different systems of signification. Its meaning derives partly from its position in a certain system of signification at a certain moment which, as Fisher explains, "challenge[s] simplistic causality" ("Thoughts").

Beginnings in Caitlin Fisher's *These Waves of Girls*

This does not mean that Web fiction narratives are devoid of authorial guidance in the form of signals or signs. In fact, most Web fiction authors are aware that their readers are in a nascent state, just as is the case with their own multimodal stories. Deena Larsen openly admits to writing for several audiences: "*People* who are approaching hypertext for the *first time*. . . . *People familiar* with hypertext/elit. . . . [and] *Scholars and analysts*." In Larsen's case, as in Fisher's, a default path is built into the narrative, suggesting both chronological sequence and plot development. While "scholars and analysts" can travel more flexible paths through the stories, first-time readers are advised to follow thematic or character links. Although Fisher does not have an introductory screen explaining these options to readers, she includes arrows that direct readers through more linear versions of the narratives. The problem with following any default reading path is the limitations they entail. In Fisher's case this means the reader cannot move beyond a selection of beginnings or endings. This position seems to point to a predicament for hypertext authors: in David Kolb's words, "How can the reader . . . be guided to such crucial nodes without unduly reducing hypertext openness?" On the one hand, Fisher includes specific predetermined points and paths in order for newer readers to ease themselves into the narrative.[3] On the other hand, those readers will not experience such a rapid onslaught of numerous narrative trajectories, nor will they be required to extensively "organize and reorganize the various data offered . . . by the text" (Iser 222).

Since Web fiction is open to manipulation, other beginnings are available. However, what every reader, scholarly or otherwise, of *These Waves of Girls* encounters is the splash page which refuses the interactive reader's desire to click to the next screen, thus obliging each reader to gaze at the streaming clouds and listen to the sustained forty seconds of female voices laughing amid the sounds of a seascape. The patient reader is rewarded with a new screen in which an "off kilter" image of a young girl in cyanotype forms the background and, at the bottom of the screen, a "play button" like that on a CD player is accompanied by the word "listen." This leads to a second node that Fisher revealingly calls "navigate," suggesting the combined roles of reader and author in the creation of the fiction.

Clicking on the button does not emit sound as expected, so here is an example at the outset of the fiction of the author challenging the reader's assumptions and making explicit a key value of the hypertextual environment: narrative is "built both by the structure . . .

and as an effect of reading" (Fisher, "Electronic" 58). Furthermore, this synesthesia reminds readers that "signifiers . . . on the computer screen . . . are only the top layer of a complex system of interrelated processes" (Hayles). Clicking on the "listen" button releases a thread that slowly but effectively unwinds, displaying eight possible entrances to the narrative. Each link is a key phrase or idea appearing in one of the eight sections of the fiction. For example, the first link is "kissing girls," the second is "school tales," the third is "I want her," and the fourth is "she was warned."

Hovering on each link brings forth a visual and textual synopsis, framed and at opposite sides of the screen. This effect serves to remind readers that without interaction the story will not develop beyond the introductory synopses. Thus, from the beginning in the discourse each reader has various options, none of which includes a chronological story beginning, all marked as analepses or prolepses.

A Default Path

Knowing, then, that none of the entry links will default to the temporal beginning of the story means that each reader must excavate and reread in order to feel "satisfied," in Jane Douglas's terms. Hovering on the phrase "I want her" elicits an image of a succulent pear on a leafy branch and a mini-synopsis: "I'm in bed with Jennie Winchester and I realize she wants me to undo her pants. She needs to be home by 11 o'clock and needs to leave my place by 10:45. I'm kissing her but opening my eyes at intervals to catch the clock. At exactly 10:43 I unbutton her Levis." The emphasis on time in this extract may be used as a paradigm for the entire text and the way the reader goes back and forth in story time. Clicking on the phrase leads the reader to a new node. In the center of the screen the synopsis from the "first" page continues, and directly below it rests an image of a female breast that becomes contorted and blurry when the reader hovers on it. The contrast of the bright yellow font and breast on the black background, reminiscent of early computer games, not only encourages the reader to squint and hesitate but also highlights the two links available from "within" this story segment. The reader can either click on "Jennie" or "drives me to school." Continuing by choosing either of these links will allow the reader to follow a more linear path within this story section. The sequential narrative thread here approximates a reading of a print fiction in that determination of the reader's options is not required. Additionally, these sequences follow, for the most part, a distinguishable temporal chronology, thus performing something akin to what Raine Koskimaa terms "horizontal episodes . . . giv[ing] the feeling of [a] continuous stripe of nodes, reaching towards some unknown limit in the east." Using the links in the sidebar ("butterfly," "tell," "watching," "camp," "crush," "Barbie," "Vanessa") means taking diversions from the default path and encountering "structures that are neither pre-defined nor clearly boundaried" (Walker, "Feral" 47). Since this is a default reading, what Douglas calls "the hypertext equivalent of channel surfing" (97), let's continue with the default link, "Jennie."

Clicking here moves us to another horizontal node giving background information on Jennie and the narrator, Tracey, who is now fifteen years old. Following this default path leads the acquiescent reader to details of summer camp, high school, and first crushes.[4] Arriving at a node titled "tell" indicates the end of this default reading; readers have the option of changing to a different narrative section or starting the reading process again from the "navigate" screen. Fittingly, the "tell" node is the most constrained, mimetic of Tracey's own lack of choice regarding her sexuality. As she says, "I always knew, early on, it's a cliché, I know, but it's also true." Broaching the topic of Tracey's sexuality, it is significant that the narrative becomes more linear while the accompanying images blur hypnotically. While Tracey is left wondering whether people "could tell, all the way from across the street, from a bus, that I'm a lesbian," the reader is also left to speculate making this a particularly incomplete version of the narrative.

A Not-So-Default Path

Going back to the initial portal to this section, "navigate," and clicking any link opens a separate window in which we can now choose from the various entrances hovering in the sidebar column. Clicking on "Vanessa" leads to a new node where each section of text is accompanied by an image. Additionally, at the top and bottom of the page readers can choose to "listen to the story."

Exerting her authorial presence and again playing with signification, Fisher does not wait for readers to accept the invitation to listen to the story. Instead, a woman's voice erupts, detailing significant episodes in Tracey's life. Listening to the story produces an entirely different reading experience (not least because the audio recitation makes reference to a character not named in this section of text). The reader must agree to give up some control in terms of link choice and allow the author to tell the story her way. As the author suggests, the reader should close his or her eyes and "listen." If the aural experience is not appealing, the reader can choose from a variety of other links and move on.

This node is one example of the significant role "sequence" plays in Fisher's fiction. Beginning at the top of the screen with Vanessa at three years old is an x-ray-like image of her. Scrolling down through the columns of bold black text we learn of Vanessa at six with an "attractive, wandering hazel eye" and see a photograph of what looks to be a six-year-old girl staring out of the screen at the reader. As we progress further down the screen, Vanessa's past unfolds; Vanessa at ten, as a "feral child," then as a young teenager. As the reader scrolls down the seemingly endless columns of text and image, Tracey's memories unfurl faster and faster. As the fleeting memories dart along the scrolling screen, they also increase with fervor. Both the reader and Tracey are plunged into a graphic sexual scene culminating with Vanessa's "lips against mine [Tracey's], sealing secrets." The palpable passion of this node is partly due to the graphic confessional text as well as the reader's constant descent into the depths of Tracey's memory (see Koskimaa). Just as Tracey constructs her story from memory fragments, so the reader pieces together Tracey's subjectivity: at the beginning (discourse level) of this node there are images of Tracey—her body, her arms, her knees, her eyes—but only at the very end of the node is there finally an image of Tracey and Vanessa in their entirety. In this specific case, words and images follow the same downward chronological path. However, Tracey does call into question this seemingly chronological route by switching between present and past tense as she tries to "think back," and wonders "where was I," eventually deciding not to "rush the process."

Are There Differences between Beginnings?

We've seen how the link "I want her" evolves; how then does this narrative section relate to the others? What if we had chosen another beginning? As Douglas says about another hyperfiction, "instead of narrowing the margins of the narrative, the further [one reads] . . . the more contingencies arise" (99). Going back to "navigate," we can choose the link "she was warned." This opens a new node with bright red lettering screaming at the reader: "Grade five we all knew what a slut was: Tammy Stevens." While Tracey is growing up as a lesbian with her own share of difficulties, she also recognizes that difficulty is synonymous with development regardless of sexuality. Although on the one hand Tracey does try to question the patriarchal perspective, she nonetheless admits her own curiosity, being both "grossed out and fascinated." For Tracey, Tammy becomes a sexual subject who signals a closeness between heterosexuality and homophobia. In fact, this node ends with the sad conclusion that "It didn't seem worth it, somehow. . . . [Tammy] was way too slutty even for him. Pierre Gitor, the guy she'd done it with, didn't want to go out with her either." Although the node ends here, the reader's quest does not. In a conscious decision to continue reading even though no path is possible from this node, the reader must go back to "navigate." Selecting a different beginning, "her collections," reveals a graphic-heavy screen with a mise-en-scène effect. In the center of the smallest frame is a diminutive white hand squeezing a blurry house. The purple text explains the image: "At six I hold a whole house in the palm of my hand from under a tree." The reader can be like Tracey and, via the mouse, also squeeze the house, watching it bend and smudge into the purple forested background. This tactility reinforces the interactive role of the reader but also offers a subtle warning: the hazy effect is emblematic of the unclear path novice readers might make through the narrative.

Following this "leaping"[5] path through *These Waves of Girls* reveals Fisher's most obvious effort to mediate the hypertextual spaces between "self" and "life." For Tracey, as for Fisher, autobiography is not an undertaking to recapture her self but to identify and gain knowledge of her present self and experiences. Tracey seems to think that her identity, or at least a coming- to-knowledge of herself, might be located at the crossroads of writing and selfhood: "I write, but it doesn't need to be my life, exactly. It lets me fill in the parts I forget. One name. One moment. A hand on my thigh that reminds me of all the other hands. Of yours." If for Tracey this slippery autobiography prepares for the encounter between writing and selfhood, then, with the unreliability of memory and of language (and image and sound), this destiny is always deferred. Tracey's autobiography reveals gaps in sequence, gaps between identities (others and her own), and gaps between the strengthening desire to represent her identity and the increasing impossibility of her doing so. In other words, self-representation reveals the impossibility of its own definition: what commences with the assumption of self-knowledge and accuracy ends in the creation of a fiction. As Tracey confesses, "The desire to write is the desire to fool you, seduce you. Here I am—again—always getting the girl, saying the right thing or (toss this in for effect) something deliciously, winsomely wrong. Look over there—that's me, at four."

Conclusion: "All the Possibilities Like a Thick Web"

On one hand, *These Waves of Girls* articulates the story of a girl maturing, becoming aware of herself and her place in society—a traditional bildungsroman. On the other hand, it is an account of the evolving story of Web-based narratives. The multimodal devices, the (sometimes chaotic) combinations of sound, image, text, and touch seem to embody and thereby "make real" (or at least experiential) the constructed, confused, manifold, and situated nature of memory and identity. In this fiction there is no underlying message that one can systematically and chronologically author one's experience. Tracey and Fisher both seem to approve of conscious creation through their fiction, creation that bears witness to the fact that life's material is made of "moments

[that] flash by." Accordingly, the protagonist of *These Waves of Girls* and her narratives are mobile, eschewing the search for permanence or constancy. Thus, meaning is created as the reader progresses through the narratives, because even with a single starting or finishing point, reading is always a provisional assemblage.

Narrative beginnings in *These Waves of Girls* conjure multiplicity, "a complex web of relationships, associations, and alternative constructions" (Douglas 16). Through the "perpetually unfinished textuality" (Landow 3) this Web fiction is able to reconfigure and problematize notions of identity and subjectivity. By implying a certain narrative ubiquity whereby readers can "go" in any direction they choose, *These Waves of Girls* suggests an alternative to Said's "primordial need for certainty at the beginning" (49). The understanding that "without at least a sense of a beginning, nothing can really be done" (49) dissolves in the light of Fisher's "scrittura mutante"[6] in which many beginnings emerge and intersect. The mutating writing, the multimodal devices, and the presence of fluid story openings help emphasize the constant state of "becoming" (Braidotti 5) pertinent to both subjectivity and reading practices.

Notes

1. Ryan Claycomb's essay in this volume, however, shows how the beginnings of dramas can be problematized.
2. Although this is changing with the advent of on-demand services and interactive television.
3. Walker ("Piecing" 112) suggests that this is the case with the default reading path in Michael Joyce's *Afternoon*.
4. Walker suggests that a default reading allows the establishment of a corpus of background information in order to "start enjoying the leaps between story lines and to understand connections" where initially there had been confusion ("Piecing" 112).
5. "Traditional reading is characterized as coherent and continuous, and hyperreading is known for *leaping*" (Zhang 24).
6. "Mutating writing"; my translation. See Osservatorio Scrittura Mutante.

Works Cited

Bolter, Jay David. "Hypertext and the Question of Visual Literacy." *Handbook of Literacy and Technology: Transformations in a Post-Typographic World*. Ed. David Reinking, Michael C. McKenna, Linda D. Labbo, and Ronald D. Kieffer. Mahwah NJ: Erlbaum, 1998. 3–13.

Braidotti, Rosi. *Nomadic Subjects: Embodiment and Sexual Difference in Contemporary Feminist Theory*. New York: Columbia University Press, 1994.

Douglas, Jane Yellowlees. *The End of Books or Books without End? Reading Interactive Narratives*. Ann Arbor: University of Michigan Press, 2001.

Fisher, Caitlin. "Electronic Literacy." *Light Onwords/Light Onwards*. Living Literacies Conference. Nov. 14–16 (2002): 57–63. http://www.nald.ca/fulltext/ltonword/complete.pdf.

———. "Some Thoughts on These Waves of Girls." Creative Writing and New Media. De Montfort University. 1 Dec. 2006. http://web.mac.com/caitlin_fisher/iWeb/Site%204/Podcast/Podcast.html.

———. *These Waves of Girls*. 2001. www.yorku.ca/caitlin/waves/.

Hayles, Katherine N. Interview with Lisa Gitelman. "Materiality Has Always Been in Play." *The Iowa Review Web*. 1 July 2002. http://www.uiowa.edu/~iareview/tirweb/feature/hayles/hayles.htm.

Iser, Wolfgang. "The Reading Process: A Phenomenological Approach." Ed. David Lodge. *Modern Criticism and Theory: A Reader*. London: Longman, York, 1991. 212–27.

Jackson, Shelly. "Stitch Bitch: The Patchwork Girl." *Transformations of the Book*. 4 Nov. 1997. MIT Communications Forum. http://web.mit.edu/comm-forum/papers/jackson.html.

James, Henry. Preface to the New York edition of *Roderick Hudson* (1907). *Literary Criticism: French Writers, Other European Writers, The Prefaces to the New York Edition*. New York: Library of America, 1984.

Kolb, David. "Twin Media: Hypertext Structure under Pressure." *Proceedings of the Fifteenth ACM Conference on Hypertext and Hypermedia*, ACM Hypertext '04. 1–2 (2004): 26–27. http://www.sigweb.org/conferences/ht-conferences-archive/ht04/hypertexts/kolb/kolb.pdf.

Koskimaa, Raine. "*These Waves of Memories*: A Hyperfiction by Caitlin Fisher." *Dichtung Digital* 3 (2004). http://www.brown.edu/Research/dichtung-digital//2004/3/Koskimaa/index.htm.

Landow, P. George. *Hypertext: The Convergence of Contemporary Critical Theory and Technology*. Baltimore: Johns Hopkins University Press, 1992.

Larsen, Deena. "Re: *Children's Time.*" Online posting. 14 Apr. 2003. http://mural.uv.es/fersam/emaildeena.html.
Nelson, Theodore H. *Computer Lib/Dream Machines.* Self-published, 1974.
Nuttall, A. D. *Openings: Narrative Beginnings from the Epic to the Novel.* Oxford: Clarendon Press, 1992.
Osservatorio Scrittura Mutante. "Concorso Scrittura Mutante 2.0." 2004. *Trovarsi in Rete.* http://www.trovarsinrete.org/concorsosm2004.htm.
Phelan, James. *Reading People, Reading Plots: Character, Progression, and the Interpretation of Narrative.* Chicago: University of Chicago Press, 1989.
Prince, Gerald. *Dictionary of Narratology.* University of Nebraska Press, 1987.
Said, Edward W. *Beginnings: Intention and Method.* New York: Columbia University Press, 1985.
Walker, Jill. "Feral Hypertext: When Hypertext Literature Escapes Control." *Proceedings of the Sixteenth acm Conference on Hypertext and Hypermedia.* ACM Hypertext '05 (2005): 46–53. http://delivery.acm.org.
———. "Piecing Together and Tearing Apart: Finding the Story in *Afternoon.*" *Proceedings of the Tenth acm Conference on Hypertext and Hypermedia: Returning To Our Diverse Roots. Feb. 21–25 1999.* ACM Hypertext '99 (1999): 111–17. http://delivery.acm.org.
Zhang, Yuejiao. "Wiki Means More: Hyperreading in Wikipedia." *Proceedings of the Seventeenth Conference on Hypertext and Hypermedia.* ACM Hypertext '06 (2006): 23–26. http://delivery.acm.org.

PART THREE

Beginnings and/as Endings

It is widely felt that beginnings are connected in significant ways to endings, though the precise nature and implications of these connections are not always agreed on. Edward Said and Peter Brooks affirm the mutually implicating relation of the two; for Said, however, the act of beginning establishes the parameters of what will follow, while for Brooks the choice of ending determines the rest of the narrative. Gerald Prince, reflecting on the retrospective nature of most fiction (i.e., the events being narrated have occurred before the actual narrating begins), suggests that "the end frequently determines the beginning at least as much as, if not more than, it is determined by it, since from the beginning the beginning is oriented by the idea of the end" (158). In her well-known critique of Brooks's model, Susan Winnett argues that ends and beginnings are much more intertwined than is generally acknowledged in masculinist narrative theory; as opposed to Brooks's postulation that narrative reproduces the entirely end-driven arousal and significant discharge of the (male) sexual act, she points out that, concerning two female kinds of detumescence and discharge, birth and breast-feeding, "their ends (in both senses of the word) are, quite literally, beginning itself" (143–44). In this volume's final essay, "Maculate Reconceptions," Winnett compellingly applies this general thesis. And as we have already seen, a number of theorists from Todorov to D. A. Miller to Emma Kafalenos postulate a general narrative trajectory that both begins with and returns to a "non-narratable" state of equilibrium or quiescence. In the more carefully constructed plots there is a clear connection between originary causes and final resolutions of the major components of the plot.

It is also increasingly evident that there need not be any such definitive relationship in all texts: picaresque novels, many forms of comedy, the *roman fleuve*, and serial fiction may well have seemingly arbitrary, "tacked-on" endings, as Ejner Jensen, Lynette Felber, and Robyn Warhol have shown. Or, as Warhol contrasts the status and function of endings in two genres: "If romance novels require an ending, serial narratives actively resist coming to closure: formally speaking, . . . [they] could have continued indefinitely" (76). After all, how does an author foreshadow the conclusion of a narrative that is not intended to come to an end?

Despite these counterexamples, in the history of the novel there has often been a desire for the ending to somehow refigure, mirror, or revisit the work's beginning. Tolstoy, for instance, expressed pride in his having "concealed the arches" that framed and supported the story of Anna Karenina. Peter Rabinowitz articulates a metarule that "leads us to expect balance in a text, to expect that somehow the ending will be prefigured by the beginning" (161), and notes a number of ways that this can be achieved, including the return in the end to the work's original dramatized consciousness (125–28). In his contribution to this volume, "The Beginning of *Beloved*: A Rhetorical Approach," James Phelan shows how the reader is led symmetrically into and out of a work of narrative fiction at four different levels, thereby disclosing a web of relations that can bind beginnings to endings. In her essay in this section, "Connecting Links: Beginnings and Endings," Armine Kotin Mortimer draws salient examples from several periods of French fiction to show the range of relations between beginnings and endings over several centuries and traces a general movement from connection to disjunction.

As Oliver Buckton demonstrates wonderfully in his essay on *Catriona*, Stevenson's sequel to *Kidnapped*, the relation between two or more books that explore the same fictional world is a most interesting one for narrative critics and theorists, particularly when, as Buckton points out, the sequel might easily not have been written. Multivolume constructions like Balzac's novels or Faulkner's Yoknapatawpha works resist closure and problematize beginnings: insofar as a novel presents a later installment of a previously developed fictional world, much of the beginning of the story will already be in place before the first word of the new text is written or read. If the later work treats an earlier period of the same world, however, it can re-create the original beginning by providing a chronologically earlier one, as the story of Ikkemotubbe in "Red Leaves," published in 1930, "begins" the story of Faulkner's fictional county anew several years after the first novel depicting it had appeared.

Meir Sternberg argues in *Expositional Modes and Temporal Ordering in Fiction* that the situation of the author returning to a preexisting fictional world is analogous to an author's re-creation of historical accounts or mythic narratives; he cautions that in all of these cases, fictional or nonfictional, the anterior "facts" can be altered or ignored (2–5). Usually, one ignores minor changes in a writer's imaginative domain as inconsequential errors, as Malcolm Cowley does certain discrepancies in Faulkner's oeuvre. Sternberg, however, "take[s] them to be deliberate and revealing deviations from previous thematic and structural conceptions"; therefore, "it is evident they constitute or call for new expositional material" (4–5). Perhaps the best solution to this dilemma is to combine both positions: a new text that returns to a previously created fictional world should be thought of as a continuous totality except in those cases in which the later book contradicts significant aspects presented in earlier volumes.

Before leaving this topic we might note a few other ways in which beginnings and endings can be brought into juxtaposition. Thomas Mann intended *Der Zauberberg* to be read twice; the book's ending is thus a preliminary act to the desired rereading of the work. In many modern narratives, the language, style, and technique of beginning and end can mirror each other: the letters of the last word of *Ulysses*, "yes," appear in reverse order in the book's first word, "Stately." The setting of the first and last episodes is a domestic residence that houses or has recently housed a usurper. The figures are just rising from or lying down in their beds. Joyce's indication of the technique of the first three chapters, "narrative (young)," "catechism (personal)," and "monologue (male)," is balanced by the opposite incarnations of the same techniques in the final three chapters: "narrative (old)," "catechism (impersonal)," and "monologue (female)" (Gilbert 30).

More radical conjunctions are also possible: there are even circular texts that literally return to their beginning, as the last sentence of the work is also its first (*Finnegans Wake,* Nabokov's "The Circle"), as an infinite narrative is assayed. We may conclude that the wide array of possible relations between beginnings and endings is impossible to circumscribe within a single conception; we would do better to identify and analyze the extensive range of possible connections and divergences.

Works Cited

Gilbert, Stuart. *James Joyce's* Ulysses: *A Study*. New York: Random, 1952.

Kafalenos, Emma. *Narrative Causalities*. Columbus: Ohio State University Press, 2006.

Prince, Gerald. *Narratology: The Form and Functioning of Narrative*. Amsterdam: Mouton, 1982.

Rabinowitz, Peter. *Before Reading: Narrative Conventions and the Politics of Interpretation*. 1987. Reprint. Columbus: Ohio State University Press, 1999.

Sternberg, Meir. *Expositional Modes and Temporal Ordering in Fiction*. Baltimore: Johns Hopkins University Press, 1978.

Warhol, Robyn. *Having a Good Cry: Effeminate Feelings and Pop-Culture Forms*. Columbus: Ohio State University Press, 2003.

Winnett, Susan. "Coming Unstrung: Women, Men, Narrative, and Principles of Pleasure." PMLA 105 (1990): 505–18.

13

The Beginning of *Beloved*

A Rhetorical Approach

JAMES PHELAN

This essay locates narrative beginnings within a rhetorical theory of narrative, develops an approach to beginnings that pays attention to both textual dynamics and readerly dynamics, and then analyzes the beginning of Toni Morrison's *Beloved*. Rhetorical theory defines narrative as somebody telling somebody else on some occasion and for some purpose(s) that something happened. The theory further postulates that narrative is a form in which an implied author draws on or invents the appropriate textual and intertextual resources to convey a multi-leveled communication about the something that happened to an implied audience. In this view, then, narrative is not just a structure of meanings but also an act that engages and seeks to influence its audience's understanding, emotions, and ethics. Rhetorical theory also notes that individual historical readers can seek to join that implied audience—or, to use Peter J. Rabinowitz's term, authorial audience—and thus share the experiences offered by narrative. Thus, when I speak of readerly dynamics here I am speaking of the activities of the authorial audience.

Narrative progression is the concept that rhetorical theory uses to refer to the double movement of narrative from its inception to its ending, a movement of characters and events (or textual dynamics) and a movement of audience response (or readerly dynamics). Progression, in this sense, is the synthesis of a narrative's textual dynamics and readerly dynamics. Thus, within a rhetorical theory of narrative, an adequate account of beginnings, middles, and ends must provide a means for giving us access to both kinds of dynamics.

I have chosen to use Toni Morrison's *Beloved* as the focus for my development of the concept of beginnings, because it provides both a welcome invitation and a healthy challenge to the rhetorical approach. It is inviting because it clearly is a narrative act that has designs on its audience, but it is just as clearly a complex act whose designs are not easy to pin down. Among the chief questions it raises are these: Why does Morrison choose a narrator who opens the novel with such a dense and difficult- to-process exposition? In particular, why does Morrison choose to make the temporality of the action and of the telling difficult to track? Does Morrison expect her audience to believe in ghosts? Why does the narrator introduce so many possible threads for the narrative to follow in such a short space? I will attempt to address these questions after setting out my rhetorical approach to beginnings in particular and progressions in general.[1]

Previous narrative theory, for the most part, has emphasized the textual rather than the readerly side of narrative beginnings. Aristotle tells us in his wonderfully logical way that a beginning is that which is not itself necessarily after anything else and that which has naturally something else after it. Structuralist theorists, following Propp, identify the beginning with the introduction of a lack. Psychoanalytic critics such as Peter Brooks view the beginning as the initiation of narrative desire. In my previous work on narrative progression, *Reading People, Reading Plots* (1989), I identified the beginning as that part of a narrative which introduces unstable relationships between characters (instabilities) or between the reader and the author or narrator (tensions). Local instabilities are those whose resolution does not signal the completeness of the progression; global instabilities are those that provide the main track of the progression and must be resolved for a narrative to attain completeness. (Of course, not all narratives seek completeness in this sense.) The first chapter of *Pride and Prejudice*, for example, uses local instabilities—the dialogue between Mr. and Mrs. Bennet about whether Mr. Bennet will visit the new tenant of Netherfield Park—even as it communicates the global instability: the arrival of the single man of good fortune into the neighborhood. The one theorist who has emphasized the readerly side of beginnings, Peter Rabinowitz, has been less concerned with identifying beginnings proper than with pointing out that, before reading, we are already equipped with conventional "rules of notice" that mark the initial features of texts—titles, first sentences, first chapters—as deserving special emphasis. These different perspectives obviously have much in common and suggest that beginnings not only set the narrative in motion but give it a particular direction.

Indeed, beginnings do more than initiate the action, as becomes apparent when we focus on readerly dynamics. Elements of exposition matter because they influence our understanding of the narrative world, which in turn influences our understanding of the meaning and consequences of the action, including our initial generic identification of the narrative and the expectations that follow from that identification. Furthermore, I propose that we need to include in a broadened concept of beginnings narrative discourse and the readerly dynamics associated with it. Sometimes the forward movement of a narrative is generated by the tensions arising in narrative discourse, but even when the forward movement is generated primarily by instabilities, our processing of the narrative discourse is a crucial component of our entry into the narrative world.

Given these considerations, I propose the following conception of narrative beginnings and the following way of sorting out the numerous terms related to beginnings.[2] *Beginning* is the technical, precise term referring to a segment of a narrative defined by four aspects. The first two aspects focus on the "aboutness" of the narrative and on the textual dynamics, while the third and fourth focus on the activity of the authorial audience, what I have been calling readerly dynamics.

1. *Exposition*: everything, including the paratexts of the front matter (illustrations, epigraphs, preludes, notices, author's or editor's introductions, etc.), that provides information about the narrative, the characters (listings of traits, past history, etc.), the setting (time and place), and events of the narrative. Exposition is the inclusive term that also covers *background* and *orientation*. Exposition may appear anywhere in a narrative; exposition that is part of a beginning includes anything prior to or immediately following and directly relevant to what I call the launch.[3]

2. *Launch*: the revelation of the first set of global instabilities or

tensions in the narrative. This moment in the narrative marks the boundary between the beginning and the middle. The launch may come early or late, but I set the boundary at the first global instability or tension because until then a narrative has not established a clear direction. This way of identifying the launch also means that, from a first-time reader's perspective, the identification will initially be a tentative one, something for which the reader will seek confirmation or disconfirmation in the subsequent progression.

3. *Initiation*: the initial rhetorical transactions among implied author and narrator, on the one hand, and flesh- and-blood and authorial audience on the other. Rabinowitz's rules of notice are especially relevant to the reader's experience of the initiation.

4. *Entrance*: the flesh-and-blood reader's multi-leveled—cognitive, emotive, ethical—movement from outside the text to a specific location in the authorial audience at the end of the launch. When the entrance is complete, the authorial audience has typically made numerous significant interpretive, ethical, and even aesthetic judgments, and these judgments influence what is arguably the most important element of the entrance: the authorial audience's hypothesis, implicit or explicit, about the direction and purpose of the whole narrative, what I will call its configuration. This hypothesis about configuration is of course subject to revision in the light of developments in the middle and even the ending.

This conception of a beginning means that it is a unit whose length will vary considerably from narrative to narrative, since some beginnings will include more exposition than others and some will take longer to establish the first set of global instabilities or tensions. In addition, this conception of a beginning naturally leads into similar conceptions of middles and endings, conceptions that also identify four aspects of each and that round out a way to describe narrative progressions.

Middles have the following aspects.

5. *Exposition*: again, information relevant to the narrative (e.g., chapter titles), especially descriptions of its setting, characters, and events.

6. *Voyage*: the development of the global instabilities and/or tensions. Sometimes the initial set of global instabilities or tensions becomes more complicated, as it does in *Beloved*; sometimes, as in many picaresque narratives, the global instabilities remain largely as they are or get only mildly complicated as the characters deal with a series of local instabilities.

7. *Interaction*: the ongoing communicative exchanges between implied author, narrator, and audience. These exchanges have significant effects on our developing responses to the characters and events as well as to our ongoing relationship with the narrator and implied author.

8. *Intermediate Configuration*: the evolving responses of the authorial audience to the overall development of the narrative. During this stage our initial hypothesis about the configuration of the whole will become more fully developed, though that development may either largely confirm or substantially revise the hypothesis formed at the entrance.

Endings have the following four aspects:

9. *Exposition/Closure*: When this information about the narrative, characters, or action includes a signal that the narrative is coming to an end, regardless of the state of the instabilities and tensions, it becomes a device of closure. Just as beginnings may include such paratextual material as epigraphs and authors' notes, endings may include epilogues, afterwords, appendixes, and the like.

10. *Arrival*: the resolution, in whole or in part, of the global instabilities and tensions. Arrival is more significant than closure in giving the audience a sense of an ending. In other words, narratives with strong closure but weak or no arrivals will seem more open-ended than those with clear arrivals but no strong signals of closure.

11. *Farewell*: the concluding exchanges among implied author, narrator, and audiences. The farewell may or may not involve a direct address to the narratee, but the final exchanges always have the potential to affect the audience's response to the whole narrative. The final section of *Beloved* is an extended farewell that has major consequences for our understanding of the whole.

12. *Completion*: the conclusion of the reader's evolving responses to the whole narrative; culmination of the effects of the previous eleven aspects of progression in the authorial audience's understanding of the multi-layered narrative act.

Another way of presenting this model is in rows and columns so that, reading across, one can see how the two aspects of textual dynamics and the two aspects of readerly dynamics develop.

BEGINNING	MIDDLE	ENDING
Exposition	Exposition	Exposition/Closure
Launch	Voyage	Arrival
Initiation	Interaction	Farewell
Entrance	Intermediate Configuration	Completion

The Beginning of *Beloved*: Front Matter and First Chapter

Morrison does not number the sections of her novel, leaving it to us to notice that part 1 has 18 sections, part 2 has 7 sections, and part 3 has 3 sections, which, when combined, gives us 1873. The first section of part 1, which I will call the first chapter, constitutes the beginning of the novel: by its end the various unstable situations and tensions introduced in the previous pages coalesce sufficiently around an event that launches the narrative forward. The first chapter also provides us with an excellent initiation into the methods of the implied author and her relations to both the protean narrator and her authorial audience. But even before we get to the first sentence of the novel, "124 was spiteful," we encounter some important paratextual front matter.

In addition to the title, the paratexts include a dedication, an epigraph, and two illustrations. Together these expository materials provide a complex backdrop against which to begin reading, a set of thematic associations that provides a context within which to understand the rest of the narrative. The dedication to "Sixty million and more" makes a link between this narrative and the genocide accompanying the slave trade, and as such it suggests that Morrison sees herself as taking on an ambitious project, something that would be worthy to dedicate to those sixty million and more. The epigraph, from Romans 9:25, not only makes a reference to the title but also foregrounds the importance of the teller in relation to the tale and the idea of paradox:

> I will call them my people
> which were not my people; and her beloved
> which was not beloved

On the title page the reader is confronted by an illustration of an apparently female angel with curly hair, a black, frowning face, and wide eyes staring directly out from the page. That stare conveys a challenge to the viewer, a challenge mixed with the sorrow in the face. On the page announcing part 1 there is another black figure, this one hairless so that the head seems more like a skull; like the first figure, this one has a frown and big, round, staring eyes. The angel-like quality is preserved in the appearance of wings behind the face. The illustrations call forth themes of race, death, angels, and unhappiness, and in so doing they reinforce the effect of the dedication and of the epigraph. The paratexts, in short, announce an ambitious narrative about difficult, even horrific subjects in American history and culture.

The first paragraph of the novel continues the exposition but does so in a way that calls attention to the remarkable quality of the initiation.

> 124 was spiteful. Full of a baby's venom. The women in the house knew it and so did the children. For years each put up with the spite in his own way, but by 1873 Sethe and her daughter Denver were its only victims. The grandmother, Baby Suggs, was dead, and the sons, Howard and Buglar, had run away by the time they were thirteen years old—as soon as merely looking in a mirror shattered it (that was the signal for Buglar); as soon as two tiny hand prints appeared in the cake (that was it for Howard). Neither boy waited to see more; another kettleful of chickpeas smoking in a heap on the floor; soda crackers crumbled and strewn in a line next to the doorsill. Nor did they wait for one of the relief periods: the weeks, months even, when nothing was disturbed. No. Each one fled at once—the moment

the house committed what was for him the one insult not to be borne or witnessed a second time. Within two months, in the dead of winter, leaving their grandmother, Baby Suggs; Sethe, their mother; and their little sister, Denver, all by themselves in the gray and white house on Bluestone Road. It didn't have a number then, because Cincinnati didn't stretch that far. In fact, Ohio had been calling itself a state only seventy years when first one brother and then the next stuffed quilt packing into his hat, snatched up his shoes, and crept away from the lively spite the house felt for them. (3)

This paragraph is, above all, disorienting. Although the narrator gives us a lot of expository information, the relation between all of it is murky at best—especially because the narrator withholds some very important information from us. The narrator moves the audience in and out of medias res, starting there early in the paragraph but, by the end, signaling her own temporal distance from the action. Concurrent with her movement in time and space is the movement of her voice. Sometimes she is distant, formal, and authoritative, "by 1873 Sethe and her daughter Denver were its only victims." Sometimes she is more intimate and informal, but she always retains the authoritative tone: "Nor did they wait for one of the relief periods: the weeks, months even, when nothing was disturbed. No." This initiation is one that requires the audience to stretch, even struggle, to keep up with the narrator and the implied author, as a closer look at the paragraph will reveal.

"124 was spiteful. Full of a baby's venom. The women in the house knew it and so did the children. For years each put up with the spite in his own way, but by 1873 Sethe and her daughter Denver were its only victims." The narrator does not say what sort of entity 124 is, though by the third sentence and certainly by the end of the paragraph we can identify it as a house. Establishing this fact calls attention to Morrison's use of personification. The house has a life apart from the people who live in it, a life very much linked with the baby's venom. Indeed, the metonymic relation established between house and baby in the first two sentences becomes metaphoric by the middle of the paragraph, when the narrator tells us that Howard and Buglar flee "the moment *the house* committed . . . the one insult not to be borne or witnessed a second time." By establishing this metaphoric relation, Morrison underlines the alienation of Sethe and Denver from their own house. This underlining suggests, in turn, that any resolution of that alienation will depend on some resolution of their relation to this venomous baby. What's striking about the situation revealed here is that it appears to be a kind of fixed instability, that is, an uneasy relationship that is now a constant in the lives of the women in the house. In that sense, this information is part of the exposition rather than the launch. The energy for the launch will need to come from some source that has the potential to alter this static disequilibrium.

Furthermore, the first three sentences incline me to align my sympathies with Sethe and Denver. They seem to be not foolish victims but people with staying power. Of course this initial alignment is fairly tentative, but it also signals something about the value structure of the story: this implied author values persistence in the face of difficulty.

The phrase "baby's venom" evokes other responses. It is disorienting because it has the ring of an oxymoron; we don't typically associate babies and venom with each other. It is also disorienting because it seems initially related to Baby Suggs and then later to a ghostly presence. Once we infer that the baby is a ghost, the phrase makes more sense, but the initial disorientation has some ongoing effects. The narrator's casual use of the phrase sends a strong signal that things that are familiar in the narrative world are not familiar in my flesh-and-blood reader's world. If baby's venom is, in some sense, a matter of course, something that can be casually invoked to explain a spiteful house, then I am in a world quite different from my own. Once I infer that the baby is a ghost, I also infer that Morrison wants me to be taken aback by the matter-of-factness of her opening and to think about the distance I must travel to enter her authorial audience.

However, not all flesh-and-blood readers will react this way. For some readers, including some segments of Morrison's African-American audience, a belief in ghosts is the norm, not the exception. This point does not alter the fact that Morrison's authorial audience can take a matter-of-fact attitude toward the presence of ghosts in the world, but it does indicate that different flesh-and-blood readers will have different relations to that audience. Some readers will feel the comfort of having their beliefs confirmed by Morrison's narrative, whereas others, like me, will have to adopt new beliefs to participate fully in that narrative.

This dimension of Morrison's approach to audience reveals an ethical dimension to the initiation she offers. Morrison uses her narration to convey both authority and pride. With neither apology nor explanatory introduction, she implicitly says, here is my narrative world; deal with it. In other words, the burden of establishing a satisfactory rhetorical relationship between author and audience here falls largely on the audience. This strategy also entails some obligations on Morrison's part, or it will end up working against her. Her obligation is simply to reward the audience that meets her challenge with a rich reading experience, one commensurate with the effort it takes to enter her world.

Reading on, we discover that "baby's venom" is apparently not so virulent: it gets manifested in a shattered mirror, hand prints in a cake, spilled chickpeas, crumbled soda crackers. Faced with such venom, I might find courage enough to qualify for a Medal of Honor, but not so the two young males in the story. Indeed, the main action summarized in the paragraph is the fleeing of Howard and Buglar, and the narrator suggests that they abandoned the women of 124: "Within two months, in the dead of winter, leaving their grandmother, Baby Suggs; Sethe, their mother; and their little sister, Denver, all by themselves in the gray and white house on Bluestone Road." The effect is to emphasize 124 as a distinctly female space and to set up the issue of gender relations as a potentially significant one for the whole narrative.

These sentences about Howard's and Buglar's flights also form part of the paragraph's disorienting discourse on time. In the fourth sentence we have two references: "for years" and "by 1873." In the fifth sentence we learn that in 1873 Baby Suggs was dead and that Howard and Buglar had run away by the time they were thirteen; the two sentences I have just discussed tell us that they left within "two months of each other" and that when they left Baby Suggs was still alive. The last two sentences, which shift the narrator's location in

The Beginning of *Beloved*   205

time, say that they left seventy years after Ohio became a state (1803), which means 1873. The narrator soon reports that Baby Suggs died right after they left and that at that point Denver is ten. But later we learn that Denver was born in 1855. What is going on? Clearly, Morrison wants to foreground the importance of time, history, and the interrelation of events in this narrative but also wants to suggest that in this world, time is a jumble, that past, present, and future easily get mixed up. I also think, however, that the implied Morrison has herself become so disoriented by the jumble of time that she got, well, temporarily confused and unwittingly introduced this mistake about the temporality.

The last two sentences of the paragraph significantly complicate exposition and initiation in other ways as well. "It didn't have a number then, because Cincinnati didn't stretch that far. In fact, Ohio had been calling itself a state only seventy years when [Howard and Buglar left]." First, these sentences underscore how important the number 124 must be to the narrative. "124 was spiteful. Full of baby's venom. The women in the house knew it and so did the children." This expository discourse seems to be describing a particular moment when the action will begin, and consequently it suggests that all the things named in that discourse are as they were at that moment—the venom, the women, the children, the house. But since the house was not then numbered, this discourse must be heavily retrospective. The narrator has not stepped all the way back into the moment in 1873, when the story will begin. The next sentence suggests that she is located in the 1980s, because it is only from a perspective considerably after 1873 that one would say "Ohio had been calling itself a state *only* seventy years." I say that the narrator's perspective is the 1980s because, in the absence of evidence to the contrary, a narrator's present will be an author's present, and Morrison published the book in 1987.

These matters of temporal perspective combine with the specific information about the numbering and location of the house in Cincinnati to emphasize the way that this narrative is very much interested in locating itself in the larger history of America. So, in conjunction with the front matter, especially the dedication, 1873 becomes important as a time shortly after the end of slavery. The narrator's location in the 1980s implies a yet-to-be-revealed relevance of the events of 1873 to those of the 1980s.

By the end of the first paragraph, then, I have had to work hard simply to understand the expository moves Morrison is making, I have developed a sympathetic disposition toward the women of 124, and I have begun to feel, despite some minor bumps, both challenged and rewarded in my relation to Morrison.

The move from the exposition and introduction of the first paragraph to the initiation and entrance does not come swiftly or easily. As I have noted, the first paragraph reveals a fixed instability, a static disequilibrium that needs to be disrupted by some new force before any significant alteration in the characters' lives will be possible. That force is Paul D Garner, who knew Sethe when both were slaves on the Kentucky plantation called Sweet Home and who has now, eighteen years after Sethe fled the plantation, made his way to 124 Bluestone Rd. Paul D's arrival is a major instability for several reasons: it introduces an adult male into the female space of 124; it signals an opportunity for Sethe to confront the past; it holds out some promise for a future different from the dismal present. But Paul D's role in the launch, which does not occur until the end of the chapter, cannot be understood apart from the whole series of instabilities and tensions established in the first chapter.

Indeed, the progression of the first chapter depends at least as much on tensions of unequal knowledge between Morrison and the narrator, on one side, and the authorial audience, on the other, as it does on instabilities. Morrison's narrator continues the exposition by giving us pieces of the past and present, but because those pieces raise more questions than they answer, the exposition allows us to establish only an unsecure foothold in this narrative world. The greatest tension surrounds the ghost: How did the baby die? Morrison alludes to the death in Sethe's memory of how her powerful love for the baby led her to trade sex for the engraving of the word "Beloved" on her tombstone: "Not only did she have to live out her years in a house palsied by the baby's fury at having her throat cut, but those ten minutes she spent pressed up against dawn-colored stone studded with star chips, her knees wide open as the grave, were longer than life, more alive, more pulsating than the baby blood that soaked her fingers like oil" (5). The glimpse, however, does not allow us to see who cut the baby's throat or the circumstances under which Sethe was able to feel the blood soaking her fingers.

There are numerous other tensions as well. Once Paul D arrives we learn pieces of the story of Sweet Home, pieces that create tensions about other parts of that story. Sethe was the only female slave among five black men; she chose to marry one called Halle and had four children in four years, the last, her daughter Denver, shortly after escaping from the plantation. Just before she left, she was assaulted by white men; first, they "held [her] down" and "took [her] milk," then when she told Mrs. Garner, they came and whipped her until they left scars in the figure of a tree on her back. But though we know these elements of the past, we also recognize that there are many gaps in our knowledge. These tensions about Sweet Home reinforce the first paragraph's emphasis on the importance of time and memory in this narrative. By the end of the chapter we know that any positive progression forward in 1873 depends in part on some working through of Sethe's past experience at Sweet Home.

The first chapter also opens the narrative out beyond the story of Sethe and Paul D by introducing instabilities and tensions involving Sethe's daughter Denver. The narrative discourse switches to her perspective and shows us that Paul D represents an overt threat and a covert hope for Denver. He makes her mother act differently, like a flirtatious girl instead of "the quiet, queenly woman Denver had known all her life" (12). Paul D and Sethe with their talk of Sweet Home and her father seem to share a world in which Denver has no place. And so she acts out, then breaks down crying in a way that she had not for nine years. The crying is not just about being shut out of the intimacy between her mother and Paul D but also about the life she is forced to have:

"I can't live here. I don't know where to go or what to do, but I can't live here. Nobody speaks to us. Nobody comes by. Boys don't like me. Girls don't either."

"Honey, honey."

> "What's she talking 'bout nobody speaks to you?," asked Paul D.
>
> "It's the house. People don't—"
>
> "It's not! It's not the house. It's us! And it's you!" (14)

Again the new information we learn here also opens up new tensions: What is it about Sethe, what is it about all of them that makes nobody want to interact with them? At the same time, even as this dialogue shows Denver's opposition to her mother, Morrison uses it to generate sympathy for each of them: for Sethe because she is genuinely concerned for Denver here, and for Denver herself because she is in such an awful situation.

Paul D's own sympathy with Sethe, and the glimpses we get of his past, position us in a similar sympathetic relation to him, even as the narrative continues to mark the importance of gender difference. Consider the dialogue that follows Sethe's narration of how she came to get the "tree" on her back.

> "Men don't know nothing much," said Paul D, tucking his pouch back into his vest pocket, "but they do know a suckling can't be away from its mother for long."
>
> "Then they know what it's like to send your children off when your breasts are full."
>
> "We was talking 'bout a tree, Sethe."
>
> "After I left you, those boys came in there and took my milk. That's what they came in there for. Held me down and took it. I told Mrs. Garner on em. . . . Them boys found out I told on em. Schoolteacher made one open up my back, and when it closed it made a tree. It grows there still."
>
> "They used cowhide on you?"
>
> "And they took my milk."
>
> "They beat you and you was pregnant."
>
> "And they took my milk!" (16–17)

Whereas Paul D focuses on what seems to him the greater physical violation of Sethe's body—the white men's beating her—Sethe emphasizes the violation to her role as mother, first in having to send her children off without feeding them, and second in having her milk taken by the white men. Again Morrison asks us to judge each character's position as valid, though her giving Sethe the last word suggests that Sethe's position will trump Paul D's. More than that, the dialogue itself reinforces the significance of gender difference for the narrative. I will return to this passage later in the chapter.

As the source of the greatest tensions, the ghost is both a powerful magnet for our interest and a great mystery, something we do not know yet know how to respond to: she is obviously a disruptive force, but she is the ghost of a baby who had her throat cut, and so a creature who deserves our sympathy. Denver is the character whom we can interpret and judge most readily, even as the narrative's move to her concerns and interests certainly complicates our response to Sethe, especially in adding the tension about how Sethe could be the reason that nobody will come to the house. In short, as the chapter develops it introduces so many tensions, so many instabilities, and it offers so much competition for our attention, interest, sympathy, and understanding, that it heightens the disorienting effect of the first paragraph.

In the final pages of the chapter, the narrative focus returns to Sethe and Paul D and then shifts to Paul D and the ghost as Morrison pulls things sufficiently together to provide the launch. Sethe tells Paul D the story of how she got the tree on her back, and he begins to comfort her physically, putting his mouth on the scars of her back and holding her breasts in his hands, an action that prompts Sethe to wonder:

> Would there be a little space . . . a little time, some way to hold off eventfulness, to push busyness into the corners of the room and just stand there a minute or two, naked from shoulder blade to waist, relieved of the weight of her breasts, smelling the stolen milk again and the pleasure of baking bread? (18)

Sethe's pleasure arouses the jealous resentment of the ghost, who exhibits a venom far greater than anything mentioned in the first paragraph. The ghost makes the whole house pitch, until Paul D, seizing a table that has been flung at him and bashing it about while screaming for the ghost to leave, succeeds in chasing the ghost from the house. The chapter ends not with a focus on Paul D and Sethe but rather with Denver missing her brothers and Baby Suggs, and thinking, "Now her mother was upstairs with the man who had gotten rid of the only other company she had. Denver dipped a bit of bread into the jelly. Slowly, methodically, miserably she ate it" (19).

With the elimination of the ghost, the static disequilibrium revealed in the first paragraph is permanently altered. This alteration constitutes the launch because it significantly complicates rather than resolves that initial unstable situation. Although the ghost is "gone," the narrator also tells us that after the battle, while "Sethe, Denver, and Paul D breathed to the same beat, like one tired person," "another breathing was just as tired" (18–19). The implicit promise of this sentence—and, indeed, of the magnetic interest surrounding the ghost throughout this section—is that she will return. Furthermore, Morrison emphasizes the complication of the instabilities by shifting to Denver and showing her unhappiness. From Denver's point of view, the house was better with the ghost and without Paul D.

By the end of the chapter, then, we have sufficient information to complete our entrance into the narrative world. We are temporally oriented toward both the present of 1873 and the past at Sweet Home. Our judgments of the characters are essentially positive and so our sympathies are with all of them, even as we recognize the unstable relations between them. We desire that Paul D's arrival at 124 will make life better for Sethe, but we don't want an improvement for Sethe that will come at the expense of her daughter. We are also aware that the ghost remains a threat to disrupt whatever positive changes Paul D might help to bring about. And we are very cognizant of the multiple thematic threads introduced into the narrative, especially the ones about slavery, death, unhappiness, time and memory, and gender. This entrance does not allow us to predict the trajectory of the narrative for either the characters or the thematic issues, but it does take us inside a compelling and difficult narrative world.

Notes

1. Although I have not found any work on *Beloved* that offers a thorough analysis of its beginning along the lines I offer here, the novel has received many excellent commentaries. I have found especially helpful those by Christian, Hirsch, Homans, Rimmon-Kenan, Travis, Wilt, and Wolfe. For more background work on the rhetorical theory of narrative, see my *Narrative as Rhetoric* and *Reading People, Reading Plots*.
2. This account of beginnings is a revision and extension of the brief account I offer in my entry on "Beginnings and Endings" in *The Encyclopedia of the Novel*.
3. See Sternberg for an impressive account of the relation between exposition and a narrative's handling of time. Sternberg uses the *fabula/syuzhet* distinction to identify exposition as "the first part" of the *fabula* (14), and he sees its function as providing the reader "with the general and specific antecedents indispensable to the understanding of what happens in [the fictive world of the story]" (1). His understanding of exposition informs my own, but my interest in the phenomenon here is different: I want to account for the role of information relevant to but different from setting, characters, and events in the *syuzhet*. By including paratexts as part of the exposition of beginning, I am including diverse kinds of relevant material, and a full rhetorical study of exposition itself would make further distinctions among these kinds.

Works Cited

Aristotle. *Poetics*. Trans. Gerald Else. Ann Arbor: University of Michigan Press, 2000.

Christian, Barbara. "Beloved, She's Ours." *Narrative* 5 (1997): 36–49.

Hirsch, Marianne. "Maternity and Rememory: Toni Morrison's *Beloved*." *Representations of Motherhood*. Ed. Donna Bassin, Margaret Honey, and Meryle Mahrer Kaplan. New Haven: Yale University Press, 1994. 92–110.

Homans, Margaret. "Feminist Fictions and Feminist Theories of Narrative." *Narrative* 2 (1994): 3–16.

Phelan, James. "Beginnings and Endings." *Encyclopedia of the Novel*. Ed. Paul Schellinger. Chicago: Fitzroy-Dearborn, 1998. 96–99.

———. *Narrative as Rhetoric: Technique, Audiences, Ethics, Ideology*. Columbus: Ohio State University Press, 1996.

———. *Reading People, Reading Plots: Character, Progression, and the*

Interpretation of Narrative. Chicago: University of Chicago Press, 1989.
Rabinowitz, Peter J. *Before Reading: Narrative Conventions and the Politics of Interpretation.* 1987. Columbus: Ohio State University Press, 1998.
———. "Truth in Fiction: A Reexamination of Audiences." *Critical Inquiry* 4 (1977): 121–41.
Rimmon-Kenan, Shlomith. *A Glance Beyond Doubt: Narration, Representation, Subjectivity.* Columbus: Ohio State University Press, 1996.
Sternberg, Meir. *Expositional Modes and Temporal Ordering in Fiction.* Baltimore: Johns Hopkins University Press, 1978.
Travis, Molly. "Speaking from the Silence of the Slave Narrative: *Beloved* and African-American Women's History." *Texas Review* 13.1–2 (1992): 69–81.
Wilt, Judith. *Abortion, Choice, and Contemporary Fiction.* Chicago: University of Chicago Press, 1989.
Wolfe, Joanna. "'Ten Minutes for Seven Letters': Song as Key to Narrative Revision in Toni Morrison's *Beloved.*" *Narrative* 12 (2004): 263–80.

14

Connecting Links

Beginnings and Endings

ARMINE KOTIN MORTIMER

In a coherent system, beginnings lead to endings, and endings determine how we understand beginnings. Our concept of the novel as the locus of a fictive world includes a strong expectation of coherence. As Peter Rabinowitz writes, "by the general rule of conclusive endings, readers are invited to revise their understanding of the beginning of the text so that the ending, which at first seems a surprise, turns out to be in fact prefigured" (305). Rabinowitz also posits an innate need for closure: "there is a general tendency in most reading to apply rules of coherence in such a way that disjunctures are smoothed over so that texts are turned into unified wholes—that is, in a way that allows us to read so that we get the satisfaction of closure. This interpretive technique is taught explicitly in school; and it may be connected to an innate psychological drive for closure" (310–11). In her inaugural work, *Poetic Closure*, Barbara Herrnstein Smith always understood that the reader's perception of closure was a function of the whole of the poem (4).

With these unifying premises in mind, I will confront beginnings and endings in examples of French novels, to describe a combined construct of "beginning-and-ending." We are no longer in the dark about narrative closure, because a large number of books and colloquia have brought considerable illumination to the topic, but the relations of beginnings to endings is less well understood. The French novelist and critic Julien Gracq (1910–2007) posed the problem of beginnings in acute terms by alluding to Archimedes' fulcrum, the ultimate starting point:

> The truth is that the sum of unredeemable decisions, whether abrupt or subtle, implied by any first page is enough to set one's head spinning.... The beginning of a work of fiction may well have no other real objective than to create something irremediable, a fixed anchor point, a fact of resistance that the mind cannot budge. For in the problematic of fiction, there is a problem that arises before all others, which is left unexamined; it is none other than Archimedes' fulcrum: from what basis can we push off to get outside the enclosure of the evasive, the substitutable, the fluctuating? (109–10)

To achieve a definite starting point by creating a fiction, the novelist can only ignore the mystery of how one can create, at the beginning of beginnings, something which can then become opaque to one's own mind—and this with nothing more than the hands, according to Gracq.

Beginnings are therefore difficult to study on their own terms, because nothing comes before. Given that the beginning is the thing that makes the ending possible at all, the initiator of the ending can be called the connecting link (the "and" of my title). Rabinowitz has identified as "the second metarule of configuration" a convention that "leads us to expect balance in a text, to expect that the ending will somehow be prefigured in the beginning" (304–5). Beginnings and endings of novels bespeak the period in which the novels were written; for instance, we can speak of "romantic closures" defining a certain style of novels of the nineteenth century or the "open endings" so characteristic of the narratives of the 1960s. An eighteenth-century novelist begins with a "genealogy" and a twentieth-century novelist plunges in in medias res, leaving it up to the reader to sort out who is speaking or what the situation is. Given that all works of fiction start and end, what is interesting is the fact that there are many different ways to start and end and to join the beginning to the ending. In an approach to addressing this relationship, I will skim some theoretical ground and discuss three different moments of French literature. But instead of examples that defy conventions, my examples will confirm them, showing how the ending is prefigured in the beginning, whatever their forms.

In Balzac's *La Comédie humaine*, the link between beginnings and endings is typically very solid. To best illustrate this, I choose from among nineteen novels and novellas that close on a *historical present* after what I have called a "composed past." For an author whose every novel proceeds either by composition or analysis, like chemistry, such endings correspond to a historical type of narration, which recomposes the past until it succeeds in arriving at a present that is by definition unchanging, ideally situating the reader in the moment when analysis begins. Such a structure defines the realism often called Balzacian. In those cases, the beginning announces a history to be composed, using a variety of opening devices, and strongly implicates the ending. As Rachel Blau DuPlessis writes, "To compose a work is to negotiate with these questions: What stories can be told? How can plots be resolved?" (284). Her concerns are with social and literary conventions, as she writes: "Any artistic resolution (especially of a linear form that must unroll in time) can . . . attempt an ideological solution to the fundamental contradictions that animate the work. Any resolution can have traces of the conflicting materials that have been processed within it" (284). But these are good questions for any *formal* structure as well: What intentions will be inscribed in the opening, what expectation or anticipation? What is narratable, to borrow the term proposed by D. A. Miller in *Narrative and Its Discontents*?

In the opening work of *La Comédie humaine*, the novella "At the Sign of the Cat and Racquet," the jump to the present tense at the ending is as abrupt as possible. As in other cases in Balzac, the present-tense diegesis in the narrative closure is at a considerable distance from the time of the rest of the plot. The last scene of the composed story (before the jump to the present-tense ending) shows the young and innocent Augustine de Sommervieux pitifully contemplating the remains of her portrait, which its painter, her aristocratic husband, Théodore, has violently destroyed, the result of a scene the narrator calls too odious to paint. From this point, we find ourselves without transition in a scene written in the historical present, in which an unnamed friend visits Augustine's gravestone at the Montmartre cemetery and sees in her tomb the untold last act of a drama—her actual death.

The scene of her death, absent from the composed past, occurs only in the imagination of this first-person narrator witness, who makes the narrative endure just as he perpetuates her memory while pursuing an analysis that formulates and finalizes the story's fundamental theme: the harm caused by the error of mismatched marriages.

Théodore's portrait of Augustine is what makes the link to the beginning strong, and doubly so. The first paragraph of the novella, a typical Balzacian opening, details the zoological and archaeological significance of Augustine's family home above her father's fabric store, seen through the amused eyes of the young, aristocratic painter, disdainful of the style of the bourgeois merchant class. The house is old and old-fashioned, rooted in bourgeois mentality, whimsical and frail, and opposed in all ways to the house where Augustine will later live after she marries Théodore and especially to the elegant salons and sumptuous boudoirs of Théodore's mistress, the duchesse de Carigliano, spaces characteristic of Balzacian noble dwellings. The story's title, "At the Sign of the Cat and Racquet," by its very oddity, focuses the reader's attention on the paragraphs after the opening one which describe the shop sign that hangs from the house, depicting a cat engaged in the aristocratic *jeu de paume* or *pelote*, a game forbidden to commoners. As a painting and as a shop sign (which Théodore finds ridiculous), it corresponds to and opposes the portrait of Augustine (shown at the salon). This ironic juxtaposition of the merchant's sign with the portrait encapsulates the central purpose or finality of the entire story: the merchant class errs in taking on aristocratic airs just as Augustine was mistaken to marry de Sommervieux. Balzac weaves enough symbolism around this sign in the beginning pages, while focusing our attention through the painter himself, that the connection to the story's closure will become clear. When in addition we read in the opening that such store signs replicate devices that, in the past, rhetorically connected the living with the dead, we are, without knowing it, close to the other painting whose destruction is a metonym for Augustine's death: "these street signs . . . are the *dead* paintings of the living tableaus with which our clever ancestors had succeeded in attracting customers to their shops" (41; emphasis added). Contrast is the chief quality of the archaeological beginning, a separation of two worlds, and it is in that abyss of misunderstanding that Augustine will founder. If her death is not actually narrated in the closing pages of the composed past, one could say it is because the narration itself stumbled into the abyss. The beginning of the story lends the only possible clue to Augustine's end, by preparing the destruction of the painting as symbolic of her death.

The link is also strong in the eighteenth-century memoir-novel, a popular and widespread genre. Strongly authoritative opening texts announce the narrator's intentions while summarizing the narrative (*Manon Lescaut*) and guide the reader's interpretation (*Les Liaisons dangereuses*), or the embedded narration goes forward until it arrives at the condition permitting the narration (*Paul and Virginia*). But the possibility of a continuation if the work pleases (given the often serial publication of this genre) makes for endings with an open door, a raised foot, stepping stones—strategies that belie the claims of the beginnings and betray an underlying refusal of closure. These examples are interesting precisely because the ending is "won" over a threatening possibility of continuation, because the authors of memoir-novels may not know how their novels will end when they start to write them, and their beginnings betray this impossibility of knowing. Against this structure characteristic of the genre, the three novels mentioned here impose their forged beginning-and-ending as a composition all the more tightly joined.

The epistolary novel *Les Liaisons dangereuses* ends twice: first it reaches closure by many devices and strategies—among them, destinies meted out to all and a closing maxim: "Farewell, my dear and excellent friend; I feel at this moment that our reason, so incapable of foreseeing our misfortunes, is still less capable of consoling us for them" (Laclos 352). Then, a footnote to the final word ("consoler") opens or reopens toward a potential new beginning, or to be more exact, it invites continuations. This "switch off–switch on" closing is the result of the opening strategies of the novel which, like many eighteenth-century novels, begins with liminary texts that purport to direct our reading: first a "Publisher's Note," then an "Editor's Preface," which both appear to be fabricated by Laclos himself. These two "documents" establish the "rules of pertinence" or what Said calls *authority* in his book *Beginnings*: certain things are admissible; others are not (16).

Rules are exactly what the first liminary text, the "Publisher's Note," is about—genre rules, to begin with, which very quickly become social rules. Preceding and preempting the self-styled "Editor" who will claim to have "put in order" a voluminous correspondence that fell into his hands, the publisher "notifies" the public that "we do not guarantee the authenticity of the collection and we have good reason to believe it is only a Novel" (1)—whose author destroyed his own attempts at verisimilitude by placing the story in the enlightened contemporary eighteenth century, which has made "all men so worthy and all women so modest and reserved." The publisher's ironic note concludes with a "triumphant and unanswerable argument," that our society has never seen "a young Lady, with an income of sixty thousand livres, become a nun, nor the wife of a Président die of grief while she is still young and pretty" (1).

Those are in fact two of the significant final destinies that wrap up the narrative closure, the first or real ending. The same "Publisher" who spoke first and had the preemptive authority to say the ending of the novel is impossible returns in the ultimate footnote to deny closure by claiming that private reasons "force us to *stop* here" (352), with the emphasis on *stop*—an apparently arbitrary cut in the narrative flow, rather than a final ending point. "For the moment," the footnote claims, "we cannot give the reader the continuation of Mademoiselle de Volange's adventures nor inform him of the sinister event which completed the misfortunes or the punishment of Madame de Merteuil"—which punishment was one of the more forceful clotural events. (As it was put by Peter Washington, in his almost uncredited excellent introduction to the translation I am using, "Nemesis duly follows hubris" [xvii].) Closure has been given and taken away, and a real question remains about who had the authority, as Said wondered, to do so. Joan DeJean has shown that the closing footnote may indeed have been written by Laclos's publisher Durand, in contradiction to Laclos's last word and his "Editor's Preface" (255).[1] The footnote implies that if the reader's taste has been molded by the story told, if the reader perchance has acquired "our reason for taking an interest in reading these matters," a continuation might "some day" allow the publisher "to complete this work." Directly recalling the first liminary text, these ironic moves place the collection of letters squarely in the tradition of novels published sequentially, in multiple volumes, in response to an enthusiastic readership. (And that is only one of the connecting links between opening and closing strategies.)

Manon Lescaut was the product of just such a publication, the *Memoirs and Adventures of a Man of Quality Retired from Society* by Prévost. *Manon Lescaut,* first published in 1731 as the seventh volume in this memoir-novel, was revised for separate publication in 1753. Its inclusion with the *Memoirs and Adventures* motivates the opening, a "Foreword by the Author of the *Memoirs of a Man of Quality*," where Prévost takes pains to justify including a story of scandalous behavior among the memoirs of this virtuous Man of Quality: "If the public have found anything to please or interest them in the story of my life, it will, I dare say, be no less satisfied with this addition. It will see, in M. Des Grieux's conduct, a terrible example of the power of the passions" (3). The precept is widespread: to instruct while entertaining does service to the public; the book will be a pleasure to read that also can "serve as an aid to moral instruction." The virtuous ending is already inscribed in the moral functions of this liminary text: bad conduct will not get rewarded—need we say it?

And yet, the overwhelming evidence of the story itself is that profane love wins hands down over the sacred, and that the pleasures of having a beautiful mistress outweigh and indeed explain away the dubious morality of the hero. But in the foreword it takes the Man of Quality another page and a half to argue that "the whole work is a moral treatise, appealingly presented as a practical example" (5). The middle, in other words, is in conflict with the moral function to which the foreword assigns the narrative. As a consequence, the beginning dwells on the moral purpose and the ending fulfills it in the most commonplace manner, starting with the death of the heroine. With nothing left to distract him from virtue, the hero can return to being a dutiful member of the aristocracy, resolved to "follow the dictates of honour alone" and to "return to my native land, and to rectify, by a wise and well-ordered life, the scandal of my past conduct" (145). Seeds of virtue are, on the last page, beginning to bear fruit, and the final sentence brings the hero as close as possible on his return trip to the bosom of his family, given that he has been sitting for 135 pages at a hotel in Calais recounting to the Man of Quality the misfortunes, suffering, transgressions, and shameful weaknesses that constitute the entire middle, his first-person narrative.

Bernardin de Saint-Pierre's 1786 short novel, *Paul and Virginia*, begins: "On the eastern slope of the mountain that rises behind the town of Port Louis on the Ile de France may be seen, on a piece of ground once under cultivation, the remains of two small cabins" (39). The rest of the opening paragraph describes a bit of the geography of the island and names Tomb Bay and the Cape of Misfortune. These place-names, the ruined cabins, the no-longer-cultivated ground, and the frank and noble old man the first-person narrator encounters there are the remains of "a touching story" the old man will tell starting at the beginning and ending again at the ruined cabins, the suggestive place-names, and the barren land. I have just described a circular structure, because we begin where we are going to arrive, but more accurately, we can say that the ending prompts the beginning: the narrator says to the old man: "Old Father, can you tell me to whom these two cabins belonged?" and the old man, having assured himself of a good narratee ("be assured that even the man who is most depraved by worldly prejudices likes to hear of the happiness provided by Nature and virtue" [40; translation modified]), launches into a linear, chronological narrative. Had there been a happy ending, there would have been no Tomb Bay, no Cape of Misfortune, and therefore no story prompted by them, for the Cape of Misfortune is where the ship bringing Virginia back from France to Paul and her island home foundered, and Tomb Bay is where her body washed ashore and was found half-buried in the sand: "The voice of the people, which says nothing of the monuments raised to the glory of kings, has given names to some parts of this island which will perpetuate the memory of Virginia's loss" (136). From her death followed all others—Paul, the two mothers, the servants, and the dog, all deaths motivated in various ways but presented as the consequence of Virginia's death—hence the ruined cabins. At no point in the old man's story can the reader expect a different outcome, even when nature and virtue seem to be conspiring so well to turn the mothers' retreat from shame into the children's earthly Eden, overcoming and negating the harm to which society condemned the two women. At every point, the faithful listener will have to anticipate a disaster. That ending is inscribed in the beginning.

A construction is equivalent to an intention, said Said quoting Valéry (*Beginnings* 61). These constructions reveal their intentions; the intentions reside in the beginning-and-end construction, the connecting link, more so than merely in the beginning. That solidification of beginnings by the connecting link becomes more significant in many modern and contemporary novels where the pure authority of beginnings, as described by Said, diminishes and is sometimes abandoned altogether, as if the authors did not really think it is possible to begin.

The post–World War II novel in France, a complete revitalization of French fiction in several stages, takes many new forms, in which the beginning-and-end construct loses some of its solidity and pertinence. The French New Novel, for instance, abandoned linear chronology, disrupted readers' comfortable sense of realism, rejected characterization, and generally ignored the idea of creating a stable mimetic universe. In such a structure, a refusal of the pure authority of beginnings corresponds to uncertain endings. Jean Ricardou, in *La Prise de Constantinople*, invented a form to redefine beginnings and endings by giving his novel a second entry: the back cover looks exactly like the front cover, except that the title is *La Prose de Constantinople*, as Ricardou explained at a 1971 colloquium:

> This book is laid out a bit like those movie theaters where you go in under a brilliant marquee but go out at the back, down some shadowy adjacent street, by way of the discreet back cover of the book.... once the single entrance is passed, the reader is called upon to follow the corridor out to the single exit, at the very end. Bringing this underlying ideology of the book to light

> by contesting it amounts to establishing a reverse course: setting up a second entrance against the first. (385)

Bernard Le Gros explains that the modern novelist is ill at ease in the role of godlike creator and that this uneasiness corresponds to the reader's refusal to believe "that characters can have the clarity of an anthropometric photograph; he [the reader] has heard of Freud and is curious about the unspoken, about the apparent randomness of people's behavior. . . . [H]e no longer wants fiction to provide a different image of reality. The author can therefore leave holes in his narrative and expect the reader to fill them any way he likes" (138). Alain Robbe-Grillet's *Jealousy* (1957) refuses linear narrativity and requires the reader's active participation to create a story with a beginning, a middle, and an end, but the interesting thing is that it is possible to rewrite the plot as a short narrative about a husband's suspicion that his wife is having an affair with their neighbor, Franck. By reordering scenes, the reader can devise a simple plot that begins with the husband's earliest and mildest suspicions, grows through more and more acute suspicions, reaches a climax in chapters 6 and 7 when the wife and Franck spend a night in the city, claiming their car broke down, and comes to a muted conclusion when it seems the affair was not very successful. The connecting link between the beginning and the ending of the novel is however also left to the reader's ingenuity to devise, because the novel does not begin at the beginning of this plot and it does not end precisely when the plot is over. Where *Jealousy* does end recalls the novel's opening, with a significant astronomical device that makes a cloutural move. Scene and setting are the same: the husband is spying on his wife from the deck. The opening words of chapter 9, the last, repeat those at the opening of the first: "Now the shadow of the pillar." With the precision of detail that shocked and fixated the first readers of Robbe-Grillet, the opening paragraph of the novel minutely sets the time of day as early to mid-afternoon. At the start of chapter 9 the time of day is late afternoon, and by the end the shadow has lengthened until it has disappeared with the sunset. It is dark in the tropics at 6:30 at night, the closing moment of the book. Close of day brings closure in spite of the crisis of uncertainty in chapters 6 and 7. The fact that this scene (the husband spying on the wife from the deck) would lie somewhere in the muddy middle of the plot makes it necessary for the reader to forge the connecting link, if the reader wishes to see the beginning lead to an ending.[2]

Georges Perec's 1965 novel, *Les Choses: Une histoire des années soixante* (*Things: A Story of the Sixties*), begins in the conditional tense: "Your eye, first of all, would glide over the grey fitted carpet in the narrow, long and high ceilinged corridor. Its walls would be cupboards, in light-coloured wood, with fittings of gleaming brass" (21). Nothing less than a provocation, this extremely unusual narrative tense initiates a promenade of tenses throughout the novel leading, almost inexorably, to the future tense, just as the events move the characters inexorably to their future. In *Beginnings*, Said underscores the "primordial need for certainty at the beginning over the usually later sense of an ending." As he says, perhaps unnecessarily, "Without at least a sense of a beginning, nothing can really be done, much less ended" (49–50). The conditional is not the tense of certainty; it appears here as the tentative sense of a beginning, the nearest one can hope to get toward this primordial need, just as the couple Jérôme and Sylvie hope, in the conditional tense, for their ideal apartment, the subject of the entire first chapter. Bringing the novel to an end, the epilogue all in the future tense also stamps uncertainty on the sense of an ending: in spite of a story narrated between the beginning and the ending, a story of the sixties, Sylvie and Jérôme have not arrived at their dream life—nor will they ever. It is not in the past tense but in the always unrealized future tense that the story is told of their getting well-paying jobs. We last see them in the dining car of the train taking them to Bordeaux for their new jobs, and the final sentence, ending with suspension points, tells us: "But the meal they will be served will be quite simply tasteless . . ." (126).[3] The social satire will go on forever, the teleology of the narrative disrupted by an obscured beginning, as Mark Workman notes (261). The conditional tense paradoxically "authorizes" the future tense and answers to the problem of the arbitrary nature of beginnings, what Gracq has succinctly called the "vice of the *incipit*" (116).[4]

I conclude with the striking example of the *broken* link: *Le Livre brisé*, a prize-winning novel of 1989 by Serge Doubrovsky, the creator of the term *autofiction*. In this autobiographical fiction of strictly real facts and events, the narrator, protagonist, and author are all the same. A real ending was made impossible by the death of Doubrovsky's real wife, Ilse; instead, for the final word, Victor Hugo's poignant poem mourning his daughter's death, "Demain, dès l'aube," speaks metonymically about Ilse's lost child and Serge's lost woman-child, while recalling the childhood memories the loss of which was the theme of the opening chapter, called "Memory Hole." The French press was quick to call this sensational novel a "livre-monstre" because the author did not hesitate to continue it and to publish it after his wife's death, but little was said about the fact that Doubrovsky had given his novel a regular, neatly constructed form that has no similarity to the chaos of real life. Intention and method, to reuse Said's terms, were evident: the first two chapters established the global theme and design that were to govern the structure of the whole book. "Memory Hole" and "From Hole to Hole" show Serge remembering (or trying to) events from his past, starting with 8 May 1945, and wondering about the facts and dates, especially about women, that he cannot remember perfectly—in particular, when was the first time he slept with a woman? The present intervenes in the third chapter, "Conjugal Novel," which introduces the writer's wife, Ilse, furious about the direction Serge's novel is heading and demanding that he write about them as a couple. Thus begins an alternating structure made of two distinct series, the first in chapters 1, 2, 4, 6, 8, 10, and 12 whose subject is Serge's quest for memory and mastery and his reading of Jean-Paul Sartre, the other in chapters 3, 5, 7, 9, 11, and 13, which narrate the more and more intimate story of Ilse.[5] In each series, the narrative takes up directly where it had stopped in the previous installment, thus giving very distinct contours to the two series.

When Ilse's death broke apart the design of composition established at the outset and pursued in the first three-quarters of the book, no ending seemed possible. The writer abandoned intention, method, and the narrative closure that was to combine the two series in a happy marriage. The writing changed. Struggling to finish the story by recounting the funeral and simultaneously, or alternatively, filling in the parts he would have told had he not abandoned his method, Doubrovsky loses more and more of the authority he had claimed, until giving up his pen to the greater poet seemed the only way to bring the broken book to a halt.

As Said wrote, humans have an imaginative and emotional need for unity that prompts them to put things in order: "Very frequently, especially when the search for a beginning is pursued within a moral and imaginative framework, the beginning implies the end—or, rather, implicates it" (41). I suspect that *implication* characterizes the beginnings of novels of the last fifty years far less than before.

Notes

1. DeJean's argument centered on the textual evidence is complex and should be consulted for the details; see DeJean 253–56.
2. Frédérique Chevillot has aptly described both the several linkages between the opening and closing scenes and the repetitions and "reopening" of the ending (69–88).
3. It is true that these are not the last words on the page, because a quote from Karl Marx follows, in italic type: "The means is as much part of the truth as the result. The quest for truth must itself be true; the true quest is the unfurling of a truth whose different parts combine in the result." There is no result, however, in Perec's *Things*.
4. "No artist, of course, can remain altogether insensitive to this vice of the *incipit*, even if he gets beyond it, which marks all the arts of organization of time—literature, music—as opposed to plastic arts, which certainly require a passage of time to be executed but which, in their fulfillment, efface all temporal reference and present themselves more purely as a closed circuit without beginning or ending" (Gracq 116).
5. This modification of an original structure seems to resemble what Gary Saul Morson has called "tempics," to identify a style of thinking (replacing poetics) about narrative as process, rather than as the unfolding of some previously ordained design. But, while giving the appearance of "making it up as he goes along," Doubrovsky has clearly made the decision, early in the structuring of this novel, to proceed with two strands. His book is processual only in appearance.

Works Cited

Balzac, Honoré de. "La maison du chat-qui-pelote." *La Comédie humaine*. Ed. Pierre-Georges Castex et al. Paris: Gallimard, 1976. 1: 39–94.

Bernardin de Saint-Pierre. *Paul and Virginia*. Trans. John Donovan. London: Peter Owen, 1982.

Chevillot, Frédérique. *La Réouverture du texte: Balzac, Beckett, Robbe-Grillet, Roussel, Aragon, Calvino, Bénabou, Hébert*. Stanford: Anma Libri, 1993.

DeJean, Joan. *Literary Fortifications: Rousseau, Laclos, Sade*. Princeton: Princeton University Press, 1984.

Doubrovsky, Serge. *Le Livre brisé*. Paris: Grasset, 1989.

DuPlessis, Rachel Blau. "Endings and Contradictions." *Narrative Dynamics: Essays on Time, Plot, Closure, and Frames*. Ed. Brian Richardson. Columbus: Ohio State University Press, 2002. 282–99.

Gracq, Julien. *En lisant en écrivant*. Paris: Corti, 1980, 1986.

Laclos, Choderlos de. *Les Liaisons dangereuses*. Trans. Richard Aldington. New York: Knopf, 1992.

Le Gros, Bernard. "A toutes fins utiles." *Fins de romans: Aspects de la conclusion dans la littérature anglaise*. Caen: Presses de l'université de Caen, 1993. 133–39.

Miller, D. A. *Narrative and Its Discontents: Problems of Closure in the Traditional Novel*. Princeton: Princeton University Press, 1981.

Morson, Gary Saul. "Essential Narrative: Tempics and the Return of Process." *Narratologies: New Perspectives on Narrative Analysis*. Ed. David Herman. Columbus: Ohio State University Press, 1999. 277–314.

Perec, Georges. *Things: A Story of the Sixties*. Trans. David Bellos. Boston: David R. Godine, 1990.

Prévost, Abbé. *The Story of the Chevalier Des Grieux and Manon Lescaut*. Trans., intro., and notes by Angela Scholar. Oxford World's Classics. Oxford: Oxford University Press, 2004.

Rabinowitz, Peter. "Reading Beginnings and Endings." *Narrative Dynamics: Essays on Time, Plot, Closure, and Frames*. Ed. Brian Richardson. Columbus: Ohio State University Press, 2002. 300–313.

Ricardou, Jean. "Naissance d'une fiction." *Nouveau Roman: Hier, aujourd'hui*. Pratiques. Paris: 10/18, 1972. 2: 379–92.

Said, Edward. *Beginnings: Intention and Method*. New York: Basic Books, 1975.
Smith, Barbara Herrnstein. *Poetic Closure: A Study of How Poems End*. Chicago: University of Chicago Press, 1968.
Workman, Mark E. "Obscured Beginnings in Personal Narratives of Sexual Jealousy and Trauma." *Narrative* 12 (2004): 249–62.

15

"Mr. Betwixt-and-Between"

The Politics of Narrative Indeterminacy in Stevenson's *Kidnapped* and *David Balfour*

OLIVER BUCKTON

Upon its publication in 1886, *Kidnapped* immediately claimed a place of high renown in Stevenson's canon. No less a critic than Henry James, writing in *Century Magazine* in April 1888, claimed of *Kidnapped* that "the execution is so serious that the idea (the idea of a boy's romantic adventures), becomes a matter of universal relations" (1236) and viewed the novel's central characters as "representing the highest point that Mr Stevenson's talent has reached" (1237). James remarks that he "may deplore in passing" the "inadequate title" of the novel (1242), yet he considers it Stevenson's "best book" (1253), one that, despite "the fiction that a production so literary as *Kidnapped* is addressed to immature minds . . . embraces every occasion that it meets to satisfy the higher criticism" (1253). Yet James's praise is not unqualified: he identifies as one of the "weak spots" in the novel the abrupt termination of the narrative: "the history stops without ending, as it were" (1253). Yet, having identified this weakness, James provides an intriguing disclaimer, excusing his friend and fellow author from artistic error: "Mr Stevenson has often to lay down his pen for reasons that have nothing to do with the failure of inspiration, and the last page of David Balfour's adventures is an honourable plea for indulgence" (1253). Alluding, one must assume, to Stevenson's fragile state of health, which often prevented him from writing, James forgives him for the "accident" on the grounds that "the remaining five-sixths of the book deserve to stand by *Henry Esmond* as a fictive autobiography in archaic form" (1253). Significantly, what allows James to overlook the novel's evident incompleteness is the "archaic form" that it adopts. I will argue in this essay that Stevenson's use of the "fictive autobiography" of the first-person narrator in both *Kidnapped* and its sequel, *David Balfour*, seeks to return to this earlier mode of fiction, to overcome or resist the commodification of "storytelling" within what Fredric Jameson calls "the corrosive effects of market relations" (220). This return "to the older fiction of the storyteller and the storytelling situation," according to Jameson, reflects "impatience with the objective yet ever intensifying alienation of the printed book" (219).[1] Hence the use of the first person signals an "attempt to conjure back the older unity of the literary institution, to return to that older concrete social situation of which narrative transmission was but a part" (220). Yet for Jameson this is a "vain attempt," as the novel becomes a commodity within the market system of capitalism.

Stevenson's romances were evidently constructed as literary commodities, being, as James observes, "originally given to the world . . . in a 'boy's paper'" (1253). Yet, equally, they evoke the fantasy of direct personal communication within a concrete historical setting. Indeed, the breaking off of David Balfour's narrative in *Kidnapped*, rather than disrupting the illusion of personal communication, helps to preserve this illusion over a longer period: the continuation of the narrative "hinges on the public fancy" (208), thereby involving the reader beyond the pages of the novel. Subsequently, the narrative continuity established by David's reappearance in *Catriona* is itself an example of what Jameson terms the strategy of containment—one of "those narrative frames . . . which seek to endow their objects of representation with formal unity" (54)—whose object is a seamless transition between two strikingly dissimilar texts: a Scott-like historical romance (*Kidnapped*) that is followed by a narrative of contemporary colonial intrigue and political corruption (*David Balfour*). The partial success of this strategy is suggested by the fact that early reviews tended to treat *Kidnapped* and *David Balfour* as a single work, as was the case with Arthur Quiller-Couch's September 1893 review in *The Speaker*, titled "First Thoughts on *Catriona*," which considered the two works together "a very big feat—a gay and gallant tale" (Stevenson, *Letters* 8: 187n). The efficacy of this union of narratives is compromised, however, by the indeterminacy of its narrator-protagonist, David Balfour, who cannot shake off the label of "Mr Betwixt- and-Between" (*Kidnapped* 53)—an indeterminacy connected to the problems of closure identified by James, and one that haunts both *Kidnapped* and the novel designated as its "sequel."[2] Referring to David in terms of "the density of that medium," James suggests the obstruction presented to the narrative's clarity by "this unfortunate though circumspect youth" (1254).

As James hints in his essay, Stevenson—the most successful and popular writer of "romances" in the late nineteenth century—had previously encountered difficulties completing his longer works of fiction.[3] Yet never before had Stevenson needed to resort to the desperate measure of abandoning a narrative in mid-plot: leaving the story incomplete, and postponing its closure to a sequel, to be written at an unspecified time in the future. Though it is now usually read as a self-contained work, *Kidnapped* (1886) is in fact only the first installment of a two-part text eventually published (posthumously) as *The Adventures of David Balfour* (1895); the second part had a double life of its own, appearing as *David Balfour* (1893) in the United States and as *Catriona* (1893) in the United Kingdom.[4] With its "bibliographic code" (McGann 85) split in two, the "adventures" of David Balfour might more accurately be described as being divided three ways, with all the confusion of naming and identity that this implies.

Although the composition of *Kidnapped* began auspiciously, there were early signs of hesitancy, as Stevenson wrote his father in March 1885 about his "new boys' story . . . which you will like, if ever I can write it, which seems almost too much to hope for" (*Letters* 5: 94).[5] Stevenson here hints at the difficulties of composition that would return to haunt him, while his admission "I have no name for it but only a title page . . . 'Memoirs of the Adventures of David Balfour'" (5: 94) reveals his difficulty defining the identity, and the central focus, of his narrative. Reflecting his tendency to think of this work in two sections, Stevenson writes later in the month, "I am now fairly in part two: the Highland part. I don't think it will be so interesting to read, but it is curious and picturesque" (5: 186).[6] This splitting of his novel into two parts, anticipates problems Stevenson would have with the form of the work as a whole, specifically with the latter parts of his novel. He writes W. E. Henley in April 1885, "I must go on and drudge at *Kidnapped*, which I hate and am unfit to do" (5: 105); while to Thomas Dixon Galpin he wrote in May, "the trouble I am having over the last chapters of *Kidnapped* is incredible. I have written one chapter seven times, and it is no great shakes now it is done" (5: 249).[7] As in prior cases, the closure of the novel proved most troublesome: Stevenson suggests that the reluctance of his protagonist ("sticks in the mud") is the cause.

These problems with concluding the novel proving insoluble, Stevenson wrote James Henderson—editor of the periodical *Young Folks*, which had agreed to serialize the novel—advising him that the fate of the story was by no means secure: "I warn you my health is not to be trusted; I may break down again, and the cup and the lip be once again divorced. Please consider this in your own interests and do as you please. Perhaps some qualified announcement, owning the uncertainty of this vile author's health would serve your end" (*Letters* 5: 187). Stevenson in effect anticipates the editorial "announcement" that would conclude the novel, though the latter does not adduce the author's health as a reason. As he wrote his father in May 1886, "The David problem has today been decided. I am to leave the door open for a sequel if the public take to it; and this will save me from butchering a lot of good material to no purpose" (5: 255).[8]

Significantly, David Balfour is left in limbo outside "the doors of the British Linen Company's bank" (208)—on the threshold (literally) of recovering his birthright, the inheritance of the House of Shaws. His physical position reveals a state of indeterminacy: being at the very doors of the bank, David is neither inside nor outside the space of wealth. He is on the brink of gaining his fortune but has not yet done so. Likewise, his triumph at becoming "a man of means" (204) is compromised by "a remorse for something wrong" (208). Emotionally and physically in limbo, David cannot provide the closure that the novel requires. Stevenson therefore abruptly terminates the novel with a "postscript" that reiterates the role of the public in ensuring the continuation of the narrative: "Just there, with his hand upon his fortune, the present editor inclines for the time to say farewell to David. How Alan escaped, and what was done about the murder, with a variety of other delectable particulars, may be some day set forth. That is a thing, however, that hinges on the public fancy" (208).[9] Revealing his dependence on public approval for his novel to continue, Stevenson joins David in a state of indeterminacy. He, in effect, kidnaps his own narrative, holding it captive until the "public" meet his demands for "ransom" in the form of commercial success. With this strategy, the problem of concluding the novel has not been resolved, however, but only deferred to a later time. The alternative is an act of textual violence that he refers to as "butchering" his own narrative: equivalent, perhaps, to Ebenezer's attempts to murder his nephew.[10]

Yet why does *Kidnapped* grind to a halt in the first place, requiring the ruse of leaving the door open for a sequel? I argue that this failure of narrative closure derives from problems inherent in the role of the central narrator and protagonist, David Balfour: problems not of psychology, but of narrative function. Stevenson had written in "A Gossip on Romance" (1882) that "a certain interest can be communicated by the art of narrative" (*Lantern-Bearers* 176) but that the appeal of "romance" depends for its effect on compelling incident: "not upon what a man shall choose to do, but on how he manages to do it; not on the passionate slips and hesitations of the conscience, but on the problems of the body and of the practical intelligence in clean, open-air adventure" (173). While these features might apply to *Kidnapped*, they do not fit David Balfour as protagonist. A brief comparison with Jim Hawkins, the protagonist-narrator of *Treasure Island*, is helpful to illustrate these problems. For Jim, though somewhat younger than David, is an active, assertive figure who knows his own interests. He proclaims from the outset that he is writing to fulfill a demand: "Squire Trelawney, Dr Livesey and the rest of these gentlemen having asked me to write down the whole particulars about Treasure Island" (11); hence his narrative is part of the commercial enterprise that includes the finding of the "treasure" itself (some of which is "not yet lifted" [11]—an allusion, perhaps, to the profits to be earned from publication). Despite his proclaimed abhorrence for "that accursed island" (208), Jim never hesitates in his pursuit of the treasure: it is he who takes the "oilskin packet" (33) containing the map and presents it to the squire and doctor, thereby initiating the quest. He shows extraordinary resourcefulness in steering the *Hispaniola* on his own and dispatching the pirate Israel Hands. Jim, who acts rather than thinks, is the ideal protagonist of a romance.

David Balfour, by contrast, takes directions from others—for example, he travels to the House of Shaws at the prompting of Minister Campbell, and is easily persuaded by his uncle to climb the lethal unfinished staircase, despite being warned that "that part of the house is no finished" (21).[11] Having been kidnapped by Captain Hoseason, he is effectively helpless until the arrival of Alan Breck Stewart, the Highland Jacobite who is picked up from the sea and does battle with the crew of the *Covenant*. James had remarked on Stevenson's "intimate acquaintance with the passive" (1244), and this is nowhere more evident than in David's languid conduct.

This physical timidity of David's—as he admits, "my heart beat like a bird's, both quick and little" (58)—is compounded by his political indeterminacy. On their first meeting, David observes that Alan's identity as an outlawed Jacobite is proclaimed by both his appearance and his discourse. His statement "I have been in France" (50) is only less of a giveaway than his appearance: "he laid a pair of fine, silver-mounted pistols on the table, and I saw that he was belted with a great sword. His manners, besides, were elegant and he pledged the captain handsomely" (50). Alan later admits, "to be quite plain with ye, I am one of those honest gentlemen that were in trouble about the years forty-five and six" (51). Yet on being asked by Alan whether he is a Whig, David evades the issue: "Betwixt and Between," he replies, a wavering answer that Alan seizes upon in dubbing him "Mr Betwixt-and-Between" (53). This exchange demonstrates David's inability (or refusal) to choose sides in the central political and historical conflict of the period, the Jacobite uprising against the Hanoverian government of George II. Of this "betwixt and between" state, Alan observes "that's naething" (53). Although he claims to be "as good a Whig as Mr Campbell could make me" (53), David will waver when it is to his advantage to do so.

David's political indeterminacy is reflected in the anomaly of a lowland loyalist traveling through the Highlands in the company of an outlawed Jacobite, determined to "avoid Whigs, Campbells, and the 'red-soldiers'" (101); and consorting with the allies of the exiled King James and Prince Charlie. Of course, one might argue that it is this fluidity of allegiance that allows David to function as a narrator, by protecting him from investment in either side of the struggle. Indeed, it is only by suppressing his loyalty to King George (e.g., when Cluny MacPherson and Alan toast "The Restoration" [150]) that David can narrate the encounter with a proclaimed traitor and enemy of the king. Yet the disavowals that allow David's adventures to begin—his shipwreck, entrapment on the islet of Earraid, and flight through the heather—also impede their conclusion, as the narrative can produce no resolution between competing ideologies. To this extent, the Jacobite plot beginning with Alan's rescue and the shipwreck of the *Covenant* is indeed a distraction from the plot of inheritance with which the novel begins—a distraction of such force that the narrative cannot contain it and conclude with David's inheritance. David's involvement with Alan haunts him even until the final image of passivity: "I let the crowd carry me to and fro; and yet all the time what I was thinking of was Alan" (208).

Yet the Jacobite plot also serves the ideological purpose of displacing the intensifying class conflicts of Victorian Britain into an earlier, "romanticized" mode of opposition. Jameson has argued in *The Political Unconscious* that the ideological function of the nineteenth-century novel as a "strategy of containment" is to provide imaginary resolutions to actual social and historical conflicts that are incapable of such closure. The strategy of containment "allows what can be thought to seem internally coherent in its own terms, while repressing the unthinkable ... which lies beyond its boundaries" (53). One can recognize in *Kidnapped* a confrontation between David's "bourgeois individualism" (Jameson 221), with its concern with the acquisition of property, and the "aristocratic" values of Breck, with his "king's name" and warrior code. To gain "two clear thirds of the yearly income of Shaws" (204) is a triumph of bourgeois individualism, yet "this good change in my case unmanned me more than any of the former evil ones" (204). David's masculinity, far from being shored up by his acquisition of property, is undone by his grief for Alan, causing him to "cry and weep like any baby" (207).[12] Hence, rather than achieving a reconciliation of the ideological differences between romantic Jacobite (Alan) and bourgeois subject (David), the narration offers an effacement or suppression of them: by displacing them into differences of individual "temperament."[13]

Indeed, the label "Mr Betwixt-and-Between" illustrates David's dependence on Alan for his identity. By (re)naming David, Alan takes control of his persona and assumes the role of his surrogate father, a role that is clearly developed by his training of David in the skills of fighting and survival. Yet, curiously, this is a naming that does not *confer* an identity on the "son" but rather highlights the *lack* of one and, moreover, prevents one from being formed. Proud that he himself, as a Stewart, bears "a king's name" (55), Alan rejects David's lowland, "whiggish" surname in favor of one that represents, even emblazons, his indeterminacy. Indeed, such a name, as Alan says, is "naething": it makes its bearer a cipher, a blank. Hence the claims to identity that David makes as narrator, by telling "the story of my adventures" (1), is undone by his reliance on a supplementary figure. David can only function, it appears, in Alan's presence. It is significant, therefore, that the suspension of *Kidnapped* occurs immediately following the separation of David and Alan as they approach Edinburgh. The language at the end of the novel confirms David's dependence: "I felt so lost and lonesome . . . all the time what I was thinking of was Alan" (207-8).[14]

I have already cited Henry James's objection to the "inadequate title" of the novel. It is striking that the term *Kidnapped*—if taken to refer to David's captivity on the *Covenant*—accurately represents less than half of the novel, for David gains his freedom from the ship in the thirteenth of thirty chapters, after which the Jacobite plot of Alan and the Appin murder dominates the narrative. I have already proposed one additional interpretation of the title: let me suggest another, that the narrative, and arguably David as narrator, is "kidnapped" by Alan, "the Jacobite" (51) who usurps the protagonist's role and whose Highland speech is the most vital part of the discourse. Aptly enough, the "editor" places Alan's name first in proposing a sequel:

"The editor has a great kindness for *both Alan and David*" (208, emphasis added). This order suggests a hierarchy in the readers' own preference for Alan's company, a preference that Stevenson wished to thwart in publishing his sequel. Responding defensively (in April 1893) to Sidney Colvin's criticism of *David Balfour*, which "cuts me" (*Letters* 8: 38), Stevenson trumpeted the merits of his titular hero: "there has been no such drawing of Scots character since Scott; and even he never drew a full length like Davie, with his shrewdness and simplicity, and stockishness and charm." However, Stevenson's ebullience soon fails him, as he anticipates the public response: "Yet you'll see, the public won't want it; they want more Alan. Well, they can't get it" (8: 38). In contrast to the ingratiating tone of the "editor" who closes *Kidnapped* with promises of more "delectable particulars" (208) of Alan's adventures, Stevenson here stymies readers' desire, insisting that they accept "Davie," whom he intends to displace the figure who had "kidnapped" his novel.

Yet for all his wish to restore David to narrative primacy in the "sequel" to *Kidnapped*—of which his preference for the title *David Balfour* is indicative—the structural problems with duality and division continue to plague Stevenson: writing Colvin on 18 February 1892, he admits that "there is no doubt there comes a break in the middle and the tale is *practically in two divisions*" (*Letters* 7: 243, emphasis added). Indeed, he elaborates (in March 1892) on his difficulty writing the sequel: "is it not characteristic of my broken tenacity of mind, that I should have left Davie Balfour some five years in the British Linen Company's office, and then fall on him at last with such vivacity?" (7: 246). In a telling letter, Stevenson indicates that he, like David, is incapable of getting along without Alan: "I have come to a collapse this morning on DB; wrote a chapter one way, half re-copied it in another, and now stand halting between the two like Buridan's donkey. These sorts of cruces always are to me the most insoluble, and I should not wonder if DB stuck there for a week or two" (7: 344). Depicting himself as stuck "between the two" versions of his novel, Stevenson appears to resemble his narrator, immured "betwixt and between" competing alternatives, neither of which he can commit to.

Yet another anxiety of the irresolute novelist appears later in the same letter: "If I had not recopied *Davie* he would now be done and dead and buried; and here I am stuck about the middle, with an immediate publication threatened and the fear before me of having after all to scamp *the essential business of the end*" (*Letters* 7: 344, emphasis added). Stevenson here identifies the closure of the novel as the most important feature. Yet the unnerving prospect of the "end," invoking death and separation, deters the author from bringing his narrative to closure. Influenced by affection for his hero—"I love my *Davy*" (7: 344)—Stevenson is reluctant to terminate his adventures, preferring to be "stuck about the middle" rather than confront "the essential business of the end." With his own fragile health—to which, we recall, he referred in his letter to Henderson as a reason for delay—Stevenson no doubt recognized that each novel he completed could be his last. Understandably concerned that Davie might be the death of him,[15] the threat that produces "fear" in Stevenson is not that of sudden death but of "immediate publication," with its commitment to satisfy the readership he had referred to as "that great, hulking, bullering whale, the public" (7: 161).

The fragmentation and incompletion that haunt the composition of *David Balfour* derive, in part, from the long hiatus since the publication of *Kidnapped*, a delay that threatens the success of the sequel: as Stevenson warns in his dedication to Charles Baxter, "it is the fate of sequels to disappoint those who have waited for them" (211). If the editor's "postscript" to *Kidnapped* had offered a contract to "the public"—whose "fancy" had the power to produce a sequel—the long lapse of time had revoked that contract, such that the protagonist "must expect his late re-appearance to be greeted with hoots, if not with missiles" (211). Anticipating public hostility, Stevenson begins *David Balfour* with a dedication that smacks of an apology. However, the dedication itself seeks to bridge the gulf with the earlier novel, which Stevenson had also dedicated to Baxter.[16] As such, this opening page is a crucial component of the narrative itself. The dedication is an example of what Jerome McGann, following the work of Gérard Genette, refers to as "paratexts": textual features "that surround the central text: like prefaces, dedications, notebooks, advertisements, footnotes, and so forth," and which are "consistently regarded as only quasi-textual, ancillary to the main textual event" (13). The paratexts of the first edition of *David Balfour* would also include the subtitle, which is placed immediately underneath the title and in bold print: "A Sequel to *Kidnapped*" and continues "Being Memoirs of the *Further Adventures* of David Balfour at Home and Abroad" (*Catriona* iii, emphasis added). These headings, which occupy a prominent place on the title page, help to highlight the text's status as a *supplement* to an original work and as an installment in an ongoing story.[17]

Presumably seeking to heal the fissures of narrative structure, Stevenson begins *David Balfour* exactly where *Kidnapped* left off, with David emerging from the doors of the British Linen Company bank in Edinburgh. Even in its sentence structure, the transition is almost seamless, an invisible edit that sutures the "new" adventures of David with the old. What this paratextual construction of the novel as a "sequel" disguises, of course, is the complete transformation of Stevenson's material circumstances since 1886. The success of *Strange Case of Dr Jekyll and Mr Hyde* in 1886 had brought him worldwide fame and increased income. Although the death of his father, Thomas Stevenson, in 1887 had been a severe emotional blow, it had left Stevenson financially independent for the first time in his life while also freeing him to travel far from Britain—something he had not done since his epic pursuit of Fanny Osburne (the woman who became his wife) to California in 1879. In 1887 Stevenson had traveled with his family to the United States and, after a nine-month stay, began a cruise to the South Sea Islands, where, on the island of Samoa, the Stevensons had eventually settled, buying a property and building a large house that became his residence until his death in 1894. Yet the Polynesian island of Samoa, far from being an untroubled paradise, was embroiled in civil strife and colonial conflict (as recorded in *A Footnote to History*, which he wrote during the same period as *David Balfour*).[18] Writing for a distant readership, Stevenson grew increasingly insecure about the popular reception of his work in Britain.

Tellingly, what has changed most noticeably at the opening of *David Balfour* is the representation of the city itself. As David's destination in *Kidnapped*, Edinburgh is a beacon of hope, a familiar landmark with its "castle on the hill" (207), to which David is brought by "the hand of Providence" (208). At the opening of *David Balfour* this has become "the tall, black city" (215), a fragmented "rabbit-warren" inhabited by "a brotherhood of spies" (216), and a site of political corruption. This transformation of Stevenson's portrayal of the city suggests what Jameson terms "the fatal trajectory from the traditional to the rationalized" society, accompanied by the "vanishing mediation of so-called charisma" (249). Embodied in "the mechanical animation of late Victorian city life, with all the smoke and conveyance inherent in new living conditions" (251), Edinburgh loses its aura of attraction. Its rationalization is also reflected in "the reorganization of operations in terms of the binary system of means and ends" (250), a process in which "the book or printed text is wrenched from its concrete position . . . and becomes a free-floating object" (220), a commodity in a system of market relations.[19]

Whereas the transformation of Stevenson's material circumstances is repressed, that of David's is highlighted in the opening paragraph: "even so late as yester-morning, I was like a beggar-man by the wayside. . . . To-day I was served heir to my position in life, a landed laird" (215). Yet, though he may be dressed in "new clothes" (231), David shows few signs in *David Balfour* of having become more single-minded: he is again caught in a political conflict that he is powerless to influence; he is again kidnapped and held in captivity (this time by government agents on the Bass Rock). The political duality of Whig and Jacobite is displaced into a romantic dilemma, as David wavers between the attractions of Barbara Grant (daughter of the Lord Chief Advocate) and Catriona Drummond (child of a disgraced Jacobite). Yet perhaps the most telling sign of his lingering indeterminacy occurs in the twelfth chapter, in which Alan Breck makes his return, David's "first sight of my friend since we were parted" (302). In trying to elicit a description of a possible foe, Alan asks if this red-headed man was "gaun fast or slow" (309), to which David's reply is "Betwixt and between" (309)—a remark that echoes their first conversation on the *Covenant* when David refuses to commit himself politically. Alan's reply then may still apply now: "And that's naething" (53). To be "betwixt and between" is to be "stuck about the middle," a narrative impasse that Stevenson seeks in vain to overcome by means of the long-deferred sequel.

Alan's role is again pivotal to the novel, yet his ideological function as David's Jacobite "other" is usurped by Catriona Drummond. David's anxiety "to endure the time till Alan should arrive, or I might hear word of Catriona" (452) indicates the supplanting of his male friend by his female counterpart. Alan, in fact, turns adviser to David on "the weemen folk" (454); he also enables David's successful courtship of Catriona, allowing her father, James More, to live only on condition that he permits the marriage of the pair.[20]

If the course of *Kidnapped* was shaped by its publication in a periodical chiefly marketed toward boys—*Young Folks*—then by contrast its sequel appeared in ten monthly installments in *Atalanta*, a serial subtitled "Every Girl's Magazine." Ironically, the novel was published in serial form as *David Balfour*, not as *Catriona*, despite the predominantly female audience to which it was directed. Long known for narrative fictions from which "women were excluded" (*Lantern-Bearers* 279), Stevenson later came to view the creation of strong, leading female characters as an advance in his narrative art: "As for women, I am no more in any fear of them: I can do a sort all right, age makes me less afraid of a petticoat; but I am a little in fear of grossness" (*Letters* 7: 284). Stevenson's fear of "grossness" or "even . . . the far more damnable *closeness*" (7: 284, emphasis in source)—his anxiety to avoid what he termed "the false fire of Hardy" (284) in *Tess of the D'Urbervilles*—accounts for the timidity of David's romantic conduct toward Catriona. Yet the narrative closure produced by their marriage can scarcely patch over the ambiguity of David's identity. Stevenson's preferred title for the sequel, *David Balfour*, seeks to maintain the masculine focus of *Kidnapped*, thereby effecting a smooth transition from one "romance" to another. Yet the narrative's structural duality is marked by a schism of gender, even as Stevenson greets the coming of the "new woman" in fiction.[21] Hence when the novel was published as *Catriona* in his native country, it was public knowledge that "Mr Betwixt-and-Between"—whose previous "adventures" had been kidnapped by the Jacobite Alan Breck—was now usurped by "a petticoat."

Notes

1. In *The Political Unconscious*, at the beginning of his influential Marxist reading of *Lord Jim*, Jameson argues that Conrad's place is "still unstable, undecidable, and his work unclassifiable ... floating uncertainly somewhere in between Proust and Robert Louis Stevenson" (206). Claiming that Conrad himself is "betwixt and between" high art and popular fiction, Jameson apparently relegates Stevenson to a position deemed unworthy of serious analysis. My objection to Jameson's sweeping judgment might be taken as part of the impetus for writing this essay, especially as Conrad was deeply influenced by Stevenson in his use of the sea as a setting ("the privileged place of the strategy of containment in Conrad," according to Jameson [210]), in his deployment of exotic locales and colonial settings, and in his use of the first-person narrator of romance. The obvious literary ancestor of Lord Jim is Stevenson's Jim Hawkins.
2. This union of the novels is continued in modern times by their publication in a single volume as part of the Oxford World's Classics series.
3. Late in life, Stevenson recalled the difficulty of finishing his first novel, *Treasure Island*: "fifteen days I stuck to it, and turned out fifteen chapters; and then, in the early paragraphs of the sixteenth, ignominiously lost hold ... there was not one word more of *Treasure Island* in my bosom" (*Lantern-Bearers* 281).
4. Published serially in *Atalanta* between December 1892 and September 1893 as *David Balfour*, the novel retained this title in the U.S. volume published by Scribner. The British publisher, Cassell, however, was concerned that a novel with this title would be confused with *Kidnapped* and therefore secured Stevenson's permission to change the title to *Catriona*. Stevenson gave permission for both the change of title and the publication of a two-volume edition of both novels under the general title *The Adventures of David Balfour*. He stipulated to Sidney Colvin, "do see that they make it a decent looking book" (*Selected Letters* 565).
5. His confidence remained into 1886, as he writes his father in January, "I think David on his feet, and (to my mind) a far better story and far sounder at heart than *Treasure Island*" (*Letters* 5: 182).
6. The novel's reviews detected a duality, reflecting Stevenson's own tendency to think of the narrative in two parts. However, the hierarchy between the two portions was reversed: Theodore Watts-Duncan, for example, felt "the story passes through two stages" and argues that "of *Kidnapped* the Highland portions alone are imagined" (*Letters* 5: 313–14n). Steven-

son responded by pointing out the economic pressure to publish: "there was the cursed beginning, and a cursed end must be appended . . . so it had to go into the world, one part . . . alive, one part mere galvanized" (5: 313–14).

7. He added later the same month, "I keep grinding out David at the rate of a page a day, with the least conceivable pleasure; but he's got to be ground out" (*Letters* 5: 215). In early May he wrote Henley that his novel was "advancing at the rate of less than a page a day; this with infinite labour and poor results as to merit" (5: 248).

8. Elaborating on this point, Stevenson wrote his father again on 23 May, "I had to give up David Balfour, but by Colvin's suggestion, left the end for a sequel, which, if the first part is successful, I should be able to do with both pleasure and effect" (*Letters* 5: 256–57).

9. The postscript itself occupies a kind of narrative no-man's-land: it is neither part of the central fiction of Jameson's "concrete social situation" (220) (it is not "spoken" by David) nor an authorial intervention. Rather, it is an utterance by the "editor" of the work, who mediates between David (as narrator of his own story) and the public (which consumes it) and here plays a role closer to an agent, representing his client's interests in negotiations with the public.

10. Stevenson refers elsewhere to violence against his texts, but it is usually described as being perpetrated by others. For example, with reference to "The Beach at Falsea," he writes J. M. Barrie in 1892 about "a story of mine, the slashed and gaping ruins of which appeared recently in the *Illustrated London News*. . . . Two little native children were described . . . running away mother-naked. . . . The celestial idiots cut it out" (*Selected Letters* 516).

11. Indeed, the unfinished" state of much of the House of Shaws seems to forewarn of the unfinished condition of the novel itself. On first sight "the house itself appeared to be a kind of ruin" (7) while David finds "stone uprights," remarking that "a main entrance it was plainly meant to be, but never finished" (8). The tower, with "nothing but emptiness beyond it" (23), is only the most extreme example of incomplete structures that mirror the curtailed narrative.

12. One might say that David sheds tears not only for the loss of a friend but also for the collapse of his narrative.

13. Their famous "quarrel"—which does dramatize a profound difference in values—is resolved through Alan's pity for David's helplessness ("I cannae draw upon ye, David. It's fair murder" [164]), and Alan's disappearance from the novel—like David's indeterminacy—prevents the reunion necessary for narrative closure.

14. One can ascribe this reaction of David's to guilt at his own good fortune as compared to that of Alan, who must flee the country as an outlaw. Yet it also registers the impossibility of concluding the narrative in the absence of its chief driving force. Ironically, Alan has himself taken a false name—Mr Thomson—with the aim of concealing his identity from the authorities. Yet it is David's status as "Mr Betwixt-and-Between" that proves the shipwreck of the novel, which can conclude only with his "drifting to the . . . doors of the British Linen Company's bank" (208). The shipwreck of the *Covenant* is of course an earlier point at which the novel dramatically changes course.

15. In fact, Stevenson died while working on *Weir of Hermiston*, a novel (posthumously published in 1896) whose incompletion results directly from the author's sudden demise.

16. By repeating, or reiterating, the dedication, Stevenson establishes Baxter as his first or preferred reader and also as he who connects him with the (Scottish) past, "the whole stream of lives flowing down there far in the north" (vi).

17. The placement of such materials contributes to what McGann terms the text's "bibliographical codes," which contain their own "hidden ideological histories" (85). Another paratext linking the two novels—one that appeared in the 1893 edition but is not usually reprinted in modern editions—was a plot summary of David's adventures in *Kidnapped*, which appeared prior to the table of contents of *David Balfour*.

18. If he attributes his return to *David Balfour* as an impulse, a "sudden passion," his account to J. M. Barrie in November 1892 indicates a more complex motive: "It is a singular thing that I should live here in the South Seas under conditions so new and so striking, and yet my imagination so continually inhabit the cold old huddle of gray hills from which we come. I have just finished *David Balfour*" (*Letters* 7: 412). The juxtaposition is revealing, for *David Balfour* allows Stevenson to travel imaginatively to his old home and reestablish the connection he had lost. The novel contributes to the illusion that time has stood still, that the world is the same in 1893 as it was in 1886.

19. Crucially, this "depersonalization of the text" is accompanied by alienation between author and audience, "the disappearance from the horizon of its readership, which will become the *public introuvable* of modernism" (Jameson 221). In the 1894 essay "My First Book," Stevenson referred to his readership as "my paymaster" (*Lantern-Bearers* 277), specifying a commercial relationship that became increasingly oppressive.

20. Hence, as John Sutherland remarks, "the match is finally brought about by the vigorous intervention of Alan Breck" (352). Catriona poses a threat to more than Alan's primacy in David's affections. Drawing attention to David's masculine deficiencies—"what was your father that he could not learn you to draw the sword?" (289)—Catriona confesses her own transgression of gender roles: "I am made this way, that I should have been a man child. In my own thoughts it is so I am always; and I go on telling myself about this thing that is to befall and that . . . and I am the boy that makes the fine speeches all through, like Mr David Balfour" (289). David unwittingly forces her into this role during the climactic swordfight between Breck and More, in which he thrusts his sword, which "encountered something yielding. It came back to me reddened. I saw the blood flow on the girl's kerchief, and stood sick" (469). The scene suggests David's sexual penetration of Catriona, prefiguring their nuptial union, yet it presents this as a violation that makes him "sick." Given the phallic significance of swordplay in both novels, one would expect this to masculinize David and confirm the feminine subordination of Catriona, yet it has the reverse effect: her initial response, "I am loving you for the pain of it," is inverted as she states, "see, you have made a man of me now. I will carry a wound like an old soldier" (470). David is displaced by "her brave nature" and confirms his heroine worship: "I embraced her, I kissed the wound" (470).
21. According to John Sutherland, "many novels of the 1890s reflected and contributed to the debate over the so-called 'new woman.'. . . The two most widely-read new women novelists were, in fact, Grant Allen . . . and Thomas Hardy" (460).

Works Cited

James, Henry. "Robert Louis Stevenson" (1888). *Literary Criticism: Essays on Literature, American Writers, English Writers*. New York: Library of America, 1984. 1231–55.

Jameson, Fredric. *The Political Unconscious: Narrative as a Socially Symbolic Act*. Ithaca: Cornell University Press, 1981.

McGann, Jerome J. *The Textual Condition*. Princeton: Princeton University Press, 1991.

Stevenson, Robert Louis. *Catriona: A Sequel to Kidnapped*. London: Cassell, 1893.

———. *A Footnote to History: Eight Years of Trouble in Samoa*. 1892. Honolulu: University of Hawaii Press, 1996.

———. *Kidnapped and Catriona*. Ed. Emma Letley. New York: Oxford University Press, 1986.

———. *The Lantern-Bearers and Other Essays*. Ed. Jeremy Treglown. New York: Cooper Square, 1999.

———. *The Letters of Robert Louis Stevenson*. Ed. Bradford A. Booth and Ernest Mehew. 8 vols. New Haven: Yale University Press, 1994–95.

———. *Selected Letters of Robert Louis Stevenson*. Ed. Ernest Mehew. New Haven: Yale University Press, 1997.

———. *Treasure Island*. Ed. Wendy Katz. The Centenary Edition. 1883. Edinburgh: Edinburgh University Press, 1998.

Sutherland, John. *The Stanford Companion to Victorian Fiction*. Stanford: Stanford University Press, 1989.

16

Maculate Reconceptions

SUSAN WINNETT

Elaine Winnett, in memoriam

Looking Back: An Open Letter

Dear Professor Polhemus,

I have just finished reading your book, *Lot's Daughters: Sex, Redemption, and Women's Quest for Authority*, and I'm trying to reconcile what you say with an article I'm writing about mothers, daughters, and narrative beginnings. You claim to find "hope" and a blueprint for "moral redemption" and "female empowerment" in the story of Lot and his daughters (xi): Lot, you remind us, is the only man whom God deems worthy of sparing in the destruction of Sodom and Gomorrah. Following the instructions of God's angelic messengers to "escape for your life; look not behind thee, neither stay thou in the plain" (Genesis 19:17), Lot leads his wife and his daughters out of the city.[1] Lot's wife looks back and is turned into a pillar of salt. Lot escapes and settles in a cave with his daughters, who believe him to be the last man on earth. On two successive evenings, they get him drunk and each "lie[s] with him" in order to "preserve [his] seed" (Genesis 19:34).

    You call this story "a grid through which to view the world . . . especially for times and texts concerned with women's subjectivity, the emergence of once marginalized people, and the nuances of social and familial power-shifts." You explain that "the Lot complex can help redress and clarify the pervasive influence of the Oedipus complex and the myth with its inherent narrative biases stressing male desire and action. . . . Oedipus features unwitting parricide and the intercourse of son and mother; Lot features the divinely ordained death of the wife and mother and the intercourse of father and daughters" (6–7).

While I welcome your attempt to "redress and clarify the pervasive influence of the Oedipus complex," I wonder about the counterscript you propose, one in which the daughter borrows the power of a father(-figure) in order to beget (male) progeny that perpetuate culture as we know it. No one denies the pervasiveness of this "complex" in our culture. For centuries, bright and ambitious women have had no choice but to hitch their wagons to the star of patriarchal power if they wanted to expand their horizons. Yet they've always paid a price for this transaction; in fact, it turns out to be a high-interest loan that the lender has the power to recall at will. And its stakes are well documented in some of the texts you enlist in your argument, such as *Mansfield Park*, *Jane Eyre*, and *Wuthering Heights*, which are far more ambivalent about it than your readings suggest.

But it's not only the daughters who pay a high price. As a mother and thus, according to your definition, an older woman, I recoil (not morally, as you suggest, but politically) at the complacency with which you sustain the demise of Lot's wife. In the passage I've quoted above, you call her death "divinely ordained." Later in the same paragraph, however, you term it "arbitrary": "[The Lot complex] presumes to figure crucially and explicitly both rational and unconscious *female* wishes, fears, and drives; and it stresses the arbitrary death and metamorphosis of the mother, the traumatic impact of her loss and absence, and the meaning of her replacement by the daughters" (7, emphasis in source).

Only, it seems to me, by calling the nature of God's will and power into question in a way that would undermine the authority of your argument could one describe Lot's wife's disappearance as *both* "divinely ordained" and "arbitrary." If this event is central to culture-making, it is because it is part of God's design, and hence illustrative of something essential about the structure of the human predicament. A reading that showed how the cultural "arbitrariness" of the mother becomes a constitutive element of a paradigm sanctioned as a matter of "divine ordination" might help us begin to interrogate the authority you attribute to this particular "map or code by which men and women can read and organize the chaotic turbulence and psychology of their relationships, activities, inner conflicts, and longings" (7). In other words, your model assumes whatever power it possesses at the underinterrogated expense of the figure whose disappearance authorizes it. Could we also say that it borrows this power and, like our culture at large, gets away without ever returning or adequately paying for it?

What happens to Lot's wife, and why? "But his wife looked back from behind him, and she became a pillar of salt" (Genesis 19:26). In the biblical text, the angels address their instructions in the second-person masculine singular to Lot: "Escape for your life; look not behind *thee*, neither stay *thou* in the plain" (Genesis 19:17, emphasis added).[2] My guess is that his wife hasn't been privy to and, hence, doesn't even know of the admonition not to look back. If she has, indeed, been paying attention, she might assume that the injunction, directed as it is to a man, has nothing to do with her. Or perhaps she interprets Lot's successful negotiation with the angels about staying in the plain as a sign that other aspects of God's message are equally negotiable. Indeed, in light of the angels' willingness to let Lot determine his own escape route, his wife might even be warranted in reading the original command figuratively: "Get the hell out of here, and fast." You write that she panics (although I find no evidence of this in the text). Maybe, in her panic (if that's what it is), she forgets what the angels said. And maybe, just maybe, she does, indeed, intentionally disobey the angels, because she has a whole set of priorities of her own. Perhaps she wants to remember where she came from or to witness the magnitude of God's punishment. (And the importance of the story of Sodom and Gomorrah suggests that she was right; Western culture has been looking back at Sodom and Gomorrah ever since.) Maybe she's dropped something. Or maybe, being a Jewish mother, she looks back to make sure her daughters are still there.

What is clear is that Lot's wife has to be gotten out of the way in order that the story of Lot and his daughters unfold as it does. In her absence, Lot's tent becomes an extralegal space where the daughters' incestuous project can be undertaken. As mothers, they, too, of course, disappear unnamed from the record; it is the birth of named male progeny that ratifies this project and reinscribes it within the genealogical history of the Jewish people.

You interpret Jesus's command to "remember Lot's wife" (Luke 17:32) as meaning, "always remember to forget . . . you must give up the past with its memories to which you are wed—the past which has mothered you—and make yourself ready, under any circumstances, to give birth to the future" [5]). Yet the admonition is more than a suggestion for dealing positively and dynamically with the future. Jesus's policing of the terrain of memory is an important ideological move without which the disciples might be tempted to try to resolve the teachings of what will come to be called the Old Testament with the tenets of what is taking its place as the New. "Don't take any baggage from the old faith with you," he warns, or "you, too, will be turned into a pillar of salt." Only under the new dispensation that is still in the making—and which cannot, perhaps, so early in its reign, hold its own against the force and habit of the old—lies the promise of eternal life. Doing away with the figure of memory—or rather, replacing the figure of memory with a memory of that figure—serves to reinforce the foundation of stone on which Jesus builds his church. And by choosing a woman to stand for what is obsolete about the past, Jesus—Luke's Jesus, at least—is both perpetuating the gender ideology of the Pentateuch and revising its terms for the Christian era.

Why am I writing this to you at the beginning of an essay on mothers, daughters, and beginnings? There's something about your thesis and your way of presenting it that gets in the way of my beginning to write about mothers and daughters. I sense you are a well-meaning person who really thinks he has found a paradigm that can compete favorably—in women's favor, that is—with the oedipal paradigm. There's nothing wrong with examining the cultural progeny of the Lot narrative, but the connection between this narrative and your advocacy of female self-empowerment remains difficult for me to grasp. In fact, to the extent that maternity is a not entirely implausible future scenario in a young woman's life, the eradication of the figure who could transmit to her the experience of this future strikes me as a severe liability rather than a necessary liberation. (Or are the patriarchs—who, after all, are the ones who have sanctioned the transmission of this story—worried about what Lot's wife would tell her daughters—about motherhood, about men?)

You mention Virginia Woolf's recollections of her violently ambivalent feelings toward her mercurial, domineering father and those moments of "acute pleasure when he . . . somehow made me feel that we two were in league together" (Woolf, "Sketch" 123; cited in Polhemus 40). You might be right in seeing in this relationship "the seed of literature and a drive for authority through authorship" and in identifying Woolf's desire to both "come to terms with her father" and to "get out of his cage" (40). But in a diary dated 28 November 1928, she writes: "Father's birthday. He would have been 96, like other people one has known; but mercifully was not. His life would have entirely ended mine. What would have happened? No writing, no books;—inconceivable" (*Diary* 3: 208).

In the same text that you cite to demonstrate Woolf's attachment to her father, I read of another powerful—even overpowering—influence on the person and writer that she would become: "[T]he presence of my mother obsessed me. I could hear her voice, see her, imagine what she would do or say as I went about my day's doings. She was one of the invisible presences who after all play so important a part in every life. This influence . . . has never been analysed in any of those Lives which I so much enjoy reading" ("Sketch" 89). Several pages later, Woolf continues: "I suspect the word 'central' gets closest to the general feeling that I had of living so completely in her atmosphere that one never got far enough away from her to see her as a person. . . . She was the whole thing. . . . She was keeping what I call in my shorthand the panoply of life—that which we all lived in common—in being" (92). If the structure of Woolf's creative agon can be considered father-identified, the substance of her creativity—what Woolf refers to as the "panoply of life"—is matricentric, matrilineal. As she famously wrote in *A Room of One's Own*, "For we think back through our mothers if we are women" (79).

"It is useless," this passage continues, "to go to the great men writers for help, however much we may go to them for pleasure" (79). The distinction Woolf makes between the pleasure we take from reading great books by men and the help we seek there in vain is an important one. As the passage above makes clear, the maternal legacy remains unmapped: "never been analysed in any of those Lives"; "the general feeling that I had of living so completely in her atmosphere that one never got far enough away from her to see her as a person." The real challenge for the woman writer and the new beginning for women's writing is the invention of a *structure*—what Woolf calls a "sentence"— that corresponds and gives expression to and hence maps the *substance* of female experience and creativity ("Room" 79–81). What Woolf seems to have learned from the agon with her father is the need for a (narrative) structure that does justice to the substance of female experience rather than submitting it to the sense-making structures of patriarchy. Only, her argument suggests, when daughters are denied access to the traditions of their foremothers—only, that is, when patriarchal structures are the only ones available to women—can such cultural contortions as the Lot complex be imagined to be liberating or enabling.[3]

You might be justified in reminding me that, realistically, patriarchal structures are, ultimately, the only ones available to anybody, but to say that you'd have to be as cynical as I, and you're not. Your naïveté is that of a decent and liberal man who's never been forced to think outside the categories in which he has no reason not to be comfortable, who finds certain aspects of the Lot complex morally, rather than politically, scandalous.

What follows is a short essay in which I begin to examine what kind of work is entailed in enabling daughters to think through their mothers. Before daughters can begin really to think through their mothers, these mothers have to come into focus, must begin to tell their own stories. How difficult this has been is well documented. What this process might look like is the subject of the two novels I discuss. This process begins, not surprisingly, when mothers risk looking back on the landscapes of their own lives in order that their daughters be able to see their own future. It's all about new beginnings and messy rebirths, about the importance of looking back in the process of rediscovering how to begin.

Beginning Reconception(s)

It is a truth universally acknowledged that the beginning of human life requires a mother. However indispensable she might be at the inception of an individual life, the stories told to make sense of this life and, indeed, of human life and society in general, tend to begin with her disappearance. In fact, many of the stories told about the beginnings of Western culture seem hell-bent on—indeed, seem to depend upon—scapegoating her and/or making her disappear.[4] Even the traditional female bildungsroman needs to repeat the matricide that Luce Irigaray sees at the origins of western culture in order for "the daughter to become woman" and to find her place in the world (Irigaray 106).[5] In the psychoanalytic paradigms that subtend most studies of the relation between family structure and narrative, the phase of a child's attachment to the mother precedes and must be superseded by the child's entrance into the structures of language, culture, and narrative. Roland Barthes thus concludes his "Introduction to the Structural Analysis of Narrative" with the suggestion that "it may be significant that it is at the same moment (around the age of three) that the little human 'invents' at once sentence, narrative, and the Oedipus" (124). If the oedipal phase initiates the boy's identification, however conflictual, with the male parent and the structures of patriarchy, for the girl this model represents the beginning of her disidentification with her mother in favor of a strong attachment first to the father, then to a male mate, and then to male progeny. The sentence she speaks, the narrative into which she enters, is written for her by patriarchy; her desire must accommodate itself to structures that construe her as the Other. In this schema, the mother must be abandoned. She is, after all, nothing but someone who has already sacrificed her own mother at the beginning of her own sojourn in the symbolic realm, and is thus a painful reminder of the daughter's own, newfound inauthenticity. And since she is schematically relegated to the prenarrative realm, her story, should she have one, has no cultural validation. Better not to listen, to turn her into a pillar of salt.

If the mother has traditionally had to disappear at the beginning of the daughter's story, two recent novels suggest an uncomfortable relation between the beginning of a mother's story and the disappearance of her daughter. Carol Shields's *Unless* (2002) and Mary Gordon's *Pearl* (2005) begin with a daughter's decision to opt out of life, and they chart the project of introspection and retrospection with which her mother attempts to understand her daughter's action and bring her back into the world.[6] In *Unless*, Norah Winters, a nineteen-year-old literature student, has cut off contact with her family and friends, stopped attending classes, and taken to sitting crosslegged on a Toronto street corner, wearing "a cardboard sign on her chest: a single word printed in black marker—GOODNESS" (11). *Pearl*'s eponymous protagonist, a nineteen-year-old American woman studying linguistics in Dublin, chains herself to a flagpole in front of the American consulate; a statement she has placed next to her on the ground explains that she is in the advanced stages of a hunger strike "because of my conviction that the only important thing I can do with my life is to offer it in witness . . . to the death of Stephen Donegan and to the goodness and importance of his life, . . . to show my support . . . for the peace agreement, and those who have worked toward it . . . to mark the human will to harm" (15–16).

On the threshold of adulthood, these two students of language abandon discursivity and offer the testimony of their bodies against the world's capacity to harm. The idiosyncratic, capriciously omniscient narrator of *Pearl* elaborates on Pearl's motivations: "She wanted to die to be out of this life, but she also wanted to use her death. Her death was the vessel of her hope. She could use her death as she could not use her life. Her death would be legible, audible. Her life, she believed, was dim and barely visible; her words feeble whispers, scratches at the door. . . . [S]he wants her death . . . as a release from being overwhelmed" (19–20). In *Unless*, immediately prior to taking up her post at the Toronto street corner, Norah tells her mother, "I'm trying to find where I fit in" (132). The traditional novel would address these daughters' predicaments by attributing their anomie to the overwhelming presence of their mothers and, were it interested in finding where the younger women "fit in," would begin by disposing of these mothers. But Shields and Gordon take another course, one that insists on the mother's collaboration in the process of discovering where her daughter "fits in," that is, on the inescapably—although entirely differently—relational nature of both the daughter's and the mother's plots.

Both novels begin with a mother's intention to prevent her daughter's end, and end with a precarious new beginning that requires a reconception of the relation between the mother's and the daughter's plots and perhaps, even, of what female plots are. Reta Winters, the narrator of *Unless*, and Pearl's mother, Maria Meyers, are shaken by their formerly docile daughters' extreme and idealistic responses to the repertoire of misery to which they, as adults, have at least partially inured themselves. In the helplessness inflicted on them by their daughters' willed inaccessibility, they reopen the past and reconstrue the narrative that has brought them into a present in which their daughters seem to have chosen a plot of self-destruction. They reexamine the extent to which they have taken refuge behind certain conventions of motherhood, and discover in themselves vulnerabilities that are not unlike the ones they suspect are behind their daughters' will to self-destruct. This process involves acknowledging the separateness of their daughters from themselves as well as contemplating their implication in the plots for which their daughters consider death appropriate closure. Not surprisingly, in the course of this reassessment they discover that they are connected to their daughters in ways that differ substantially from the ways in which their daughters are connected to them. Reta discovers a melancholy in herself that she (possibly wrongly, it turns out) thinks is mirrored in her daughter's abjection. Maria is forced to recognize in herself the same readiness to save her daughter at all costs for which she punished her father with an estrangement that lasted until his death. In order to look forward toward new beginnings for their daughters, Reta and Maria look back and risk either discovering that the edifice they've inhabited has gone up in flames or turning into a pillar of salt. That such catastrophes are averted is due to Shields's and Gordon's refusals to let go of either the daughter's or the mother's plot, their insistence on the relational nature of both and on the need to defy the end of this relation by allowing it to reconceive itself.

In both novels, the daughters are rescued from postadolescent "behavioral interludes" that are regarded as particularly female (Shields 214). Their acts of abjection turn out to be mappable, traceable responses to trauma: Norah has tried, unsuccessfully, to rescue a Moslem woman from self-immolation, and Pearl blames herself for the death of a feeble-minded boy she's befriended and then, to her mind, betrayed. The novels suggest that for the daughters, the crisis can be resolved—through therapy, travel, change of university major—into the trajectory of *Bildung*: Pearl announces her desire to go to Cambodia in search of traces of the father she never knew, a Cambodian doctor who most likely perished at the hands of the Khmer Rouge. At the end of *Unless*, Reta reports that Norah is "recovering at home, awakening atom by atom, and shyly planning her way on a conjectural map.... She may do science next fall at McGill, or else linguistics. She is still considering this. Right now she is sleeping" (320).

While the narrative (*récit*) of the girls' recoveries belongs to the mothers, their fathers feature prominently in the story (*histoire*) of their rescue. Pearl resolves to "look for something connected to my father. Try and find records, something" (351). Unlike her self-abjection to the melancholy of Irish history, the trip to Cambodia represents the opportunity to mourn for an appropriate object, to add the script of her own experience to the myth of her father that she has inherited from her mother. While Reta attributes her daughter's situation to "an accretion of discouragement . . . understanding at last how little she would be allowed to say" (309), Norah's father, a doctor, correctly suspects a connection between her behavior and some single traumatic event in the real world: "and mostly he was right. It was a case of pinning things down, pairing the incident with a missing day in our daughter's life.... It was a moment in history; it was reported in the newspapers ... recorded on videotape, so that we ... understand how its force usurped the life of a young woman and threw her into an ellipsis of mourning" (309). Through her father's reading of her symptoms, Norah is reinserted into a sense-making narrative and hence into a community that understands her action and can share her burden: "It's all right, Norah. We know now, Norah. You can put this behind you. You are allowed to forget. We'll remember it for you, a memory of a memory, we'll do this gladly" (315).

To a certain, inevitable, extent, then, both novels acknowledge the persistence and the power, both to destroy and to heal, of a traditional plot that involves the agency of and desire for the father, and both deliberately demonstrate how mothers are implicated in this narrative. But both *Unless* and *Pearl* insist upon a counterpoint between the official narrative that resolves a "behavioral interlude" into a *Bildungsgeschichte* and an equally authoritative maternal narrative that calls official history into question and which, on the level of *récit*, challenges the closure of the *histoire*.[7] Reta's and Maria's involvement in their daughters' crises is characterized by a profound and disorienting identification which sets into motion a radical revision of the conventions that make sense of personal history.

The narrative implications of this identification are clearest in *Unless*. The event that the *histoire* of *Unless* enables Norah to "put behind her" initiates precisely that gesture of "looking behind" that the Lot complex genders female (or more properly: maternal) and repudiates. Reta's commitment to "remembering" Norah's crisis involves putting it together in her way, transforming it into a mother's narrative. Reta is a novelist, and her first-person, largely present-tense narrative foregrounds the relation between the mechanics of storytelling and the gender of the story. In one of a series of unmailed letters—not unlike the open letter that begins this essay—that Reta writes to men who represent the aggressively unreflecting androcentrism that she deems responsible for both her daughter's self-destructive idealism and her own inability to redress it, she foregrounds her own situation and explains how her daughter's action has caused her to view it from another perspective:

"I am a forty-four-year-old woman who was under the impression that society was moving forward and who carries the memory of a belief in wholeness. Now, suddenly, I see it from the point of view of my nineteen-year-old daughter" (165–66).

Since *Unless* honors Norah's refusal to communicate, it is through her mother's sense of the shape of the world and of her narrative's attempt to map it that the contours of Norah's failure to "fit in" emerge: "Somehow she had encountered a surfeit of what the world offered, and had taken an overdose she is not going to be able to survive.... It sometimes occurs to me that there is for Norah not too much but too little; a gaping absence, a near starvation.... [The] world ... does not belong to her as she has been told.... She is prohibited from entering. From now on life will seem less and less like life" (133–34). By the end of this passage, the reader no longer knows to whose life it refers. Reta's reading of her daughter's malaise is a matter of projection; it is impossible to separate Norah's putative recognition of a fundamental dissociation between herself and "life" from her mother's recognition of a fundamental dissociation between herself and her daughter. In this highly charged space of silence, Reta discovers that she is telling her own story: "It is ... probable that I was weighing her down with my own fears, ... that I had found myself, in the middle of my life, in the middle of the continent, on the side of the disfavoured, and it may be that I am partly right and partly wrong" (310). In discovering her misreading of her daughter's motivations, Reta has gained a clearer notion of her own situation, and particularly of her daughter's separateness from herself.[8] (Visiting Norah on her street corner, Reta accuses herself of "voyeurism" [26]). What Reta has lost in unreflected connection is compensated by the narrative of this loss; writing, she discovers, enables her to "stand outside [her] child's absence" (109).

Reta's present-tense maternal narrative voice enters into dialogue with the past, incorporating, contextualizing, and sometimes even making sense of random, fragmentary recollections of her mother, her friends, and her mother-in-law. Cataloging what she knows about these woman, Reta begins to discern the contours of "this watercolor blob that means mother" (28). But she also recognizes that this "blob" can only come into focus through time, experience, loss, and the narrative that acknowledges them. Her daughters, she recognizes, are unwittingly in the "midst of editing the childhood they want to remember and getting ready to live as we all have to live eventually, without our mothers" (158). The narrative that begins when Reta is forced to see her daughter as a unique, endangered, even alien, person annotates that edited text of childhood and communicates the plurality and self-contradiction of the maternal experience. The text that comes to an end with Norah's return to health has a provisional, formal closure that it borrows from the institution of the novel: "It does not mean that all will be well for ever and ever, amen; it means that for five minutes a balance has been achieved at the margin of the novel's thin textual plane; make that five seconds; make that the millionth part of a nanosecond" (318). In its provisional shaping of the maternal life, however, Reta's narrative represents an alternative to the pillar of salt, one to which her children might choose to refer when they become women and begin to think back through their mother(s).

Whereas in *Unless* Reta responds to her daughter's crisis by beginning to write, in *Pearl*, Maria reacts to the news of Pearl's actions by beginning to act herself. She flies to Dublin with the intention of rescuing her daughter, but discovers that the situation thwarts the impulse to act that has gotten her through life: "There is nothing for her to do because no one will let her do anything.... They are keeping Maria in chains. Her daughter, they told her, has been in chains. Pearl's chains have been cut; hers have not" (184). Trapped in a passivity that suits her daughter's character more than her own, Maria reviews her assumptions about motherhood and about herself as a mother: "To come to terms with the strangeness of the idea that her daughter is someone she doesn't know.... There is the terror that her daughter could die; there is the grief that Pearl didn't confide in her" (190–91).

Maria's mother died when she was two. Unlike Reta, who often refers to her mother in her attempt to understand her own predicament vis-à-vis Norah, Maria has no one to "think back through." She estranged herself from her father after he used his influence to prevent her from being arrested during a 1968 police raid on her radical Harvard boyfriend's house. Having refused to mourn her father when he died, Maria is unable to recognize the similarity between his need to protect her from the police and her own ruthless commitment to her daughter's life: "I will not permit you to choose death. . . . I don't care what you want. You are my child. I will not allow you your own life if all you want to do is throw it away. . . . Having once come from my body, you will bend to my superior, my far more ancient will—not only mine but every mother's throughout history. You will succumb and once again be more mine than your own" (191–92).

The forgiveness upon which Pearl's recovery depends involves both fully and pitilessly acknowledging responsibility for one's past behavior and reconstruing it in the context of the present. As Maria comes to understand what it would mean to lose a daughter, she realizes that "because of her, her father lost a daughter. She understands for the first time what the weight of that loss might be" (320). She contemplates the stakes of both forgiving and begging forgiveness of her father: "Suppose the dead can forgive and be forgiven? How would the story end in that case? And what would that mean about what the story always was? If she is to think about it, she will have to stand—or sit, perhaps—in an unbearable place, the place of unbearable grief and loss. She will have to be in this place for a time if the story isn't over" (320). Maria realizes that by forgiving her father she can give her daughter a model for self-forgiveness that will enable her to contemplate a new beginning: "So why not act as if the story weren't over?" This new beginning, however, requires first that Maria herself be reborn. "Roll[ing] back the stone" that has separated her from her mourning, "[s]he lies weeping, helpless, the child she always refused to allow herself to be" (321).

Maria's tears of grief are transformed into tears of laughter when, several pages later, her daughter affectionately mocks the knee-jerk activism that she's now able to regard with critical affection:

> Pearl laughs. It's the first time she's laughed hard for a very long time, and it hurts her throat. Her mother is absurd. . . . Ridiculous, her mother's sense of possibility, her endless belief in the goodness of change. An old instinct tells her that her mother must be wrong. But what if she isn't? . . . [N]ow her mother's

> combination of consistency and inconsistency amuses her, delights her.... Her mother is her mother. My mother is my mother and I am I. This seems quite amusing; she could repeat it to herself just for the pleasure of the words....
>
> "Mama," she says. "Slow down."
>
> Maria looks at her daughter and blinks, as if she's just heard the most intriguing sentence of her life. And then they both begin to laugh. (345)

The narrator notes the absence of laughter in culture's repertoire of mother-daughter scenarios ("desperate loyalties; struggles to the death, struggles against death; bosoms of comfort; choking hands; get out of the house, stay in the house; find yourself a man, no man will ever love you" [345]). This precarious moment in the novel has not superseded these scenarios as much as it has suspended them, suggesting a possible outcome beyond the plots that have already been written. The novel ends, "And we will leave Pearl and Maria to themselves. We will hope for the best" (346).

Like that of *Unless*, *Pearl*'s ending is open; there is no promise except that of a beginning that has been shown to be, necessarily, a continuation not only of the novel but of the unwritten narrative that preceded the novel's beginning. To the extent that a mother's narrative is defined through its relation to the existence of another person, its trajectory remains determined both by the vicissitudes of the mother's life and by those of a person who, even as an adult, remains her child. Grounded in the present tense, both *Unless* and *Pearl* suggest that looking back and reconception are reciprocal processes in a narrative committed to saving the lives of daughters and their mothers.

Notes

1. In Biblical Hebrew, the imperative verb form distinguishes the gender and number of the addressee. Here, the verb describes the angels' addressee as masculine and singular. It is thus clear that Lot's wife is excluded from the exchange between the angels and Lot. My thanks to Professor Ste-

fan Timm for sharing his knowledge of Biblical Hebrew and of the Hebrew Bible.
2. My citations of Genesis 19 and Luke 17 are, like Polhemus's, taken from the King James Bible (see Polhemus 16–18).
3. In her discussion of the maternal plot in Toni Morrison's *Sula*, Marianne Hirsch writes: "For women who reject unconditionally the lives and the stories of their mothers, who attempt to perform what [Adrienne] Rich called 'radical surgery,' there is nowhere to go" (185).
4. See, e.g., Apollo's argument, in *The Eumenides*, in favor of Orestes' exoneration for the murder of his mother: "The woman you call the mother of the child / is not the parent, just a nurse to the seed, / the new-grown seed that grows and swells inside her. / The man is the source of life—the one who mounts. / She, like a stranger for a stranger, keeps / the shoot alive" (Aeschylus 260). For a thorough discussion of the classical paradigms, see Hirsch 28–39.
5. For further discussion of this pattern see Hirsch 43–88.
6. There is, of course, a paradigmatic classical text that tells this same story. The Homeric "Hymn to Demeter" is about a mother's attempt to get her daughter back from the underworld. But in the Homeric hymn the temptation that draws the daughter toward death is erotic, whereas in these two novels the daughter abandons erotic involvement for political martyrdom.
7. This might be the place to note that *Pearl* is explicit in its repudiation of the Lot complex: as Pearl begins to reorient herself toward life, she is visited by Joseph, a widower whose mother was Maria's father's housekeeper, and who has always been like a brother to Maria and an uncle to Pearl. Joseph has decided that Pearl's rescue depends on his active intervention; he resolves to marry her and to live with her chastely in order to "keep her safe." When Joseph reveals his plan to the convalescent Pearl, she recoils, thrashing, horrified at the transformation in this man "who [had always] stood beside her, so she always knew that if she fell, she'd be caught. . . . It was what having a father meant. Now he says he doesn't want to be a father but a husband. . . . She must be rid of him; he is a danger" (313).
8. Reta's middle daughter, Christine, rehearses this theme in a major key when, on her mother's birthday, she says, "Thank you for releasing me from your loins" (153). While it's clear that her daughter is thanking her for giving birth to her, she is also thanking her, in advance, as it were, for the permission to separate.

Works Cited

Aeschylus. *The Eumenides*. Trans. Robert Fagles. Harmondsworth: Penguin, 1977.
Barthes, Roland. "Introduction to the Structural Analysis of Narrative." *Image Music Text*. Trans. Stephen Heath. New York: Noonday Press, 1977. 74–124.
Gordon, Mary. *Pearl*. New York: Pantheon, 2005.
Hirsch, Marianne. *The Mother-Daughter Plot: Narrative, Psychoanalysis, Feminism*. Bloomington: Indiana University Press, 1989.
Irigaray, Luce. *Ethique de la différence sexuelle*. Paris: Minuit, 1984.
Polhemus, Robert. *Lot's Daughters: Sex, Redemption, and Women's Quest for Authority*. Stanford: Stanford University Press, 2005.
Shields, Carol. *Unless*. London: Fourth Estate, 2002.
Woolf, Virginia. *The Diary of Virginia Woolf*. Ed. Anne Olivier Bell and Andrew McNellie. 5 vols. London: Hogarth, 1977–84.
———. *A Room of One's Own*. San Diego, New York, London: Harcourt Brace Jovanovich, 1957.
———. "A Sketch of the Past." *Moments of Being*. Ed. Jean Schulkind. London: Grafton Books, 1989. 69–172.

Further Reading on Narrative Beginnings

Adams, Hazard, ed. *Critical Theory since Plato*. New York: Harcourt Brace Jovanovich, 1971.

———. "Titles, Titling, and Entitlement To." *Antithetical Essays in Literary Criticism and Liberal Education*. Tallahassee: Florida State University Press, 1990. 111–43.

Aguirre, Manuel, Roberta Quance, and Philip Sutton. *Margins and Thresholds: An Inquiry into the Concept of Liminality in Text Studies*. Madrid: Gateway, 2000.

Aristotle. *Poetics*. Adams, *Critical Theory* 48–66.

Berkhofer, Robert F. "Beginnings, Middles, and Endings." *Beyond the Great Story: History as Text and Discourse* Cambridge: Harvard University Press, 1995. 120–25.

Bharata-Muni. *The Natyasastra: A Treatise on Ancient Hindu Dramaturgy and Histrionics*. Ed. and trans. Manomohan Ghosh. Rev. ed. 2 vols. Calcutta: The Asiatic Society and Granthalaya, 1956–67. Vol. 1, § 21.

Buckton, Oliver. *Cruising with Robert Louis Stevenson: Travel, Narrative, and the Colonial Body*. Columbus: Ohio State University Press, 2007. 126–47.

Byala, Gregory. "Samuel Beckett and the Problem of Beginning." Diss. Yale University, 2006.

Chatman, Seymour. *Story and Discourse: Narrative Structure in Fiction and Film*. Ithaca: Cornell University Press, 1978. 63.

Corneille, Pierre, "Of the Three Unities of Action, Time, and Place." Adams, *Critical Theory* 219–26.

Del Lungo, Andrea. "Pour une poétique de l'incipit." *Poétique* 94 (1993): 131–52.

Dryden, John. "An Essay of Dramatic Poesy." Adams, *Critical Theory* 228–57.

Dunn, Francis M., and Thomas Cole, eds. *Beginnings in Classical Literature*. Yale Classical Studies 29. Cambridge: Cambridge University Press, 1992.

Fisher, John, "Entitling." *Critical Inquiry* 11.2 (1984) 286–98.

Freytag, Gustav. *Freytag's Technique of the Drama*. Trans. Elias J. MacEwan. 2nd ed. Chicago: S. C. Griggs, 1896.

Genette, Gérard. *Paratexts: Thresholds of Interpretation*. Trans. Jane E. Lewin. Cambridge: Cambridge University Press, 1997.

Gillespie, Michael Patrick. "'In the Buginning Is the Woid': Opening Lines and the Protocols of Reading." *Pedagogy, Praxis,* Ulysses: *Using Joyce's Text to Transform the Classroom.* Ed. Robert Newman. Ann Arbor: U of Michigan Press, 1996. 9–20.

Henry, Freeman G., ed. *Beginnings in French Literature.* French Literature Series 29. Amsterdam: Rodopi, 2002.

Horace. *The Art of Poetry.* Adams, *Critical Theory* 68–75.

Keen, Suzanne, *Narrative Form.* New York: Palgrave Macmillan, 2003. 75–78.

Kellman, Steven G. "Grand Openings and Plain: On the Poetics of Opening Lines." *Sub-Stance* 17 (1977): 139–47.

Levinson, Jerrold. "Titles." *Journal of Aesthetics and Art Criticism* 44.1 (1985): 29–39.

Mallios, Peter. "Untimely *Nostromo.*" *Conradiana* 40.3 (2008).

Martin, Wallace. "Endings and Beginnings in Life, Literature, and Myth." *Recent Theories of Narrative.* Ithaca: Cornell University Press, 1986. 85–90.

Miller, J. Hillis. "Beginnings." *Reading Narrative.* Norman: University of Oklahoma Press, 1998. 57–60.

Morhange, Jean-Louis. "Incipit Narratives." *Poétique* 104 (1995): 387–410.

Nuttall, A. D. *Openings: Narrative Beginnings from the Epic to the Novel.* Oxford: Oxford University Press, 1992.

Oz, Amos. *The Story Begins: Essays on Literature.* Trans. Maggie Bar-Tura. New York: Harcourt. 1999.

Phelan, James. "Beginnings and Endings: Theories and Typologies of How Novels Open and Close." *Encyclopedia of the Novel.* Ed. Paul Schellinger. Chicago: Fitzroy Dearborn, 1998. 96–99.

Prince, Gerald. "Beginning." *A Dictionary of Narratology.* 2nd ed. Lincoln: University of Nebraska Press, 2003.

———. *Narratology: The Form and Functioning of Narrative.* Amsterdam: Mouton, 1982. 150–58.

Rabinowitz, Peter. "Reading Beginnings and Endings." Richardson 300–313.

Richardson, Brian. "Introduction: Openings and Closure." Richardson 249–51.

———, ed. *Narrative Dynamics: Essays on Time, Plot, Closure and Frames.* Columbus: Ohio State University Press, 2002.

Romagnolo, Catherine. "Narrative Beginnings in Amy Tan's *The Joy Luck Club*: A Feminist Study." *Studies in the Novel* 35.1 (2003):89–107.

Roof, Judith. *Come as You Are: Sexuality and Narrative*. New York: Columbia University Press, 1996. 13–18.
Said, Edward. *Beginnings: Intention and Method*. New York: Basic Books, 1975.
Shen, Dan. "Broadening the Horizon: On J. Hillis Miller's Anarratology." *Provocation to Reading*. Ed. Barbara Cohen and Dragan Kujundžić. New York: Fordham University Press. 14–29.
Spoo, Robert. "Genders of History in 'Nestor.'" *Ulysses: En-Gendered Perspectives*. Ed. Kimberly J. Devlin and Marilyn Reizbaum. Columbia: University of South Carolina Press, 1999. 20–29.
Springer, Norman, "The Language of Literary Openings: Hemingway's 'Cat in the Rain.'" *Narrative Poetics*. Ed. James Phelan. *Papers in Comparative Studies* 5 (1986–87): 103–14.
Stein, Nancy L., and Margaret Policastro. "The Concept of a Story: A Comparison between Children's and Teacher's Viewpoints." *Learning and Comprehension of Text*. Ed. Heinz Mandl, Nancy L. Stein, and Tom Trabasso. Hillsdale NJ: Erlbaum, 1984. 113–55.
Sternberg, Meir. *Expositional Modes and Temporal Ordering in Fiction*. Baltimore: Johns Hopkins University Press, 1978.
Sutherland, John. *How to Read a Novel: A User's Guide*. New York: St. Martin's, 2006.
Todorov, Tzvetan. *Poetics of Prose*. Trans. Richard Howard. Minneapolis: University of Minnesota Press, 1981.
Verrier, Jean. *Les débuts des romans*. Paris: Bertrand-Lacoste, 1988.
Watt, Ian. "The First Paragraph of *The Ambassadors*: An Explication." *Essays in Criticism* 10 (1960) 250–74.
Whitman, Jon. "Thinking Backward and Forward: Narrative Order and the Beginnings of Romance." *Partial Answers: Journal of Literature and the History of Ideas* 4.2 (2006): 131–50.
Winnett, Susan. "Coming Unstrung: Women, Men, Narrative, and Principles of Pleasure." Richardson 138–58.
Wofford, Susanne. "Epics and the Politics of the Origin Tale: Virgil, Ovid, Spenser, and Native American Aetiology." *Epic Traditions in the Contemporary World: The Poetics of Community*. Ed. Margaret Beissinger, Jane Tylus, and Susanne Wofford. Berkeley: University of California Press, 1999. 239–69.
Wolf, Werner, and Walter Bernhart, eds. *Framing Borders in Literature and Other Media*. Amsterdam: Rodopi, 2006.

For additional items see Bennet, J. R. "Beginning and Ending: A Bibliography." *Style* 10 (1976): 184–88.

Contributors

OLIVER S. BUCKTON is Associate Professor of English at Florida Atlantic University, where he teaches Victorian literature, critical theory, and film. He is the author of *Secret Selves: Confession and Same-Sex Desire in Victorian Autobiography* (1998) and *Cruising with Robert Louis Stevenson: Travel, Narrative, and the Colonial Body* (2007). He has published essays on Dickens, Wilde, and Schreiner, among others, and is currently working on a project tracing the responses of British Victorian writers to the Italian body as "other."

PHILIPPE CARRARD is Professor of French, Emeritus, at the University of Vermont and a Visiting Scholar in the Program of Comparative Literature at Dartmouth College. He is the author of *Poetics of the New History: French Historical Discourse from Braudel to Chartier* (1995) and several essays on conventions of writing in factual, nonfictional narrative. He is currently working on a book about the memoirs of the French who fought for Germany during World War II.

TITA CHICO teaches in the English Department of the University of Maryland. She is the author of *Designing Women: The Dressing Room in Eighteenth-Century English Literature and Culture* (2005) and has published a variety of articles on eighteenth-century British literature and culture. She also edits *The Eighteenth Century: Theory and Interpretation*.

RYAN CLAYCOMB is Assistant Professor of Literature at West Virginia University, where he teaches courses on modern drama, gender studies, and twentieth-century British literature. He has published several articles on the intersection of narrative, gender, and performance in such journals as *JNT, Modern Drama*, and *Journal of Dramatic Theory and Criticism*. He is currently at work on a book on life writing and contemporary feminist drama and is editing a collection on writing and antidisciplinarity.

MELBA CUDDY-KEANE is Professor of English at the University of Toronto and the author of *Virginia Woolf, the Intellectual, and the Public Sphere* (2003). Her most recent work includes "Narratological Approaches" in Palgrave, *Advances in Virginia Woolf Studies* (2007); "Global Modernisms" in *A Companion to Modernist Literature and Culture* (2006); and "Modernist Soundscapes and the Intelligent Ear: An Approach to Narrative through Auditory Perception" in *A Companion to Narrative Theory* (2005). Her annotated edition of Virginia Woolf's *Between the Acts* is forthcoming from Harcourt, and she is writing a book on modernism, globalism, and the sphere of tolerance.

MARILYN EDELSTEIN is Associate Professor of English and also a faculty member in the Women's and Gender Studies Program at Santa Clara University. She teaches courses on contemporary American literature, feminist theory, literary and cultural theory, postmodernism, and multicultural literature and theory. She has published articles and book chapters on Vladimir Nabokov, John Barth, bell hooks, Julia Kristeva, feminist theory and postmodernism, literature and ethics, and multiculturalism. She is working on a book on ethics in/and feminism, postmodernism, and multiculturalism.

PATRICK COLM HOGAN is a Professor in the Department of English and the Program in Cognitive Science at the University of Connecticut. He is the author of *The Politics of Interpretation* (1990), *Colonialism and Cultural Identity* (2000), *The Culture of Conformism* (2001), *The Mind and Its Stories* (2003), *Cognitive Science, Literature, and the Arts* (2003), *Empire and Poetic Voice* (2004), and *Understanding Nationalism: Narrative Identity* and *Cognitive Science* (both forthcoming). He is currently editing *The Cambridge Encyclopedia of the Language Sciences*.

JESSICA LACCETTI completed her PhD at the Institute of Creative Technologies at De Montfort University. Her thesis examines Web fictions within a narrative and feminist context. She lectures at the undergraduate and postgraduate levels on media and new media. She is also involved with the Narrative Laboratory, where she helped organize Europe's first conference on women, business, and blogging (www.nlabwomen.com). Her work has been published on- and offline, and she has presented papers and given workshops in the United Kingdom, Europe, and Canada. Website: www.jesslaccetti.co.uk/musings.htm

NIELS BUCH LEANDER is Carlsberg Assistant Research Professor in Comparative Literature at the University of Copenhagen, Denmark. He has published various articles and book chapters on French literary theory with a particular focus on intertextuality and the role of the author, for instance, in the volume *Les Arrière-gardes au XXe siècle: L'autre face de la modernité esthétique* (2004). He has also written on postcolonialism in literature and criticism of the modernist period and on contemporary criticism of African film. He is currently working on a book tentatively titled *The Sense of a Beginning: Theory of the Literary Opening*.

ARMINE KOTIN MORTIMER is Professor of French Literature and of Criticism and Interpretive Theory at the University of Illinois at Urbana-Champaign. Since August 2004 she has been Head of that department. Her teaching and research are in the areas of narrative literature; she has published a significant body of work on Balzac, on Barthes, and on Sollers's novels, especially *Paradis*. She is the author of six books, including *La Clôture narrative* (1985) and *Writing Realism: Representations in French Fiction* (2000), and is the coeditor, with Katherine Kolb, of *Proust in Perspective: Visions and Revisions* (2002). Her articles have appeared in numerous journals. Her book-length study on *Paradis* appeared in *L'Infini* (fall 2004).

GAURA SHANKAR NARAYAN teaches at Purchase College SUNY. She has presented papers on Anita Desai, Assia Djebar, and Jamaica Kincaid. She is completing a book tentatively titled *The Gender Identity of the Romantic Imagination*.

JAMES PHELAN is Humanities Distinguished Professor of English at Ohio State University. He has written five books of narrative theory, the most recent of which are *Living to Tell about It: A Rhetoric and Ethics of Character Narration* (2005) and *Experiencing Fiction: Judgments, Progressions, and the Rhetorical Theory of Narrative* (2007).

In addition, he edits *Narrative*, the journal of the Society for the Study of Narrative Literature, and coedits the Theory and Interpretation of Narrative series for Ohio State University Press.

BRIAN RICHARDSON is a Professor in the English Department of the University of Maryland. He is the author of *Unlikely Stories: Causality and the Nature of Modern Narrative* (1997) and *Unnatural Voices: Extreme Narration in Modern and Contemporary Fiction* (2006). He edited the anthology *Narrative Dynamics: Essays on Time, Plot, Closure, and Frames* (2002) and a special issue of *Style* on "Concepts of Narrative" (2000). He has published several articles on different aspects of narrative theory, including plot, time, causality, closure, character, narration, and reflexivity.

CARLOS RIOBÓ is Assistant Professor of Spanish at The City College of The City University of New York. An expert in twentieth-century Argentine and Cuban literatures and cultures, he has done field research in Havana and Europe. He has published articles and reviews on Manuel Puig, Severo Sarduy, Sigüenza y Góngora, and nineteenth-century Argentine literature. His book manuscript is tentatively titled *Alternative Identities: Puig and Sarduy's Unauthorized Archives*.

CATHERINE ROMAGNOLO is an Assistant Professor of English and American Studies at Lebanon Valley College. In her research she seeks to explore and expand the convergence of narrative theory, ethnic studies, and feminist theory. She is currently completing a book-length project on narrative beginnings tentatively titled *Opening Acts: Narrative Beginnings from a Feminist Perspective*.

SUSAN WINNETT teaches at the Institute for English and American Studies at the University of Hamburg. She is the author of *Terrible Sociability: The Text of Manners in Laclos, Goethe, and James* (1993) and *Writing Back: American Expatriates' Narratives of Return* (forthcoming), as well as numerous articles on gender and narrative.

Index

Absalom, Absalom! (Faulkner), 97–98
Ada (Nabokov), 6
Adams, George, 93–94
Adams, Hazard, 13
agency attribution, familiarity and, 54, 59n10
Alice in Wonderland (Carroll), 19
Alvarez, Julia, 150–51, 156–63
The Ambassadors (H. James), 80, 114
analepses, 67, 71–72, 101, 183
Anscombe, G. E. M., 52
antetext. *See* extratextual material; paratext
Anzaldúa, Gloria, 156
The Archaeology of Knowledge (Foucault), 129
archive, 135n2, 136n4, 136n5; Latin American narrative and, 127–35; power and, 130–31
Archive Fever (Derrida), 136n4
Aristotle, 6–7, 25, 30, 124, 196; definition of beginning and, 74, 116; narrative components and, 49
Ars Poetica (Horace), 21
Artaud, Antonin, Theatre of Cruelty and, 169
artificial vs. natural beginnings, 15
Ashcroft, Bill, 141
At Swim-Two-Birds (O'Brien), 5
"At the Sign of the Cat and Racquet" (Balzac), 215–17
Austen, Jane, 117, 196

author, 18, 30–40
Autobiography of an Ex-Colored Man (J. W. Johnson), 118
autofiction, 224–25

Bader, Julia, 37
Bal, Mieke, 114
Ballard, J. G., 13
Balzac, Honoré de, 124, 192–93, 215–17
Barak, Julie, 151
Barth, John, 26
Barthes, Roland, 18, 116–17, 252
Bauer, Eddy, 68
Beckett, Samuel, 5, 115, 120–24
beginnings, 1–9; ambiguous or arbitrary, 70–74, 121–23, 166–67, 202, 223; autobiography and, 9, 116; causal events as, 16–17, 56, 69, 116–17, 153–54, 160–62; chronological, 164n6; discursive, 152–54, 163n4, 197; disruptive, 177; eighteenth century, 87, 92, 217–21; elusiveness of, 19–20, 181; endings as, 107–8, 119–20, 213, 254; in epic, 13–14; false, 3, 6, 119–24; feminist approaches to, 144–63, 163n1, 179–88, 246–60; fictional nature of, 18–21, 25–27, 124–25; historical narrative and, 44–78, 124, 137–47; incomplete, 167, 180; memories and, 252; modernism and, 97–99, 116–17; multiple, 104, 110n7,

272 INDEX

beginnings (*cont.*)
119–20, 155–59, 163n5, 176, 249; myth and, 13–14; in the narrative middle, 21, 67–68, 72, 98–101, 145–46; need for, 20–21, 188, 223; nineteenth century, 4–5; origin(s) and, 16–18, 26, 159; postmodernism and, 5–6, 221–25; science and, 17; self–negating, 97–109, 167–77; theater and, 2–3, 166–77; as unstable situation, 196–98, 204; web fiction and, 179–88

Beginnings (Said), 149, 218, 223

beginning sentences, 1, 24, 71, 99–103, 200–206

Beloved (Morrison), 149, 195–96, 200–210

Bend Sinister (Nabokov), 33–34

Bennington, Geoff, 59n6

Benveniste, Émile, 180

Bergson, Henri, 104

Berkhofer, Robert, 74

Bernardin de Saint-Pierre, Jacques-Henri, 220–21

Bernhart, Walter, 12

Between the Acts (Woolf), 107–9, 110n9

Bhabha, Homi K., 44, 147n6

Bharata (Sanskrit poetician), 7

bija (seed; initiating elements), 7

birth as narrative beginning, 84, 127–31, 137, 139–41; problems with, 15–16, 21–24

Bleak House (Dickens), 18

Bolter, Jay, 179

Booth, Wayne, 31–33

Borges, Jorge Luis, 129

Boyd, Brian, 32

Boyer, Pascal, 53–55

Brecht, Bertolt, Epic Theatre and, 169

Breuilly, John, 45, 59n6

Brontë, Charlotte, 153

Brooks, Peter, 116–17, 163n1, 191, 196

Byron, George Gordon, Lord, 2, 21–22

Cacioppo, John, 52

"The Calmative" (Beckett), 120

Calvino, Italo, 6, 166–67

Calvocoressi, Peter, 73

Camus, Albert, 1

Carpentier, Alejo, 128–29

Carroll, Lewis, 19

Castells, Ricardo, 151

Castillo, Ana, 113

Catriona. See *David Balfour (Catriona)*

causal events as beginnings, 116

causal sequences, 47, 49, 55, 57

causes, 46–58, 116–17

Céré, Robert, 66

Ceremony (Silko), 149

Cervantes, Miguel de, 25

Chatman, Seymour, 116–17

Chekhov, Anton, 2, 119

Cheng, Vincent, 118

Choses (Things) (Perec), 223

chronology, 65; reverse, 159

Churchill, Caryl, 3

Churchill, Winston, 66

Cicero, 29

"The Circle" (Nabokov), 194

classical rhetoric, 29

INDEX 273

Clore, Gerald L., 50
Coetzee, J. M., ix
Cohen, Sande, 72–74
Colvin, Sidney, 236
Comédia humaine (Balzac), 215
Composition #1 (Saporta), 113
"Composition as Explanation" (Stein), 6
The Connection (Gelber), 3
Corneille, Pierre, 7
Cortàzar, Julio, 113, 180
The Counterfeiters (Gide), 124
Cowley, Malcolm, 193
creation myth(s), 8–9, 110n3; beginnings and, 97, 102, 110n7; Native American autobiographies and, 116
Critical Understanding (Booth), 32–33
culture, shared, 103
"The Custom House" (Hawthorne), 119
Cymbeline (Shakespeare), 3

Damasio, Antonio R., 51–52
Daniel Deronda (G. Eliot), 20
Dante Alighieri, 21
Danto, Arthur, 76
David Balfour (Catriona) (Stevenson), 229–30, 236–40, 241n1; paratext and, 243n17
David Copperfield (Dickens), 22–25
"The Dead" (Joyce), 114, 116–17, 119
"Death of the Author" (Barthes), 18
The Death of Virgil (Broch), 5

deconstruction, 70
DeJean, Joan, 218
Derrida, Jacques, 12–13, 17–18, 129, 136n4
detail, narrative, 86–90, 93n4, 93n5, 93n6
Das Deutsche Reich und der Zweite Weltkrieg (Diest, et al.), 66
Dickens, Charles, 18, 22–23
A Dictionary of Narratology (Prince), 97, 116
digressive narrative, 88–91
discontinuous narrative, 134, 139; Virginia Woolf and, 106
Discourse and Ideology in Nabokov's Prose (Larmour), 39
discursive beginnings, 4
Divine Comedy (Dante), 21
Don Juan (Byron), 21–22
Don Quixote (Cervantes), 25
Double or Nothing (Federman), 5
Doubrovsky, Serge, 223–25
Douglas, Jane, 182–83, 186, 188
Dryden, John, 7–8
DuPlessis, Rachel Blau, 215
During, Simon, 45
The Dutchess of Malfi (Webster), 2–3

Elam, Keir, 99, 168
Eliot, George, 20–21
Eliot, T. S., 104, 109
Elizabeth Costello (Coetzee), ix
emotions, 45–48, 50–58, 58n2, 59n8
Endgame (Beckett), 120
endings, 159, 191–200, 213–25, 228–40, 252–60; as beginnings, 107–9, 120, 193

epics, 14
"Epics and the Politics of the Origin Tale" (Wofford), 13–14
epitext, 12
Escape into Aesthetics (Stegner), 33
"Essay of Dramatic Poesy" (Dryden), 8
exposition, 3, 79–80, 197, 200–206
Expositional Modes and Temporal Ordering in Fiction (Sternberg), 79–80, 114, 193
extrafictional materials, 30
extratextual material, 113, 119
The Eye (Nabokov), 33

Faas, Ekbert, 7
fabula and *syuzhet*, 64–73, 83–86, 89, 99–103, 113–18, 152–54, 158–60, 211n3
factual narrative, 8, 44–78, 137–47. *See also* histoire and recit; historical narrative; history as framework for fictional narrative
false beginnings, 3, 6
Faulkner, William, 5, 97–98, 110n2, 124, 192–93
Faust (Goethe), 7
feminist approaches to literature, 99–100, 144–63, 179–88, 246–60
Ferro, Marc, 64
fiction, experimental, 69
fictive autobiography, 229
Field, Andrew, 36
Fielding, Henry, 4, 93n3
Finnegans Wake (Joyce), 119, 194
Fischer-Lichte, Erika, 171–72
Fisher, Caitlin, 180–88

Fisher, John, 13
"Fizzle 4" (Beckett), 5, 120
"Fizzle 8" (Beckett), 120
flashbacks. *See* analepses
Flaubert, Gustave, 64–65
A Footnote to History (Stevenson), 238
Forster, E. M., 124
Foucault, Michel, 17–19, 129
Four Quartets (T. S. Eliot), 109
Framing Borders in Literature and Other Media (Wolf and Bernhart), 12
French New Novel, 221
Freytag, Gustav, 8, 153–54
Frijda, Nico, 52n8
Fuentes, Carlos, 128–29
Fulgens and Lucrece (Medwall), 172–73

García Márquez, Gabriel, 127–29
Garner, Stanton B., Jr., 176–77
Gay, Peter, 72–73
gender, 144–63, 179–88, 239–40, 244n20, 246–60; in *Beloved*, 204, 208
Genesis, multiple beginnings and, 9
Genette, Gérard, 12, 30–31, 41n13, 63, 85–86, 119, 237–38
Geneva School, 17
Geronimo, 9, 116
Gide, André, 124
Gilbert, Daniel T., 51
Gilbert, Stuart, 193
The Glass Menagerie (Williams), 3
Glory (Nabokov), 33
Goethe, Johan Wolfgang von, 7
Gonzàlez Echevarría, Roberto, 128–30

Goodhart, Sandor, 115
Gordon, Mary, 253–60
"A Gossip on Romance" (Stevenson), 232
Gracq, Julien, 213–14, 225n4
Gray, Alasdair, 6
Griffiths, Gareth, 141

Handke, Peter, 174–77
Handler, Daniel, 5
Hankin, James, 44
Hardy, Thomas, 4, 240
Hawaii (Michener), 116
Hawthorne, Nathaniel, 119
"Heart of Darkness" (Conrad), 5
Heartbreak Tango (Boquitas pintadas) (Puig), 127, 130–35
"Heart's Desire" (C. Churchill), 3
Hegel, Georg Wilhelm Friedrich, 20
Heilbrun, Caroline, 118
Herman, David, 64
Herman, Edward S., 58n2
Herzfeld, Michael, 55
Hirsch, Marianne, 261n3
histoire and recit, 255–57
historical narrative, open-ended nature of, 76
history as framework for fictional narrative, 127–31, 137–39, 141, 229, 234
Homer, 7, 25, 83
Hooke, Robert, 87
Hopscotch (Cortàzar), 113
Horace, 7, 21, 83
How the Garcia Girls Lost Their Accents (Alvarez), 150–55
hypertext, beginnings and, 179–88

I, the Supreme (Roa Bastos), 128–29
ideological positioning, 11
If on a winter's night a traveler (Calvino), 6, 166
Iliad (Homer), 7
India, 138–39
In-group/out-group divisions: emotions and, 54–57
In Search of Lost Time (Proust), 5, 121
interpretive conventions, 12
Introduction to the Structural Analysis of Narrative" (Barthes), 252
Inuit and lack of creation myth, 8
Invitation to a Beheading (Nabokov), 33–34
Irigaray, Luce, 252
Iser, Wolfgang, 85–86, 182
Ito, Tiffany, 52

Jackson, Shelley, 180
Jacob's Room (Woolf), 99–101, 106–7
Jacquou le croquant (Le Roy), 25
James, Henry, 8, 79–80, 124, 181, 228, 230, 235; preface and, 31
James, William, 104–5, 109, 110n5
Jameson, Fredric, 229, 234, 241n1
Jane Eyre (C. Brontë), 153–55, 247
Jealousy (Robbé-Grillet), 222–23
Je suis né (Perec), 22
John Ray, Jr. (fictional character), 32, 34–38, 41n10
Johnson, James Weldon, 118
Joyce, James, 98, 114
Joyce, Michael, 179
The Joy Luck Club (Tan), 149

Kalidasa (Indian playwright), 7
Kaplan, Amy, 150
Kauffman, Linda, 39
Kellman, Steven, 81, 161n1, 168, 177
Kershaw, Baz, 169, 173
Kidnapped (Stevenson), 228–40; paratext and, 237–38, 242n9, 243n17
King, Queen, Knave (Nabokov), 33
King, Thomas, 110n3
Kolb, David, 182
Koskimaa, Raine, 183
Kyd, Thomas, 173

Laclos, Choderlos de, 217
Lady Chatterly's Lover (Lawrence), 118
Lanarck (Gray), 6
Landow, George, 188
Lanser, Susan Sniader, 30, 32, 39
Larsen, Deena, 181–82
Latin American narrative, 127–35; archive and, 127–35; Boom writers and, 127–31; popular culture and, 132–35; search for origins as narrative, 127–31
Laughter in the Dark (Nabokov), 118
Lawrence, D. H., 118
"The Leaning Tower" (Woolf), 96, 106
Le Gros, Bernard, 222
Le Roy, Eugène, 25
Levinson, Jerrold, 13
Les Liaisons dangereuses (Laclos), 217–19
Liddel Hart, Basil George, 68

Lily Briscoe (fictional character), 2
Le Livre brisé (Doubrovsky), 223–25
Lolita (Nabokov), 29–32, 34–40
Look at the Harlequins! (Nabokov), 118
Lord Jim (Conrad), 241n1
Lost in the Funhouse (Barth), 26
Lost Steps (Carpentier), 128–29
Lot's Daughters (Polhemus), 246–60
Luis, William, 151

Madame Bovary (Flaubert), 64–65
Mahabharata, 6
The Maids (Genet), 3
Makbeth (play), 170
Malone Dies (Beckett), 120–22
Mandler, J. M., 79
Mann, Thomas, 193
Manon Lescaut (Prévost), 219–20
Mansfield Park (Austen), 247
The Man without Qualities (Musil), 5
Marx, Karl, 225n3
Marxist theory, 241n1
McHale, Brian, 5, 41n9, 175
Medwall, Henry, 172
Memoir-novel, eighteenth-century, 217, 219–20
Memoirs and Adventures of a Man of Quality Retired from Society (Prévost), 219–20
memories, beginnings and, 252
Michener, James A., 116
Micrographia (Hooke), 87
microscopy, 87–88, 94n7, 94n8
middles, narrative, 68, 163n5, 198–99, 219–20

Midnight's Children (Rushdie), 6, 80, 137–47
Miller, D. A., 215
Miller, J. Hillis, 17–18, 70–71, 81, 86, 88, 155–56
The Mixquiahuala Letters (Castillo), 113
modernism, 4–5, 97–99, 116–17, 124, 222; the individual in, 25
Moglen, Helen, 93n1
Molloy (Beckett), 120–23
Monroe, Kristen R., 44
Montagnon, Pierre, 67
The Moor's Last Sigh (Rushdie), 145–46, 147n5
morality and ethics, 37–39, 47–49, 54–57, 218–19
Morrison, Toni, 149–50, 195, 200–210
Mrs. Dalloway (Woolf), 2, 5, 101–2
mukha (opening), 7
multiple beginnings, 7, 104, 110n7, 119–20; Genesis and, 9; postmodernism and, 5; *Tristram Shandy* and, 83–84
Mumby, Dennis, 45
Murphy (Beckett), 115
Musil, Robert, 5
Myth and Archive (Gonzàlez Echevarría), 129

Nabokov, Vladimir, 29–39, 40n4, 41n10, 118
narrative, 179–88; discontinuous, 106, 187, 222; factual, 181–85; nationalism and, 44–45, 57; nonlinear, 85–86, 91–92, 145–46; as ongoing process, 98–105, 124–30, 155–63, 164n8, 225n5, 236–38, 260; regressive, 2–3, 6, 67–68, 89–91, 254–55, 257; rhetorical theory and, 195; as search for identity or origins, 127–31, 138, 142–43, 156–62, 187, 235; web fiction and, 179–88. *See also* factual narrative
The Narrative Act (Lanser), 30
Narrative and Its Discontents (Miller), 215
Narrative and Social Control (Mumby), 45
narrative components, 58n6; Aristotle and, 49
narrative perspective, 24–26, 45–46
narrative pluralism, 107–9; Virginia Woolf and, 107; William James and, 104–5
nation and nationalism, 44–46, 57, 127–35, 137–47, 156–63, 233–34
Native American autobiographies, 9, 116
Natyashastra (Bharata), 7
La nausée (Sartre), 19
Nelson, Theodore H., 181
Neveux, Georges, 174
nonlinear narrative, 91–92, 145–46
"Notes towards a Mental Breakdown" (Ballard), 13
novels, eighteenth-century, 216–21
novelty, 103–5
Nussbaum, Martha C., 48
Nuttall, Anthony, 15, 24, 26, 81, 151, 179

Oatley, Keith, 55
objectivity, pretense to, 73
O'Brien, Flann, 5
Oedipus Rex (Sophocles), 114–15
"Offending the Audience" (Handke), 174–77
"Of the Three Unities" (Corneille), 7
One Hundred Years of Solitude (García Márquez), 128–29
On the Eve (Turgenev), 4
Openings (Nuttall), 81
origin(s), 8, 13–14, 46–46, 66, 137–47; beginnings as, 16–18, 26; search for origins as narrative, 127–31, 138, 142–43, 156–62, 187, 235
origin narratives, 8–9, 14, 124, 150. *See also* creation myth(s)
Ortony, Andrew, 50
Other, the, 253
Overy, Richard, 64
Oz, Amos, 70–72, 115–16

Panksepp, Jaak, 51–52
paratext, 2–3, 12–13, 113, 118–23, 197, 200–201, 253; discursive beginnings and, 153; factual narrative and, 64, 69–70; novels, eighteenth-century and, 217–19; theater and, 167–68; Vladimir Nabokov and, 29–40, 40n1, 40n3, 41n10
Paratexts (Genette), 30
Paradise Lost (Milton), 13
parody, beginnings as, 6, 36
patriarchal matrix, 157–59, 162, 186, 246–47. *See also* gender

Paul and Virginia (Bernardin de Saint-Pierre), 219–20
Pearl (Gordon), 253–60, 261n7
Pendennis (Thackeray), 4
Perec, Georges, 22, 223
The Performance Group, 170
peritext, 12
Peterson, Dale, 33
Phelan, James, 63, 116–17, 151–52, 163n2, 166–68, 173–74, 179
Pirandello, Luigi, 173–74, 177
Poetic Closure (Smith), 213
Poetics (Aristotle), 6–7
Polhemus, Robert, 246–60
The Political Unconscious (Jameson), 234
popular culture, Latin American narrative and, 132–35
A Portrait of the Artist as a Young Man (Joyce), 98
postmodernism, 5–6, 41n9, 179–80, 221–25; theater and, 175
Poulet, Georges, 17–18
Pound, Ezra, 98
prarambha (beginning), 7
preface, 29–40, 40n1, 41n11, 217–19. *See also* paratext
Prévost, Abbé, 219
Pride and Prejudice (Austen), 196
Prince, Gerald, 97, 116, 151, 160, 179, 191
La Prise de Constantinople (Ricardou), 221–22
Propp, Vladimir, 79, 196
prototype, 47–48, 58n3; expectations and, 49–50, 59n8
Proust, Marcel, 121

Puig, Manuel, 127–35
Pushkin, Alexander, 2
Pygmalion (Shaw), 168–69

Questions sur la IIe Guerre mondiale (Ferro), 64
Quiller-Couch, Arthur, 229

Rabinowitz, Peter, 11–12, 174, 192, 195–98, 214
Ramayana, 6
reading as a provisional assemblage, 188
Reading People, Reading Plots (Phelan), 196
realism, nineteenth-century, 4, 215–17
The Real Thing (Stoppard), 3
"reference time," 64–68, 76
regressive narrative, 2–3, 6, 67–68, 89–91; *Tristram Shandy* and, 83–86; Woolf and, 100–102
Return of the Native (Hardy), 4
Reynolds, Joshua, 86
rhetorical theory, narrative and, 195
The Rhetoric of Fiction (Booth), 31
Ricardou, Jean, 221
Richardson, Samuel, 93n3
The Rise of the Novel (Watt), 93n4
The Rivals (Sheridan), 3
Roa Bastos, Augusto, 128–29
Robbe-Grillet, Alain, 23, 222–23
Roderick Hudson (H. James), 8
Rohy, Valerie, 118
Romagnolo, Catherine, 116–17
Ronsard, Pierre de, 21
A Room of One's Own (Woolf), 96, 99–101, 108, 251

Rushdie, Salman, 2, 6, 80, 137–47

Said, Edward, 8, 13, 73, 80, 93, 149–50, 180–81, 188, 191, 219, 221, 223, 225
Saporta, Marc, 113
Sarte, Jean Paul, 19, 124
The Scarlet Letter (Hawthorne), 119
Schechner, Richard, environmental theater and, 169–70, 173
Schleef, Einar, 171
Schor, Naomi, 86
The Second World War (W. Churchill), 66
serials, 130–35, 231
Shakuntala (Kalidasa), 7
Shaw, George Bernard, 3, 168
Sherman, Stuart, 86
Shields, Carol, 253
"A Short Political History of the Weimar Republic" (Gay), 72–73
Silko, Leslie Marmon, 149
Six Characters in Search of an Author (Pirandello), 173–77
"A Sketch of the Past" (Woolf), 100
Smith, Barbara Herrnstein, 213
Smith, Bradley, 75–76
Smith, D. Vance, 17
Solome (Wilde), 171–72
Some Problems on Philosophy (W. James), 104
Sophocles, 114
The Spanish Tragedy (Kyd), 3, 173
De Spectaculis (Tertullian), 173
Sprechstück (Handke), 175
Springer, Norman, 155
Stegner, Page, 33, 36

Stein, Gertrude, 6
Stein, Nancy, 79
Sternberg, Meir, 64, 79–80, 114, 152–53, 170, 193, 211n3
Sterne, Laurence, 1–2, 83–85, 119, 180
Stevenson, Robert Louis, 228–40
The Strange Case of Dr Jekyll and Mr Hyde (Stevenson), 238
The Stranger (Camus), 1
Strong Opinions (Nabokov), 32
structuralism, 79, 196
Summer (Wharton), 149
supporting narrative, need for, 19–21
Swift, Jonathan, 92–93
syuzhet, 7, 64, 113, 118–19, 211n3; *Molloy* and, 121; *Tristram Shandy* and, 83–84

A Tale of a Tub (Swift), 92–93
Talley's Folly (Wilson), 3
Tan, Amy, 149
Tan, Ed, 49
The Technique of the Drama (Freytag), 8
Terra Nostra (Fuentes), 129
Tertullian, 173
Tess of the D'Urbervilles (Hardy), 240
textual beginnings, 5
Thackeray, William Makepeace, 4
theater, beginnings and, 2–3, 166–77
These Waves of Girls (Fisher), 180–88
"Thoughts" (Fisher), 180–81
Tiffin, Helen, 141

time of day, beginnings and, 5, 67, 222–23
titles, varieties and functions of, 12–13
Todorov, Tzvetan, 79
Tolstoy, Lev, 191–92
Tomashevsky, Boris, 116–17
Tom Jones (Fielding), 4
Total War (Calvocoressi et al.), 73
To the Lighthouse (Woolf), 2, 99–101, 108–9, 110n10, 149
Treasure Island (Stevenson), 233
The Trial (Kafka), 5
Tristram Shandy (Sterne), 13, 23–26, 83–85, 119
Turgenev, Ivan, 4

Ulysses (Joyce), 5, 118, 193, 261n8
The Unfortunates (Johnson), 113
Unless (Shields), 253–60
The Unnamable (Beckett), 121
The Use of Poetry and the Use of Criticism (T. S. Eliot), 104

Valéry, Paul, 13
Van Vechten, Renée, 44
The Voyage Out (Woolf), 110n6

Wald, Priscilla, 150
Walker, Jill, 184
Wall, Cynthia, 86
Walpole, Horace, on *Tristram Shandy*, 83–84, 88
Walton, Timothy D., 51
Warhol, Robyn, 192
war narratives, 46–49, 56–58, 63–76, 184
The War's Long Shadow (Smith), 75

Washington, Peter, 218
Watch Your Mouth (Handler), 5
Watt, Ian, 93n4
The Waves (Woolf), 26, 102, 110n7
web fiction, 179–88
Webster, John, 3
Weinberg, Gerhard, 74–75
Wharton, Edith, 149
White, Hayden, 63
Why the Allies Won (Overy), 64
Wilde, Oscar, 171
Wilson, Lanford, 3
Wilson, Timothy D., 51
Winnett, Susan, 163n1, 191
Wofford, Susanne, 13–14
Wolf, Werner, 12
Wong, Hertha D. Sweet, 9
Woolf, Leonard, 98
Woolf, Virginia, 26, 96, 98–109, 149, 250–51
Workman, Mark, 223
A World in Arms (Weinberg), 74
World War II, 63–64
Worstward Ho (Beckett), 120
Worthen, William B., 177
Wright, Gordon, 67
writers, 72–73, 251
Wuthering Heights (E. Brontë), 247

The Years (Woolf), 107–9

Zajonc, Robert B., 47–48, 50, 59n10
Der Zauberberg (Mann), 193

IN THE FRONTIERS OF NARRATIVE SERIES:

Unnatural Narrative: Impossible Worlds in Fiction and Drama
by Jan Alber

Useful Fictions: Evolution, Anxiety, and the Origins of Literature
by Michael Austin

Possible Worlds Theory and Contemporary Narratology
edited by Alice Bell and Marie-Laure Ryan

Stories and Minds: Cognitive Approaches to Literary Narrative
edited by Lars Bernaerts, Dirk De Geest, Luc Herman, and Bart Vervaeck

Telling Children's Stories: Narrative Theory and Children's Literature
edited by Mike Cadden

Strange Narrators in Contemporary Fiction: Explorations in Readers' Engagement with Characters
by Marco Caracciolo

Refiguring Minds in Narrative Media
by David Ciccoricco

Coincidence and Counterfactuality: Plotting Time and Space in Narrative Fiction
by Hilary P. Dannenberg

The Emergence of Mind: Representations of Consciousness in Narrative Discourse in English
edited by David Herman

Story Logic: Problems and Possibilities of Narrative
by David Herman

Handbook of Narrative Analysis
by Luc Herman and Bart Vervaeck

Affective Narratology: The Emotional Structure of Stories
by Patrick Colm Hogan

Imagining Kashmir: Emplotment and Colonialism
by Patrick Colm Hogan

Spaces of the Mind: Narrative and Community in the American West
by Elaine A. Jahner

The Storyworld Accord: Econarratology and Postcolonial Narratives
by Erin James

Talk Fiction: Literature and the Talk Explosion
by Irene Kacandes

Ethos and Narrative Interpretation: The Negotiation of Values in Fiction
by Liesbeth Korthals Altes

Contemporary Comics Storytelling
by Karin Kukkonen

The Cruft of Fiction: Mega-Novels and the Science of Paying Attention
by David Letzler

The Imagined Moment: Time, Narrative, and Computation
by Inderjeet Mani

Storying Domestic Violence: Constructions and Stereotypes of Abuse in the Discourse of General Practitioners
by Jarmila Mildorf

New Narratives: Stories and Storytelling in the Digital Age
edited by Ruth Page and Bronwen Thomas

Fictional Minds
by Alan Palmer

Writing at the Limit: The Novel in the New Media Ecology
by Daniel Punday

Narrative Beginnings: Theories and Practices
edited by Brian Richardson

Opening Acts: Narrative Beginnings in Twentieth-Century Feminist Fiction
by Catherine Romagnolo

Narrative across Media: The Languages of Storytelling
edited by Marie-Laure Ryan

Storyworlds across Media: Toward a Media-Conscious Narratology
edited by Marie-Laure Ryan and Jan-Noël Thon

Fictional Dialogue: Speech and Conversation in the Modern and Postmodern Novel
by Bronwen Thomas

Transmedial Narratology and Contemporary Media Culture
by Jan-Noël Thon

The Story of "Me": Contemporary American Autofiction
by Marjorie Worthington

To order or obtain more information on these or other University of Nebraska Press titles, visit nebraskapress.unl.edu.